Staying Alive

Judgments of personal identity stand at the heart of our daily transactions. Family life, friendships, institutions of justice, and systems of compensation all rely on our ability to reidentify people. It is not as obvious as it might at first appear just how to express this relation between facts about personal identity and practical interests in a philosophical account of personal identity. A natural thought is that whatever relation is proposed as the one which constitutes the sameness of a person must be important to us in just the way identity is. This simple understanding of the connection between personal identity and practical concerns has serious difficulties, however. One is that the relations that underlie our practical judgments do not seem suited to providing a metaphysical account of the basic, literal continuation of an entity. Another is that the practical interests we associate with identity are many and varied and it seems impossible that a single relation could simultaneously capture what is necessary and sufficient for all of them. *Staying Alive* offers a new way of thinking about the relation between personal identity and practical interests which allows us to overcome these difficulties and to offer a view in which the most basic and literal facts about personal identity are inherently connected to practical concerns. This account, the 'Person Life View', sees persons as unified loci of practical interaction, and defines the identity of a person in terms of the unity of a characteristic kind of life made up of dynamic interactions among biological, psychological, and social attributes and functions mediated through social and cultural infrastructure.

Marya Schechtman is a Professor of Philosophy and member of the Laboratory of Integrative Neuroscience at the University of Illinois at Chicago.

Staying Alive

Personal Identity, Practical Concerns, and the Unity of a Life

Marya Schechtman

OXFORD

UNIVERSITY PRESS

Great Clarendon Street, Oxford, OX2 6DP,
United Kingdom

Oxford University Press is a department of the University of Oxford.
It furthers the University's objective of excellence in research, scholarship,
and education by publishing worldwide. Oxford is a registered trade mark of
Oxford University Press in the UK and in certain other countries

First published 2014
First published in paperback 2017

Published in the United States of America by Oxford University Press
198 Madison Avenue, New York, NY 10016, United States of America

British Library Cataloguing in Publication Data
Data available

Library of Congress Cataloging in Publication Data
Data available

ISBN 978-0-19-968487-8 (Hbk.)
ISBN 978-0-19-880127-6 (Pbk.)

To John F. and John M.

Acknowledgements

This project took shape over several years, and along the way I have benefitted immensely from the input and support of many people. At its inception I received important feedback on the ideas developed here at a conference on Practical Identity and Narrative Agency at Macquarie University in 2006. I want especially to thank Catriona Mackenzie, Kim Atkins, and Jacqui Poltera, for their questions, comments, and suggestions. In the spring of 2011, I presented an earlier draft of this manuscript to my graduate seminar, and I am indebted to participants Janella Baxter, Cleber Correa, Joseph Gottlieb, Marcello Grigolo, Michael Hurwitz, and James Virtel for spirited discussion and probing questions, which significantly impacted both the structure and content of this work. Throughout the conception and writing of this book I have relied upon conversations, comments, suggestions, and encouragement from my colleagues at UIC and elsewhere. Among the many who have had an important impact I want to mention Sam Fleischacker, Jessica Gordon-Roth, David Hilbert, Peter Hylton, Mark Jenkins, Fleur Jongepier, Colin Klein, Tony Laden, Connie Meinwald, Milosz Pawlowski, Sally Sedgwick, David Shoemaker, Miriam Solomon, and Marc Slors. I also want to thank Valerie Brown and Charlotte Jackson. They have been there for me during this process in more ways than I can count. Thanks are due also to my colleagues in the Office of the College of Liberal Arts and Sciences at UIC, especially Agnes Herget, Rachel Leamon, and Astrida Tantillo, who were relentlessly encouraging and supportive, maintaining the highest good humor even during the madness of clusters. The manuscript was improved immeasurably by the input of my editor Peter Momtchiloff and by the comments and suggestions of three anonymous reviewers, each of whom read and generously commented on an earlier draft with great sympathy, care, and insight. I also owe a special debt to my teacher, Stanley Cavell, the depth of whose influence I am only now beginning to appreciate decades later. Aleks Zarnitsyn has been an important partner in this project almost since the beginning, and has been a trusted aide and respected influence every step of the way. His keen intellect and hard work have been crucial to its completion. Finally, I give profound thanks to my family, especially my husband John Marko and my son John Schechtman-Marko, who have embraced my work wholeheartedly, and helped and supported me in just about every way it is possible for one human person to help or support another.

Contents

Introduction

Everyday life is filled with judgments of personal identity. These judgments occur spontaneously and often with very little effort. A good thing, too, since if they did not the kinds of lives we lead would be impossible. Without the ability quickly and accurately to recognize our partners, parents, or children, family life would be incoherent; if we could not identify our colleagues or employers, collaboration would go nowhere and getting paid would be a problem; if we were unable to determine whether the person climbing a ladder to the second story of our house is the person we hired to clean the gutters we would not know when to call the police.

Despite the commonness of such judgments, giving an account of just what is asserted when we make them has proved exceedingly difficult. This is not in itself terribly surprising. It is well accepted by now that we can have competencies whose basis we cannot articulate, and the history of philosophy makes it clear that providing a general definition of something is a very different task from recognizing paradigmatic instances of it. In the case of persons, however, we can say something more specific about why a satisfying general theory is so hard to come by. The special problems encountered here stem from the very ubiquity of identity judgments. Other people are integrated into our lives so deeply, and in so many different ways, that we make our judgments of identity in a host of different contexts and for a wide variety of different purposes. As it turns out, different considerations underlie these judgments in these different circumstances, and this has important implications for the project of providing a general philosophical account of the relation that constitutes personal identity.

The method most commonly used to develop such an account involves reflection on hypothetical scenarios that separate in thought the different relations that are present in paradigmatic instances of personal identity. The idea is that our judgments about what happens to the person in these cases will reveal which of the many different relations present in cases where judgments of identity are uncontroversial is the one that actually constitutes that identity. In order to focus our response to these cases we are often asked to think about some of the practical implications that follow from judgments of identity and to consider whether and how they apply in the case depicted. For instance, after being asked to imagine a person having her psychological life transferred into a different body we may be instructed to reflect on whether the resulting person is rightly held responsible for the original person's actions or whether it is rational for the original person to have prudential concern for the resulting person's well-being, or whether the resulting person is the appropriate person to receive compensation for the original person's sacrifices. In this way the contexts in which we make our everyday judgments of identity are brought into play to help guide our reactions to the hypothetical cases.

This method is bound to encounter difficulty, however, since, as I mentioned above, we employ different considerations to make our everyday judgments of identity in response to different practical demands. If we are conducting clinical trials or checking vaccination records we are going to be interested in determining whether we are encountering the same biological entity as we did before. If we are assessing praise or blame, or holding someone to a promise, we will want to know whether we are addressing the same agent. If we are calculating the trade-offs between present sacrifices and future benefits our question is whether we are dealing with the same experiencing subject, and when we are trying to reconnect with a friend from decades past, or to predict how someone will behave, we will be interested in knowing whether there is continuity of personality or character. In everyday life we use the word "person" in many different ways. Sometimes it means "human animal," sometimes "moral agent," sometimes "rational, self-conscious subject," sometimes "possessor of particular rights," sometimes "being with a defined personality or character," and there are many other senses as well. Each of these conceptions of *person* has its own corresponding criterion of personal identity, and there is no reason to assume that we can find some single relation which underlies our judgments about the identity of a "person" in every context.

If we apply the standard method for investigating questions of personal identity broadly and assiduously enough, devising a range of hypothetical cases that allows us to consider questions of identity from different angles and in different circumstances, we will inevitably end up with a variety of different candidates for our criterion of personal identity arising from the different practical questions we consider. Each of these proposed criteria will have some legitimacy, since it will capture one of the conceptions of personhood and personal identity we employ. But it will also be possible to develop compelling counterexamples to each proposed criterion by considering other practical contexts involving judgments of identity in which this particular criterion does not apply. If we seek to define the limits of a person by determining the limits of the applicability of particular practical judgments, as the standard method does, the fact that there are so many different kinds of practical judgments associated with facts about personal identity appears to present an insurmountable obstacle. In light of these observations it thus seems that we need to reconsider our approach to the question of personal identity.

The difficulty described here stems from the multiplicity of different conceptions of personhood and personal identity connected with the various practical contexts in which judgments of personal identity occur. Two obvious possibilities for alternative approaches thus present themselves. One is to accept the multiplicity of conceptions of personal identity and give up on the project of providing a single, unified account; the other is to reject the assumption that practical considerations should be consulted in developing an account of personal identity, thereby relieving ourselves of the burden of simultaneously expressing the competing intuitions generated by different kinds of practical judgment.

Consider first the possibility of embracing multiplicity. This alternative acknowledges that our many different conceptions of personhood raise different questions of personal identity. Although these are all called (somewhat misleadingly) by the same name, they are, on this view, distinct questions and must be considered separately.[1] There is obviously something useful in this approach, and it is undeniably valuable to disentangle and sort through the different questions that get called "questions of personal identity," considering each in its own terms. Each of these questions (e.g., the question about the identity of the human animal, of the agent, of the self-conscious subject, of the sentient being, of the character or personality) is interesting and important in its own right. As a stopping point, however, this multi-pronged approach is not satisfying. The fracturing of the contexts in which we make identity judgments does not imply a corresponding fracturing of the people in our lives. The people with whom we interact are unified individuals, albeit extremely complex ones. We care about these individuals in different ways in different circumstances, but at the end of the day the people in our lives—our parents and children and friends; the butcher, the baker, and the candlestick maker—are single beings to whom all of the different questions and concerns associated with personal identity can be applied. Our world is not populated with human persons and agent persons, and self-conscious subject persons, and sentient being persons, and personality/character persons; it is populated with individual people who are, in paradigmatic cases, all of these things.[2] The person I expect to keep his promise may well also be the one whose medical test results I am anxiously awaiting and whose behavior I hope to predict with relative accuracy.

---

[1] David Shoemaker suggests something like this. See "Personal Identity and Practical Concerns," *Mind*, 116 (462), April 2007, p. 339. His is not, however, exactly the approach I have described here. We will discuss Shoemaker's view in Chapter 3.

[2] I will expand on this observation and defend it more fully in Chapter 3.

Since people are ultimately unitary individuals there is a meaningful general question to be raised about the conditions under which these individuals continue to exist. The answer to the question "was that your colleague I saw on television last night?" cannot, in the final analysis, be "well, it depends," but must be "yes" or "no." A "yes" answer can be qualified, of course (e.g., "Yes, it was my colleague but he's changed a great deal since you last saw him." Or "Yes, it was my colleague, but he was hypnotized at the time so nothing he said or did really came from him."). There nevertheless remains a fundamental question about *who* it was who has changed or was hypnotized. In other words, there is a basic, *literal* question about whether the person to whom I am pointing now is the same person as some earlier person which must be answered first, and then there are a host of other questions of "personal identity" that can be asked about that person once she has been properly individuated.

This analysis makes the second alternative described above, disconnecting practical considerations from the attempt to provide a criterion of personal identity, particularly attractive. Perhaps what we need to do is to individuate persons first by some other means and then direct our various practical questions and concerns to this individual.[3] On this approach the considerations used to produce a criterion of the literal continuation of an individual person will be purely theoretical and unrelated to the many practical interests and concerns we have about personal identity in everyday life. While there may indeed be many different questions of "personal identity" that carry significance for us, on this view these concern "identity" in only a metaphorical sense, and do not actually speak to the individuation and persistence of the individual people who populate our world. We can thus consider the question of literal identity as a metaphysical question without practical admixture, independently of the many metaphorical questions of "personal identity" that are tied to particular practical concerns. In this way the multiplicity of practical contexts no longer poses a problem for generating a single account of personal identity.

There is something very attractive about this analysis, but it also has its costs. According to this approach there is on the one hand the relation that constitutes an individual person, and on the other a variety of relations that are of great practical significance to us, and there need be no inherent connection between the former and the latter. This leaves us without any explanation of why people as a kind

---

[3] Something like this view has gained a great deal of traction recently, especially in conjunction with the biological approach to identity or "animalism." The animalist view is not, however, exactly the view I describe here. We will discuss animalism in Chapter 2 and return to it throughout the remainder of the book.

are so important to us, since what makes them individuals and what makes them important are only contingently related. As I will argue throughout the book, however, we do not see the people in our lives as things that merely happen to have features that make us interested in them in particular ways. Other people are, by their very nature, beings that are significant to us in a wide variety of ways. An understanding of these entities that does not see this significance as part of their intrinsic nature is therefore incomplete. This is not an uncontroversial claim, but it is one I will defend as the discussion unfolds. For the moment, we can think about it this way. In introducing this alternative, I described it as the view that we needed first to delimit an individual and then to ask our particular practical questions or make our particular practical judgments about that individual. If the relation that defines the unity of the individual is truly independent of the relations that provide a basis for our practical judgments, however, there is no obvious reason that these practical questions should be asked *about* that individual. The basis for the unity of the individual and the basis for the practical judgments might turn out to be completely orthogonal to one another.

Here, then, is our situation: If we are to explain the fact that the people who populate our world are genuine individuals, we need an account of identity that defines a single, unified entity which is the target of all of the many practical questions and concerns that are associated with personal identity. If we are to understand these individuals fully, the relation that constitutes their identity must be connected to their practical significance inherently and not just accidentally. Since our practical questions and concerns about persons are so multifarious, however, it is not immediately obvious how a single relation can be inherently connected to all of them. None of the alternatives we have looked at so far completely addresses this situation, and so it seems that yet another approach must be found if we are to produce a satisfying account of personal identity.

The main work of this book is to develop such an approach and to use it to provide a viable and attractive account of personal identity in which facts about our literal identity are inherently connected to practical concerns. The book breaks roughly into three parts. The first four chapters gather insights from a wide range of existing views of personal identity and use them to get a picture of the basic structure that an account of identity based on practical considerations must have. This involves determining which practical concerns are intrinsically related to facts about our identity and explaining the nature of that relationship. In both of these particulars I depart from standard views. I suggest associating a wider range of practical concerns with identity than is usually the case and invoke a more complicated conception of the relation between these concerns and identity than is typically presupposed. Chapters 5 and 6 use the general schema that comes out of the first four chapters to develop an account of our identity that is inherently practical. This view, which I call the "person life view," defines the identity of a person in terms of the unity of a characteristic kind of life. Chapter 7 defends the claim that the person life view should be seen as an account of our *literal* identity and says more about precisely what this designation means.

More specifically, Chapter 1 uses a discussion of John Locke and of present-day psychological continuity theories to introduce the general form of the relation between personal identity and practical concerns I will employ in developing my view. Locke offers one of the most famous and influential accounts of personhood and personal identity. It is, moreover, an account that links identity to practical concerns by defining "person" as a "forensic term." Locke is usually taken to hold the view that judgments of identity should directly coincide with forensic judgments. I will argue that he can be read as instead providing a more complicated understanding of the connection between these two types of judgments. The significance of this feature of Locke's account is demonstrated by looking at present-day psychological continuity theories which emulate his view in some respects but lose sight of his sophisticated picture of the relation between personal identity and the practical, leaving them open to a serious objection.

Chapter 2 considers the possibility that literal questions about personal identity should be sharply distinguished from practical questions and that the two kinds of questions should be pursued entirely separately. The agential identity theory of Christine Korsgaard represents this point of view from the perspective of value theory, and Eric Olson's defense of a biological account of personal identity from the perspective of metaphysics. Although there is a great deal that is attractive in this approach I do not think that it can ultimately provide an adequate picture of the literal identity of beings like us. I will not yet have all the resources I need to make the case fully in Chapter 2. As a preliminary step, however, I will show that both Korsgaard and Olson need to allow for a unit of practical concern which is the appropriate target of our various person-related concerns and practices. This unit is inherently practical and to answer the question of how such units are individuated we must necessarily make reference to practical considerations. Since the question of what constitutes the identity of the forensic unit has the logical structure of a question of numerical identity, reflection on this question represents a potential route to developing an inherently practical conception of personal identity.

Chapters 1 and 2 develop the structure we will use for thinking about the relation between personal identity and practical considerations. Chapter 3 turns to the question of which practical considerations we should focus on in trying to understand personal identity. Drawing on the work of Hilde Lindemann I argue for the need to expand our conception of the practical importance of personal identity beyond the forensic concerns we inherit from Locke. An implication is that many individuals who would not be considered persons on the Lockean conception (e.g., infants or those with severe dementia or cognitive impairments) will be considered persons on the expanded view. Bringing together the conclusions reached to this point we are left with a conception of persons as individual loci of practical interaction to which the whole set of practical interests and concerns associated with personhood are appropriately directed. Given the wide range of practical interests we have in persons, however, it is not immediately evident how to define a single locus that is an inherently appropriate target of all of these interests, at least if the designation "appropriate" is to have any bite. This is the problem described above. Chapter 3 concludes by further explicating this challenge, which I call the "problem of multiplicity."

Chapter 4 offers resources for meeting the problem of multiplicity. Using Jeff McMahan's theory of time-relative interests as a starting point it describes how a typical mature person can be defined in terms of a single relation that makes her a strongly unified target of the full range of practical questions and concerns that apply to persons. An analysis of my own Narrative Self-Constitution View, developed in *The Constitution of Selves*,[4] offers the resources necessary to answer the challenge as it applies over time, explaining how infants and adults can be inherently appropriate loci of the same set of practical concerns as one another despite possessing very different attributes. The key element I take from the Narrative Self-Constitution View is a diachronic holism according to which personhood and personal identity are defined in terms of an unfolding developmental structure rather than in terms of relations between individual moments. This discussion will also offer the opportunity to describe the relation between the view I am defending here and my earlier views on personal identity, explaining which aspects of those views I see as compatible with my current position and which I now reject.

Chapter 5 uses the insights and resources collected in the first four chapters to begin developing my positive account of personal identity—the person life view. According to this view persons are entities that live characteristic kinds of lives, "person lives." To be a person is to live a person life; particular persons are individuated by individuating person lives; and sameness of person over time is defined in terms of the sameness of a person life. There are, of course, many questions about this view which need to be answered. Among other important challenges it is necessary to defend the plausibility of the assumption that there is such a thing as the characteristic life of a person. This chapter makes the case that there

---

[4] Marya Schechtman, *The Constitution of Selves*, Ithaca: Cornell University Press, 1996.

is, sketching a basic picture of this life as a dynamic interaction between biological, psychological, and social functions and attributes. Crucial to this sketch is the idea that the lives of persons are inherently social, and that living the life of a person involves occupying a space within a social or cultural infrastructure of the sort that beings like us naturally develop. The social aspect of the view raises a specter of conventionalism, and this is addressed through the consideration of a variety of particular cases.

With a general picture of what a person life is like in hand, Chapter 6 considers how the person life view delimits and tracks individual persons. Here I argue that we should understand personhood in terms of a cluster of mutually reinforcing properties, relations, and functions. This means that there is no single relation (or small set of relations) whose holding is necessary and sufficient for the continuation of a person life; instead, there are a variety of different combinations of relations which can work together to maintain a single, integrated unit of interaction. To show more concretely how this model works within the context of the person life view I revisit some of the standard puzzle cases from the philosophical literature on personal identity, and describe how the view evaluates them.

Chapter 7 shows that the person life view is rightly considered an account of literal identity. To make this argument it is necessary to answer challenges raised by defenders of a biological approach ("animalism"). These challenges suggest that if we take *person* as a concept that picks out a basic kind of entity, or substance, we will have trouble explaining the relation between human persons and human organisms. Animalists thus argue that questions about the continuation of a person *as* a person should be taken to be questions of "identity" in only a figurative sense, and not as literal, metaphysical identity questions. I argue that the person life view can avoid these challenges and the animalist conclusion via one of two methods. One is to employ an adapted version of the constitution model of the relation between human persons and human animals developed by Lynne Baker. The other is to concede that persons are not metaphysical substances of the sort defined by animalists, but to argue that within the ontological framework favored by animalism there is room for questions of identity that are legitimately considered questions about the literal continuation of entities even though they are not about metaphysical substances as these theorists understand them. Finally, a brief conclusion will review the major arguments and accomplishments of the discussion and offer some final thoughts.

To finish these preliminaries, I should say a brief word about the idea of "literal identity" that I have been employing here and will continue to employ throughout the book. In the philosophical context "literal identity" is most naturally understood as numerical identity and for much of what follows it can be safely read in this way. Persons as I wish to define them are individual loci which serve as appropriate targets of various particular kinds of interests, concerns, and interactions. When we want to know about their literal identity we are seeking the conditions under which there continues to be a unified locus that can play this role. This question, I will argue, is reasonably described as a question about our literal continuation. Whether it is also a question about numerical identity depends upon exactly what we think questions of numerical identity look like when applied to complex objects like us. Literal identity is like numerical identity in logical structure. It does not permit branching or admit of degrees, and if this is all that talk of numerical identity implies the terms are interchangeable. The notion of numerical identity is sometimes used in a way that carries metaphysical as well as logical content, however, and when it is, the question of whether literal identity is the same as numerical identity depends upon exactly what content it is taken to carry. The connection between literal identity and numerical identity will be raised briefly in Chapter 3 and discussed extensively in Chapter 7, where we will look at some of the more metaphysically-loaded understandings of numerical identity.

1

Locke and the Psychological Continuity Theorists

Our ultimate aim is to develop and defend an account of personal identity according to which facts about the literal identity of beings like us are inherently connected to practical considerations. All of the key terms in the statement of this goal cry out for clarification, and each will eventually be made more precise. This chapter speaks to the question of what it means for a practical concern to be "inherently connected" to facts about our identity, offering a preliminary picture of the relevant connection that will continue to be refined throughout the next three chapters.

In this undertaking, as in most to do with questions of personal identity, it is helpful to start with John Locke's discussion in the *Essay Concerning Human Understanding*. His is one of the most famous and widely influential of all accounts of personal identity. It is, moreover, an account that explicitly links facts about personal identity to practical judgments, and does so in a way that is especially useful for our purposes. Locke's conception of the role of practical judgments in determining a criterion of personal identity can, I will argue, be read as a more complicated one than it is usually thought to be. Rather than a view in which the limits of a person are coincident with the limits of the attribution of moral responsibility and other "forensic" relations, Locke can be seen as defining the limits of a person as the limits within which specific questions about responsibility are appropriately raised.

Appreciating the complexity of Locke's view is very important for our purposes since it does not seem possible for an account that takes the simpler view of the connection between personal identity and practical considerations to yield an account of our literal identity. The significance of this more complex understanding for our endeavor can be demonstrated by looking at the consequences of its absence. Present-day psychological continuity theorists offer accounts of personal identity that are in many ways inspired by Locke's, and they borrow a great deal from Locke's methodology in defending their own views. They do not, however, employ his picture of the relation between facts about personal identity and practical considerations, and as a result they are subject to a serious objection which I interpret as an expression of the fact that they have not provided a plausible account of literal identity. In the end I think that Locke's conception of the relevant practical concerns is too narrow (I will argue for this claim in Chapter 3) and that for this reason, as well as others, his is ultimately not a satisfying practically-based account of literal identity (i.e., an account in which facts about our literal identity are inherently connected to practical considerations). The understanding of the connection between personal identity and practical concerns his work provides is, however, invaluable in the development of such an account.

1.1   Locke on Identity and the Practical

In a well-known passage Locke tells us that to inquire effectively into the identity conditions for any entity we must first be clear on the kind of entity whose identity is in question—"to conceive, and judge of [identity] aright," he says, " we must consider what *Idea* the Word it is applied to stands for."[1] Different kinds of entities have different kinds of identity conditions. The identity of an atom consists in its continuous path through space and time, for instance, and the identity of a mass made up of a group of atoms consists in the continuation of the very same atoms grouped together. According to Locke, the identity of a living thing, unlike that of a mass of atoms, consists not in continuation of the same matter, but rather in the continuation of a single life in which different bits of matter participate at different times. This is true for a plant which "continues to be the same Plant, as long as it partakes of the same Life, though that Life be communicated to new Particles of Matter vitally united to the living plant," and for a man (human), whose identity consists "in nothing but a participation of the same continued Life, by constantly fleeting Particles of Matter, in succession, vitally united to the same organized Body."[2]

Although this is not always sufficiently appreciated, Locke says, the idea *person* is not the same as the idea *man*, and so the identity criteria for men and persons are distinct. To find the identity criterion for persons we thus need to know what idea *person* stands for. Locke gives two famous definitions. First he tells us that a *person* is, "a thinking intelligent Being, that has reason and reflection, and can

---

[1] John Locke, *An Essay Concerning Human Understanding*, ed. P. Nidditch, Oxford: Clarendon Press, 1975, p. 332.
[2] Locke, *Human Understanding*, pp. 331–2.

consider it self as it self, the same thinking thing in different times and places...,"[3] concluding that personal identity consists in sameness of consciousness because it is consciousness "that makes everyone to be, what he calls *self*; and thereby distinguishes himself from all other thinking things."[4] Later, and perhaps even more famously, Locke says that *person* is "a Forensick Term appropriating Actions and their Merit; and so belongs only to intelligent Agents capable of a Law, and Happiness and Misery."[5] He tells us further that "*Self* is that conscious thinking thing, (whatever Substance, made up of, whether Spiritual, or Material, Simple, or Compounded, it matters not) which is sensible, or conscious of Pleasure and Pain, capable of Happiness or Misery, and so is concern'd for it *self* as far as that consciousness extends."[6] Once again reflection on the idea of *Person* leads to an understanding of personal identity in terms of sameness of consciousness, and so Locke concludes: "This may shew us wherein *personal Identity* consists, not in the Identity of Substance, but, as I have said, in the Identity of *consciousness....*"[7]

There is no ambiguity about Locke's claim that sameness of person does not require sameness of substance but it is worth taking a bit of time to consider exactly how he argues for this view. The fundamental argument seems to be something like the following: persons are beings who can legitimately be held responsible for what they do. For this to be the case (at least according to Locke) they must be able to follow a law, and to be recipients of just punishment and reward. Reward and punishment can apply, however, only where there is a conscious subject. These practices necessitate that the recipient be able to experience pain and pleasure and care about which she experiences. They also require, as does following a law, that someone be able to understand herself as a persisting being whose past actions are connected to what she experiences now, and whose future experiences depend in certain ways on present actions. She must, that is, be able to appreciate the idea that actions have consequences. For reward and punishment to be *just*, moreover, it is essential that the very same consciousness involved in the execution of an action be the one that experiences the pain or pleasure of reward and punishment. Whatever actions a present self cannot appropriate to its consciousness, Locke says, it "can be no more concerned in, than if they had never been done: And to receive Pleasure or Pain; i.e. Reward or Punishment, on the account of any such Action, is all one, as to be made happy or miserable in its first being, without any demerit at all." He continues, "For supposing a Man Punish'd now, for what he did

[3] Locke, *Human Understanding*, p. 335.   [4] Locke, *Human Understanding*, p. 335.
[5] Locke, *Human Understanding*, p. 346.   [6] Locke, *Human Understanding*, p. 341.
[7] Locke, *Human Understanding*, p. 342.

in another Life, whereof he could be made to have no consciousness at all, what difference is there between that Punishment, and being created miserable?"[8]

To bring the point home, Locke offers a series of hypothetical cases in which we separate sameness of consciousness and sameness of substance (both material and immaterial; human animal and immaterial soul) and asks us to think about how we would make forensic judgments in these cases. He assumes that we will find that these judgments track sameness of consciousness rather than sameness of body or soul, giving us, for instance, the iconic case in which the soul of a prince (with all consciousness of his past life) enters and informs the body of a cobbler, and telling us that "every one sees, he would be the same Person with the Prince, accountable only for the Prince's Actions."[9] We are similarly instructed to imagine someone with the soul of Nestor or Thersites but no consciousness of either of their pasts and conclude that such a person could not be "concerned in" either of their actions.[10] There is also a man who switches consciousness by day and by night, and a little finger that comes apart from a human body, all of the consciousness going with the finger, and other, similar, scenarios. In each case when we think of rights, privileges, and responsibilities, he believes, we will conclude that they follow consciousness and not substance.

It is obvious that practical considerations play a key role in providing an account of personal identity for Locke. Persons are forensic entities, and sameness of person must be defined in such a way that to be the *same* person is to be the *same* forensic entity. The question we need to consider in more depth, however, is exactly how we are to think about what this actually amounts to. The basic idea may seem straightforward. Locke provides us with cases in which we are supposed to make judgments about accountability; where these apply we can conclude that we have the same person (i.e., the person with the cobbler's body and prince's consciousness is responsible for the prince's earlier actions and so is the same person as the prince) and where they do not apply we can conclude there is not (i.e., the person with the prince's body and cobbler's consciousness is not responsible for the prince's earlier actions and so is not the prince). It would thus seem that this view holds that the limits of the person should coincide with the limits of justified attributions of responsibility. But things are not quite so simple. There is an ambiguity in talk about whether a judgment of accountability "applies" in a certain case, and correspondingly different ways in which we can think about the connection between personal identity and practical concerns.

---

[8] Locke, *Human Understanding*, pp. 346–7.   [9] Locke, *Human Understanding*, p. 340.
[10] Locke, *Human Understanding*, p. 339.

To reveal this ambiguity we can, somewhat artificially, break judgments of accountability into two steps. First there is a basic question of attribution—when Mother comes into the living room to find Dick, Jane, and Spot next to the broken lamp there is an initial question of which one of them actually came into contact with the lamp and knocked it over. Suppose that Mother determines that the proximate cause of the lamp's being knocked over was contact with Jane's body. Another step is still needed, most people feel, before we judge that Jane should be held fully culpable. Perhaps Jane willfully pushed the lamp over during a tantrum, or was careless again despite several warnings, but perhaps she had one of her seizures or fainting spells and flailed into the lamp, or perhaps Spot ran in and knocked her over, or perhaps she is only eighteen months old and has no idea of the consequences of putting her hands on the lamp.

Most views of responsibility acknowledge a distance between an action's being attributable to a person in a basic, literal way and her being rightly held responsible, or punished, for it. We distinguish between basic attribution and strong practical relations in everyday life, and this distinction has also received a great deal of philosophical attention. In both philosophy and everyday speech, the distance between attribution and responsibility is often described in terms of personal identity. Although the action of breaking the lamp is attributable to Jane in, to use Harry Frankfurt's words, some "gross, literal" sense,[11] in some other sense it may not be. In the right circumstances we may want to say that it was not really *Jane* who acted here, but that the knocking over of the lamp was something that happened *through* her, a mere event in her history. This kind of view distinguishes between persons and human animals and does so on the basis of the actions for which someone is rightly praised or blamed, seeing only the latter as internal to the *person*, and to this extent it is superficially like Locke's view, which also uses such practical considerations to distinguish "person" from "man." It is crucial to recognize, however, that the distinction between humans and persons being made in these views of "true identity" is not the one Locke uses to distinguish between persons and humans, or to define personal identity.

There are two different ways in which we can think of personal identity in forensic terms. One is to set the limits of a single person as the limits within which questions about responsibility and self-interest are appropriately raised. Here the person is considered as a "forensic unit"—a suitable target about which particular forensic questions can be raised and judgments made. The other way to think of a person in forensic terms is to see the limits of a single person as set by the very

[11] Harry Frankfurt, "Identification and Externality," in *The Importance of What we Care About,* Cambridge: Cambridge University Press, 1988, p. 61.

LOCKE AND THE PSYCHOLOGICAL CONTINUITY THEORISTS 15

actions and experiences for which she is in fact held rightly accountable—those events in which questions of accountability are answered in the affirmative. I will call this the conception of *person* as "moral self." The forensic unit as I construe it here is envisioned as a kind of entity that can sometimes rightly be rewarded or punished for its actions;[12] the moral self, on the other hand, is construed more as a characterization of the true and fundamental moral nature of an entity.

My suggestion is that Locke's account of personal identity in terms of sameness of consciousness is an account of the identity conditions for the forensic unit, and not for the moral self. To see what I have in mind here we need to return to the distinction between questions about the basic, literal attribution of actions to an individual and a more full-blown kind of attribution that implies moral responsibility. Without reflection, it is easy to implicitly assume that basic, literal attribution of an action to a person is a metaphysical fact without any immediate practical significance, and that the fuller sense of attribution associated with the moral self is what speaks to our practical concerns. (We will consider views that take this position in the next chapter.) But, this move is too quick. Basic, literal attribution is not necessarily *irrelevant* to these practical judgments because it is an answer to the basic question of attribution that tells us where we can look to start asking questions about the more full-blown sense, the answers to which constitute these judgments. If Jane is the one who knocked the lamp over in the gross, literal sense, then it is to Jane that the more nuanced inquiries apply. Dick and Spot can be excused while Mother investigates Jane's circumstances further.[13] There thus seems to be a basic question of attribution that must be answered before the more nuanced one about full-blown attribution can profitably be raised.

The examples given so far imply that the more basic question is settled by sameness of human animal, while answers to the more nuanced question depend upon

---

[12] Here "entity" is not yet meant to have any particular ontological significance but just to mean something like "unified and identifiable locus." Locke does, of course, argue that sameness of person does not *require* sameness of basic substance, but it remains a matter of dispute whether he might nevertheless think that a person is a kind of substance (see, for instance, Alston and Bennett, "Locke on People and Substances," *The Philosophical Review* 97(1), January 1988, pp. 25–46; Jessica Gordon-Roth also provides a nice discussion of this debate in "A Reconsideration of Locke on Persons as Modes," unpublished doctoral thesis, and relevant material can be found in William Uzgalis, "Relative Identity and Locke's Principle of Individuation," *History of Philosophy Quarterly*, 7(3), 1990, pp.283–97 and Galen Strawson, *Locke on Personal Identity: Consciousness and Concernment*, Princeton: Princeton University Press, 2011). We will return later (and repeatedly) to the question of the sense in which a person should be considered an entity in the latter half of the book. Since our main interest here is in the broader issues and not in interpreting Locke, we can leave the sense of "entity" at work vague for now and fill it in later.

[13] There are, of course, complications—Jane may have knocked the lamp over because Dick pushed her or put her up to it. If so there are questions about the way in which Dick can be held responsible—indirectly—for breaking the lamp. For our purposes these can safely be ignored.

psychological factors. This is a common—and commonsensical—view of these matters (and one we will consider in detail later). What Mother needs to know first is whose body actually impacted the lamp, just as the police must first check to see if they have the right man using tools like fingerprints and DNA analysis before deciding whether the accused should be evaluated by a psychiatrist to determine whether he is competent to be held culpable. What I take Locke's view to be, however, is that it is this *first, basic* kind of attribution that must be defined in terms of sameness of consciousness.

In ordinary life, self-conscious subjects do not change bodies and if they did we would not be in a position to verify that they had. Human justice, Locke therefore allows, must be based on sameness of man. He insists, however, that sameness of human animal is not what really determines attribution even in the more basic sense, and that it is not the criterion of justice God would use.[14] Locke's idea thus need not be read as the view that we must define identity in such a way that judgments of identity are *coextensive with* judgments of moral responsibility, but can be read as the view that we must define it in such a way that it makes sense that it is *persons* about whom these judgments are made. The argument for a definition of personal identity in terms of sameness of consciousness rests not on the claim that the presence of sameness of consciousness settles the question of whether a person should be held culpable for the action of which he is conscious or whether it is rational for him to be egoistically concerned about some future experience, but rather on the fact that it must be in place before questions of responsibility can be coherently raised. Locke, as I am reading him, is thus proposing that sameness of consciousness and not of basic substance should play the role in determining responsibility that sameness of human animal is usually taken to do when, e.g., mother chooses *Jane* as the child to question or the District Attorney turns *this* individual over to the forensic psychiatrist to have his competency determined. In an ideal world the police would look not for the right man, but for the right person.

To get clear on the content of this claim we can consider two scenarios that are representative of two different types of hypothetical case that appear frequently in philosophical work on personal identity. The first is just a version of Locke's prince and cobbler case; the second is a kind of case that is used in defending views that draw a more direct connection between personal identity and moral responsibility, seeking to define the moral self.

[14] Locke, *Human Understanding*, pp. 343–4.

THE TRANSFER

Ben's cerebrum, carrying all of Ben's thoughts, memories, values, and desires, is transplanted into Jack's decerebrated skull, resulting in a person, J.B., who has Ben's psychology in (the bulk of) Jack's body. In reflecting on this case we are to consider whether J.B. is more properly charged with Ben's evil deeds or lauded for Jack's heroism; whether, in anticipation of the operation, it would be rational for Ben to arrange for J.B. to get his hands on Ben's resources; whether Jack, a sworn enemy of Ben, should endeavor to keep Jack's resources out of the hands of J.B., and so on.

THE TRANSFORMATION

After years of abuse and torment at the hands of her stepfather teenage Kate ultimately lashes out and kills him. Kate serves prison time for the crime, after which she undergoes intensive psychotherapy, joins support groups, and becomes a mature and well-grounded woman. She is remorseful about her past actions, but also understands them as a product of the abusive environment in which she was living. At age 28 she has resolved to put the past behind her and look constructively toward the future, seeking only to find ways to make the world a better place. We are to consider whether Kate, the woman before us now, engaging only in good deeds, has become a "different person" from teenage Kate, and is therefore not rightly held responsible for her crimes.

Putting these cases side by side we can see clearly the difference between basic questions of attribution and more nuanced ones. We can also see that the transfer case, although it relies on intuitions about practical judgments to define personal identity, relies on them in a very different way than the transformation case does, and is aimed most directly at answering questions of basic attribution rather than specific questions about moral culpability or rational self-interest.

These differences are especially clear if we offer a third case that merges the features of the other two. Imagine that it is Kate rather than Ben who has her cerebrum transplanted (some prison experiment, perhaps, that will get her sentence reduced) into Juliet's body. The result of this surgery is K.J., who is psychologically continuous with Kate and has no psychological continuity whatsoever with Juliet, although she has the bulk of Juliet's body. If our judgments are what Locke assumes they will be, we will judge that K.J. is the same person as Kate and not Juliet, and the fact that she is rightly held responsible for Kate's actions rather than Juliet's is part of what supports this judgment. What is crucial to appreciate here is that deciding this does not yet tell us whether K.J. should be held responsible for teenage Kate's crimes. If we were uncertain in the original transformation case about whether the reformed twenty-eight-year-old Kate in the original body is the same moral self who carried out the crime of teenage Kate, deciding that after the transplant K.J. is the same person as sixteen-year-old Kate rather than sixteen-year-old Juliet won't help us settle the question of whether K.J. should be held responsible. It does tell us that if *anyone* is to be held responsible it is K.J., and that in investigating the impact of the early abuse K.J. is the person to talk to. But it does not tell us whether the psychological changes now expressed in K.J.'s psyche are sufficient or of the right kind for us to say that she is no longer responsible for teenage Kate's crime. Our judgment of personal identity in the transfer case tells us where to look to answer these particular moral (or other practical) questions, but not how to answer them.

Cases involving vicissitudes of psychological life that potentially raise questions of personal identity are common in the literature. But now we can see an important distinction between cases that describe the wholesale loss or transfer of psychological life (a change of location), and cases that involve changes in the features of psychological life (a change of details). When the former ask for our moral judgments as an aid to defining identity they are looking to delimit the locus within which practical questions of this sort are appropriately raised; when the latter ask for these judgments they are attempting to settle the practical questions themselves.

All of the cases Locke provides are of the first sort, and this is one of the reasons I think his view is more naturally read as an account of the identity of the forensic unit than of the moral self. There are other reasons as well. It seems to me that there are three key elements in Locke's argument. One is consciousness (which is for him self-consciousness), one is concern for the quality of one's experience (the preference of pleasure to pain, happiness to misery), and the last is accountability (justified attributions of praise or blame). It is evident that for Locke wherever there is sameness of consciousness there is concern for the quality of consciousness, and so that someone must feel egoistic concern for whatever experiences are appropriated to her consciousness. It is not evident, however, that responsibility for an action follows immediately from the fact that it is in one's consciousness. There is thus room to read Locke as arguing that personal identity cannot be defined in terms of sameness of substance because the unity of a substance does not provide the right kind of continuity to tell us where to look when we want to ask questions about responsibility for a particular past action (a question which is at least conceptually prior to the question of whether the person who is the target of the inquiry really is responsible). The forensic unit must be a unit that links the quality of experience at the time of action to the quality of experience when its consequences occur, and that must be sameness of consciousness since only within the sphere of egoistic interest can particular judgments of responsibility be just. Crucially, however, on this understanding judgments of identity and judgments of moral responsibility need not coincide.

On this reading, then, Locke's claim that *person* is a forensic term is not a claim that the limits of a person are determined by those actions for which she is rightly held morally responsible or those experiences for which it is rational for her to feel egoistic concern.[15] It is rather the claim that the limits of a person are set by those actions for which she is (in the sense indicated above) *potentially* responsible or those experiences towards which it is *potentially* rational for her to experience egoistic concern. By looking at cases like the transfer case Locke concludes that contrary to what we might think before reflecting on the matter, it is not sameness of body, or even soul, that sets the limits of a forensic unit; it is rather sameness of consciousness.

I do not insist that this is exactly what Locke has in mind. Sometimes he does sound as if he thinks sameness of consciousness is sufficient for judgments of accountability (for instance when he says he is "as much concern'd, and as justly accountable, for *any* Action was done a thousand Years since, appropriated to me now by this self-consciousness, as I am, for what I did the last moment"[16]), or that he is speaking of the moral self (as, for instance, when he tells us that evidence for the fact that the mad man is a different person from the sober man can be found in the common expression that "one is *not himself,* or is *besides himself*" in such cases[17]). My claim is thus not that Locke himself is explicitly trying to draw the distinction I draw, only that the totality of his discussion is at the very least compatible with this reading and, I think, points toward it. It seems that what he means to define is a target of forensic concern which is a unity in something like the same way that a living thing is a unity, constituting a continuing whole through change of either material or immaterial substance by the participation of that matter in a single consciousness in a way analogous to the way an organism constitutes a whole out of changing matter through participation in a single life. He makes this analogy himself, telling us that "Different Substances, by the same consciousness (where they do partake in it) being united into one Person; as well as different Bodies, by the same Life are united into one Animal, whose *Identity* is preserved, in that change of Substances, by the unity of one continued life."[18]

---

[15] There is potential for some confusion here. The limits within which we can appropriately ask specific questions about moral responsibility on this view are set by the limits of what someone experiences, and so cares about. This may seem to imply that the forensic unit coincides exactly with the limits of egoistic concern, but not with the limits of assessment of moral responsibility. That is not so, however, given how I am using the term here. "Egoistic concern" as I am now understanding it is something more than the concern that automatically attends consciousness; it is more like rational prudence and so requires higher-order connections. Kate, for instance, may know that she will feel angry impulses in her future but want with all her might not to act on them since she knows that doing so will only lead to heartache. In the sense at issue here she does not have egoistic concern in acting on those impulses, even though failing to act on them may cause her some discomfort. In the transfer case, K.J. is the one who will experience the discomfort of these rages but she will also have no egoistic concern in seeing them carried out. We will see a different and more basic understanding of "egoistic concern" in our discussion of Jeff McMahan's work in Chapter 4.

[16] Locke, *Human Understanding*, p. 341, emphasis added.

[17] Locke, *Human Understanding*, p. 343.

[18] Locke, *Human Understanding*, p. 336.

Locke's view of personal identity sits, however, within a complicated meta-physical system, and ultimately must be interpreted within that broader context, and this is a project well outside of the scope of the present discussion. Whatever Locke's own position, the material he provides in presenting it is suggestive of the possibility of a distinction between questions about the identity of a forensic locus and questions about the identity of the moral self, and this distinction is important for our purposes because it gives us a model of a question of personal identity that is inherently tied to practical concerns without being automatically coincident with particular practical judgments. The question of the identity of the forensic locus is inherently bound to practical concerns because it is a requirement that the unity of this locus be defined in terms of a relation that makes it an appropriate unit within which to raise particular kinds of questions. For Locke, unity of mate-rial or immaterial substance does not carry any practical significance whatsoever, and so it cannot define the unity of such a locus. Sameness of consciousness, how-ever, by underlying the capacity to experience pleasure and pain, and to care about which one, is an appropriate relation to delimit the sphere within which particular questions of responsibility can be raised.

The importance of the notion of a forensic unit can be seen by looking at what happens in its absence. Present-day psychological continuity theorists of personal identity owe a great deal to Locke, but their views are also very different from his in important respects. Many of these differences are put in place to avoid difficulties with Locke's own view, and in many ways these views are much easier to defend than Locke's original account. But they also face a very serious and stubborn objec-tion which is, I argue, the result of not maintaining a clear distinction between questions about the identity of the moral self and questions about the identity of the forensic locus. Looking at these views and their susceptibility to this objection will help to further clarify the notion of a forensic unit and show its value.

1.2 Neo-Lockean Psychological Continuity Theorists

Over the last half-century or so there has been a great deal of interest in producing and defending psychological accounts of personal identity.[19] These accounts are like Locke's in holding that personal identity must be defined in terms of psychological

[19] See, e.g., David Lewis, "Survival and Identity," in *Philosophical Papers*, Vol. 1, New York: Oxford University Press, 1983; Derek Parfit, *Reasons and Persons*, Oxford: Clarendon Press, 1984; John Perry, "The Importance of Being Identical," in A. Rorty, ed., *The Identities of Persons*, Berkeley: University of California Press, 1976; Sydney Shoemaker, "Personal Identity: A Materialist's Account," in Sydney Shoemaker and Richard Swinburne, *Personal Identity*, Oxford: Blackwell, 1984.

relations rather than in terms of sameness of substance,[20] but they diverge from his account in many different ways. It should also be acknowledged at the outset that these views also differ from one another. There are, by now, dozens of versions of the psychological continuity theory and many able defenders of the general approach. For present purposes I am more interested in what the views have in common than in how they differ, particularly their understanding (sometimes implicit, sometimes explicit) of the relation between facts about personal identity and practical considerations which is, I argue, quite different from that found in Locke.

In the early development of this view, its defenders found themselves faced with the task of defining the precise nature of the psychological relation that constitutes personal identity. Locke calls it "sameness of consciousness," but this is a rather mysterious notion. However much we may (or may not) feel we have an intuitive grasp on this concept, it stands in need of further explication if it is to provide a developed account of personal identity. An obvious way of glossing sameness of consciousness is in terms of memory. To be conscious now of some past experience or action as my experience or action is just to remember it, one might think, and so Locke's view should be read as the view that a person at one time is the same as a person at some earlier time just in case the later person can remember actions or experiences of the first person from the inside. This reading has been and continues to be a standard interpretation of Locke's view. In 1785 Thomas Reid says, "Mr. Locke attributes to consciousness the conviction we have of our past actions, as if a man may now be conscious of what he did twenty years ago." Reid continues, "It is impossible to understand the meaning of this, unless by consciousness be meant memory, the only faculty by which we have an immediate knowledge of our past actions."[21] Almost 200 years later in John Perry's important 1975 anthology Locke's chapter on personal identity is reprinted in a section entitled "Versions of the Memory Theory."[22] I (among others) have argued elsewhere for a slightly different reading of Locke,[23] but for our current purposes what is important is not Locke's own view but the understanding of his view that has influenced the development of the personal identity debate.

A simple memory theory of this sort has a great many serious deficits, and critics have been quick to point them out. Psychological continuity theorists thus seek to take the basic sensibility behind this approach and alter it in ways that will

---

[20] Although, as we will see in a moment, some of them require the continued functioning of the same brain.

[21] Thomas Reid, "Of Mr. Locke's Account of our Personal Identity," in J. Perry, ed., *Personal Identity*, Berkeley: University of California Press, 1975, p. 115.

[22] John Perry, ed., *Personal Identity*, Berkeley: University of California Press, 1975, table of contents.

[23] Marya Schechtman, *The Constitution of Selves*, Ithaca: Cornell University Press, 1996, pp. 105–12.

avoid the objections to a memory approach and in general provide a stronger view. As they do so they do not distinguish between the identity of the forensic unit and the identity of the moral self. Of course Locke did not make this distinction explicitly either, but the two concepts are run together in psychological continuity theories—both in the content of the views and in the arguments for them—in a way that they are not in Locke. Largely this is the result of the fact that attempts to flesh out the notion of identity-constituting psychological connections increasingly make use of intuitions about what stands behind the applicability of particular practical judgments rather than about what stands behind the general appropriateness of judgments of a certain kind. As a result, it seems as if these accounts are meant to simultaneously define the conditions of the continuity of the moral self and the continuity of the forensic unit. This double duty puts very strong demands on the view, demands which, I will argue, it is ultimately unable to meet.

To see how this happens, it will be necessary to delve a bit into the details of these views. I will do this in stages. First I will look at early versions of the psychological continuity theory, showing how it is initially developed from the simple memory theory. In this discussion I will describe the ways in which this development blurs the distinction between questions about the identity of the forensic unit and questions about the identity of the moral self. Next I will show how this blurring has led to a serious difficulty for this approach.

1.2.1 Early development

There are three standard revisions to a simple memory theory that are found in the work of almost every psychological continuity theorist. The first seeks to avoid the objection that a memory criterion of personal identity is viciously circular. In order to have any plausibility at all, the objection runs, a memory criterion must distinguish between genuine memories and delusional, pseudo-memories. It seems, however, that the difference is just that genuine memories are of an experience the rememberer actually had, while delusions are apparent memories of an experience that was not had by the person seeming to remember. Since the memory criterion must define identity in terms of *real* memories, and real memories are defined in terms of personal identity, the criterion ultimately defines identity in terms of itself. To answer the circularity objection psychological continuity theorists introduce "quasi-memory." Quasi-memories are memory-like experiences that are caused in the appropriate way by the experiences of which they are memories. Ordinary memories of our own experiences are degenerate cases of quasi-memories, but nothing in the definition of quasi-memory presupposes personal identity.[24] The difference between delusional and non-delusional memory-like experiences is now defined in terms of the cause of the apparent memory rather than the identity of the quasi-rememberer with the experiencer of the episode quasi-remembered. Defending identity in terms of quasi-memory rather than memory, it is claimed, provides a criterion that can capture what seems relevant to the constitution of identity in actual memory without being circular.

The second change is in response to an objection famously raised by Thomas Reid, who charges the view with absurdity arising from the intransitivity of memory.[25] Reid describes a young man who is flogged for robbing an orchard, a later brave officer who remembers robbing the orchard and being flogged for it during a battle in which he captures an enemy standard, and an old general who remembers capturing the enemy standard as a young officer but has no recollection whatsoever of the incident in the orchard. According to the memory theory, Reid argues, the general is the same person as the young officer, and the young officer the same person as the boy, but the general and the boy are different people, and this is a *reductio* of the position. Reid's objection is answered by replacing the requirement of memory connection with the requirement of the ancestral of memory connection. When this is put together with the change just described this means that in order for a past experience or action to be mine I do not need to be able to directly quasi-remember it, but only to be able to quasi-remember a time at which I could quasi-remember a time…at which I could quasi-remember a time, at which I could quasi-remember the experience. I need only, that is, to be connected to the experience by an overlapping chain of quasi-memories.

The third change is the addition of connections other than autobiographical memory to the developing criterion of personal identity. There is no reason to believe that memory should be the *only* relation that contributes to identity, psychological continuity theorists argue; connections between intentions and the actions that carry them out, and between the different temporal portions of a persisting belief, value, desire, or trait should also be counted. In order to be the same as some past person, then, I need to have a significant number of psychological connections to her, but they need not all be memories. Indeed none of them needs to be.[26] The modifications made with respect to memory are applied also to the other kinds of psychological connections added to the criterion of personal identity.

---

[24] I have argued that in fact quasi-memory cannot make this distinction without presupposing identity ("Personhood and Personal Identity," *The Journal of Philosophy*, 87(2), February 1990, pp.71–92), but here I am primarily interested in exploring rather than evaluating the common views on these matters, so I limit myself to describing the standard use of quasi-memory.

[25] Reid, "Of Mr. Locke's Account," p. 114.

[26] Sydney Shoemaker, for instance, tells us that memory theorists may be right to judge amnesia to be death if amnesia is understood as a complete "brain zap"—the total destruction of all of the effects of the person's past "experience, learning, reasoning, deliberation and so on." Shoemaker suggests,

The memory theory attributed to Locke is thus transformed into the view that a person at time t_1 is the same person as a person at time t_2 just in case the person at t_2 is connected to the person at t_1 by an overlapping chain of quasi-psychological connections. A fully-developed version of this view can be found in Derek Parfit's famous criterion. Parfit first defines some terms. *Psychological connectedness* is the holding of particular direct psychological connections. *Strong psychological connectedness* is the holding of at least half the number of psychological connections that are present in the life of nearly all adult humans nearly every day. *Psychological continuity* is the holding of overlapping chains of *strong connectedness*. He then offers the following criterion of personal identity:

The Psychological Criterion: (1) There is *psychological continuity* if and only if there are overlapping chains of strong connectedness. X today is one and the same person as Y at some past time if and only if (2) X is psychologically continuous with Y, (3) this continuity has the right kind of cause, and (4) there does not exist a different person who is also psychologically continuous with Y. (5) Personal identity over time just consists in the holding of facts like (2) to (4).[27]

This criterion includes all of the features just described as well as a few additional elements—the definition of continuity in terms of strong connectedness and the requirement of uniqueness in clause (4). We will discuss the motivations for and significance of these additional elements shortly.

Looking more carefully at these changes we can see that they ultimately mix the conception of *person* as forensic unit and the conception of *person* as moral self and, in so doing, run together different roles for practical concerns in determining the boundaries of personal identity. Consider first the use of quasi-memory. There are many things to be said about the legitimacy and application of this concept but my interest here is in the question of why we should think that the cause of a psychological connection should contribute to its ability to constitute personal identity. Quasi-memory is, after all, not only supposed to make the view non-circular, but to do so in a way that makes it a plausible criterion of personal identity. If

---

however, that amnesia need not be thought of as such a radical psychological transformation. "A person's personality, character, tastes, interests, and so on are," he says, "the product (at least in part) of his past experience, and it is not obvious that the loss of all memories would necessarily involve the loss of all such traits as these." A person might be able to remember nothing of her past, Shoemaker suggests, and yet remain psychologically similar along all other dimensions. In such a case, he says, judgments of survival are less clear. If such traits of personality could survive, "such a loss of memory would not necessarily amount to a total brain zap; and then it becomes more plausible to suppose that such a loss of memory is something a person could survive—in which case the memory theory. . . is false." Shoemaker, "A Materialist's Account," pp. 87–8.

[27]   Derek Parfit, *Reasons and Persons*, pp. 206–7.

merely having a memory-like experience is not enough to constitute identity we need to know how the requirement of appropriate cause helps.

This depends, of course, on how "appropriate cause" is understood. This requirement is left surprisingly vague. In most (but, as we will see, not all) views, it is generally described as the "normal physiological cause." Our question, then, is why being caused by the ordinary physiological mechanisms should make a memory-experience more suitable as part of a criterion of personal identity.[28] Since these views are fueled by the same intuitions as Locke's, the mere fact that the usual cause involves the persistence of a single physical substance (the brain) will not do as an answer to this question. Locke's point is precisely that sameness of substance cannot do that kind of work and this intuition is precisely the impetus for offering a relational view of personal identity rather than one that defines it in terms of continuity of substance. If the addition of the requirement of appropriate cause is going to help shore up Locke's insight, it will need to do so by guaranteeing that the proper kind of psychological connection is in place. Looking at the contexts in which this requirement is invoked by psychological continuity theorists we will see that the notion of "proper psychological connection" here seems sometimes to mean sameness of self-conscious subject (and so forensic unit) and sometimes to mean sameness of moral self.

For an example of the former kind of context we can look to the role the requirement of quasi-memory plays in explaining different intuitive reactions to the case of teleportation as opposed to the case of a brain transplant. These are both hypothetical cases which separate in thought the continuity of psychological life from biological continuity, and they are meant to support a psychological approach to identity insofar as our judgment is that the person goes with the psychological life rather than with the biological life. In the former case a person's body is scanned and recreated elsewhere out of new matter after the original body is destroyed; in the latter a person's brain, carrying with it all of the person's psychological life, is transplanted into a new body. As it turns out, many more people are comfortable with the conclusion that a person would survive a brain transplant than with the conclusion that she would survive teleportation, despite the stipulation that the product in both cases has contents of consciousness qualitatively identical to those

---

[28] Parfit in fact argues that it does not, and although he introduces and describes the requirement of appropriate cause (I will in fact make use of his descriptions in the next few paragraphs) he ultimately decides that in fact *any* cause is the right cause (Parfit, *Reasons and Persons*, pp. 207–9)—which is essentially to do away with the requirement altogether. He is very much in the minority in this regard, however, and his reconstruction of the motivations for requiring normal physiological cause is representative of the views of many psychological continuity theorists. We will discuss Parfit's version of the view toward the end of the chapter. Another exception here is Sydney Shoemaker, who offers a functionalist account of appropriate cause. See Sydney Shoemaker, "A Materialist's Account," pp. 67–132.

of the original person. Although some psychological theorists reject the intuition that these two cases are relevantly different,[29] many also endorse it and it is this kind of intuition that frequently stands behind the requirement that psychological continuity must have its normal cause if it is to be identity-constituting. In this context the relevant concern is with whether the same experiencing subject will continue and hence whether there is really continuity of consciousness.

Presumably the intuition that brain transplants preserve identity while teleportation does not is related to the fear that in teleportation one first-person point of view is extinguished and a new, qualitatively identical one, created. Psychological continuity with normal physiological cause is generated by the mechanism that reliably produces a continuing experiencing subject in everyday life, but the mere stipulation that there is qualitative sameness of mental states of the sort found in teleportation does not seem to guarantee this kind of continuity. I will not try to resolve the question of whether there is really a relevant difference between brain transplant and teleportation cases or, if so, whether requiring normal physiological cause can capture its import (although I will say somewhat more about this matter in a few moments). The significance of these observations for present purposes is that those who do see a difference between these two cases see a difference that concerns sameness of self-conscious subject, which they feel confident is present in the one case but worry is absent in the other. Insofar as the causal requirement is taken to play a role in constituting personal identity in this context, it does so by impacting the continuity of self-consciousness, and so of the forensic unit.

This is not, however, the only context in which the causal requirement is invoked. Explaining the rationale behind such a requirement, for instance, Parfit points out that "some changes of character are deliberately brought about; others are the natural consequence of growing older; others are the natural response to certain kinds of experience. But there would not be continuity of character if radical and unwanted changes were produced by abnormal interference, such as direct tampering with the brain."[30] Here we are looking not at the causes of psychological *continuity*, but rather at the causes of psychological *change*, and we are told that a causal requirement is needed to make sure that these changes are brought about in a way that guarantees "continuity of character," where this kind of continuity is connected with deliberation and responding appropriately to the environment. Even though tampering with the brain is mentioned here, it seems clear that what is really at issue is not so much the physiological cause of change but the psychological cause.

---

[29]   Notably Parfit, as we will see in the next section (see note 28 above).
[30]   Parfit, *Reasons and Persons*, p. 207.

The concerns being invoked in this context are not about the continuation of the same self-conscious subject. There is no suggestion at all that these unwanted changes interfere with the flow of conscious awareness. This is a transformation case and not a transfer case. The need for appropriate cause in this instance is thus linked to concerns about preserving the sameness of the moral self, and insofar as it is used to help set the limits of identity, sees those limits as coextensive with our practical judgments. Think, for instance, of the case of Kate. At her original trial her attorney might argue that she should not be held responsible for the murder because she was driven mad by abuse. He might even argue that the abuse caused a head injury that interfered with her impulse control. Quite independent of any brain transplants or disruptions in continuity of consciousness these considerations might be used to argue that Kate was "not herself" when she committed the murder and so that these should not be considered truly her actions. These are important considerations but, as we discussed in the last section, they are aimed at a different question than those that arise when considering teleportation. The requirement of appropriate cause is thus used in at least two different ways. Sometimes it seeks to guarantee the identity of the moral self and capture the limits of our particular moral judgments, while at other times it seeks to guarantee the unity of the self-conscious subject which is the appropriate locus about which such judgments are made.

The mixing of the two roles for practical judgments appears in a somewhat simpler form in the change from a requirement of direct memory connections to the requirement of overlapping chains of memory connection. Whatever the ultimate difficulties of the memory theory attributed to Locke, we can understand why someone might think that direct memory connections could constitute the continuity of a self-conscious subject. Memories of past experiences provide present consciousness with direct access to past experiences, one might argue, making the current subject simultaneously aware of the present and the past, and of her existence at both times. Autobiographical memories are one of the chief vehicles through which we see ourselves as the same experiencing subjects at different times and places, and so a memory theory might be seen to be at least aimed at defining sameness of self-conscious subject (and hence, on a Lockean view, forensic unit).

The ancestral of memory connection, however, offers no such access to consciousness at other times. By supposition the old general in Reid's example has lost any awareness of the experiences of the young boy beyond the possibility of retrieval. Overlapping chains of memory connections thus do not seem to contribute in any clear way to sameness of consciousness. What they do support is stability of character and behavior, which is more immediately relevant to questions of moral identity. Defining personal identity in terms of direct connections thus seems appropriate if we are thinking of the continuation of the person as a forensic unit, while defining personal identity in terms of overlapping chains of connections seems more appropriate if our focus is on persons as moral selves.

The mixture of considerations relevant to defining the forensic unit and relations relevant to defining the moral self is perhaps clearest in the addition of psychological connections besides memory to psychological identity criteria. As we have just discussed we can see some reason to think that memory connections might be relevant to the identity of a forensic unit because of the role they might be thought to play in constituting sameness of self-conscious subject. It is by no means obvious that the other kinds of connections psychological continuity theorists add to their identity criteria are directly relevant at all to sameness of forensic unit, however. They are once again the kinds of connections that lead to stability of personality or character. Of course, this kind of stability is often described as being connected to "personal identity" but when it is it is the identity of the moral self and not of the forensic unit that is being invoked. These kinds of connections are precisely the kinds that are lacking when we wonder, for instance, whether it is right to hold Kate responsible for her teenage crimes, or the jailhouse convert for her vicious actions.[31]

Memory connections thus seem to contribute (or can be taken to contribute) directly to the identity of persons as forensic units, while the other connections added by neo-Lockean psychological continuity theories seem to contribute more to the identity of persons as moral selves. Here, too, psychological continuity theorists do not distinguish between these two kinds of connections, implying that both contribute to personal identity in the same way. The general approach is nicely illustrated in David Lewis's imaginary case of Methuselah-like people who live for thousands of years. Lewis asks us to imagine the life of one such person to be "punctuated by frequent amnesias, brainwashings, psychoanalyses, conversions, and what not, each of which is almost (but not quite) enough to turn him into a different person."[32] Here it is implied that the kinds of changes brought about by amnesia affect identity in the same way as those that change character in one way or another (psychoanalyses and conversions) or interfere with agency (brainwashing). This equation of the contributions of memory and other kinds of psychological connections is also seen in Parfit's defense of the addition of non-memory connections to his account of personal identity: "We shall then claim, what Locke

---

[31] David Velleman makes a point roughly like this in "Self to Self," *The Philosophical Review*, 105 (1), January 1996, pp. 39–76.
[32] Lewis, *Philosophical Papers*, p. 66.

denied, that a person can continue to exist even if he suffers from complete amnesia. I would rather suffer amnesia than have surgery that would give me a quite different and obnoxious character."[33] Here the losses associated with amnesia and those associated with an unwanted change in character are seen as equivalent so far as identity is concerned.

The failure of psychological continuity theorists to distinguish considerations related to questions about the identity of a forensic unit from those related to questions about the moral self can be seen not only in the details of their views, but also in the arguments used to support them. As I have said, psychological continuity theorists, like Locke, use hypothetical cases to defend their accounts. The range of cases they employ is, however, much broader than in Locke's own discussion. Consider two cases that appear in Parfit's development of his version of the psychological continuity theory. The first is Teletransportation, which is just the kind of teleportation described earlier (in which a person's brain and body are scanned and an exact replica built out of new matter as the original brain and body are destroyed). The other is the case of the Nineteenth-Century Russian. In this case a young Russian nobleman who has a great deal of sympathy for the peasants knows that he will someday inherit land. He plans to give the land to the peasants, but fears that wealth will corrupt him. For this reason he draws up a legal document that gives the land directly to the peasants, a document that can be revoked only with his wife's permission. (One wonders why he needed such a clause if he is so sure he wants to give the land to the peasants, but that is a question for another day.) He tells her not to give that permission, no matter how much he begs, explaining "I regard my ideals as essential to me. If I lose these ideals, I want you to think that I cease to exist. I want you to regard your husband then, not as me, the man who asks you for this promise, but only as his corrupted later self." The question here is about how the wife best honors the wishes of the man she married should the anticipated changes occur.[34]

Although Parfit uses these cases for somewhat different purposes, they both contribute to the definition and defense of his psychological account of personal identity, and they are certainly not taken to apply to different questions of personal identity. Looking at these cases in light of the previous discussion, however, we can see that they do not necessarily address the same question. As we discussed earlier, Teletransportation and related cases in which psychology is transferred wholesale raise questions about the identity of forensic units, while cases that describe

---

radical or unwanted changes in psychological make-up, like the case of the Nineteenth-Century Russian, raise questions about the identity of moral selves.

The observations assembled in this section show that there is considerable difference between Locke's original theory and psychological continuity theories with respect to how they use practical concerns in defining personal identity. On Locke's account it is at least possible to draw a distinction between the question of the identity of the forensic unit and the question of the identity of the moral self. This possibility is present because Locke talks about the sameness of consciousness as if "a consciousness" is a unit. This allows us to think first about whether awareness of a particular action is in a consciousness or not and then, if it is, to investigate particular connections to other elements also within that consciousness. Correspondingly, the imaginary cases he uses always involve this consciousness moving as a unit from one body or soul to another. In psychological continuity theories, however, the relation that defines identity is made up from the beginning of particular relations among individual states and this blurs the distinction between what is tested for in transfer cases and transformation cases. We no longer have a simple question about whether a particular event is or is not one of which someone is conscious, but rather a more complex question about her exact relation to that event.

The mixing of these two types of practical considerations is, of course, not necessarily a defect. Perhaps psychological continuity theories are accounts of *both* forensic units and moral selves, and perhaps the insight being expressed is that these two are, in the end, one and the same. This is, of course, a position one might take, but as we will see, failure to make this distinction leads to some fairly serious problems.

1.2.2 *Reductionism and what matters*

Before turning to the difficulties psychological continuity theorists face as a result of blurring the line between the identity of the forensic unit and the identity of the moral self it will be helpful to focus on one more feature of these views that has important implications for questions concerning the relation between personal identity and practical considerations. This is the fact that psychological continuity theories entail a *reductionist* view of personal identity. To be a reductionist about personal identity is, as Parfit explains, to hold:

(1) that the fact of a person's identity over time just consists in the holding of certain more particular facts, and

(2) that these facts can be described without either presupposing the identity of this person, or explicitly claiming that the experiences in this person's life are

had by this person, or even explicitly claiming that this person exists. These facts can be described in an *impersonal* way.[35]

In the case of the psychological continuity theory, the "certain more particular facts" are the existence of a sufficient number of psychological connections and/or continuity (unique and appropriately caused). There is no further fact about identity on the reductionist approach; talk of "identity" is just a way of describing the holding of these more basic connections.

A consequence of a reductionist view about identity in general is that sometimes questions about whether something has continued can be "empty." Empty questions are questions that cannot be given a decisive answer, not for lack of pertinent information, but simply because there is no fact of the matter. When a question is empty we know everything there is to know about the state of affairs and this does not provide decisive reasons to judge one way or the other. At this point the only question that remains is how we wish to describe the situation. To explicate this notion Parfit gives the example of a club. Suppose at some point in a club's history most members cease to attend but a few continue meeting. They convene in a different location, change the procedures a bit, add new members, and take up new topics. We might ask if the current club is the same as the original or whether the original club has disbanded and some of its members started a new and distinct club. It is not really clear how we could give a definitive answer to this question— not because there is something we do not know, but because the question is, Parfit says, an empty one. Affirming and denying that the current club is the same as the original are just two different ways of describing the same state of affairs. What we are arguing about is word choice, not a deep metaphysical fact.[36]

Since the psychological continuity theory is a reductionist account of personal identity, it must allow that questions of personal identity can be similarly empty. This is because psychological connectedness, the relation which constitutes identity according to this view, can hold to almost any degree. Where there are a large number of psychological connections between a person at time t_1 and a person at time t_2, as in paradigmatic cases of identity, we get a clear verdict of identity; where there are no connections or only a very few, the psychological continuity theory renders a clear verdict of lack of identity. In the middle ranges, however, we are in the same situation with respect to a judgment of personal identity that we were in with respect to our judgment about the identity of the club in the earlier example; we know what the situation is, but it is not clear how we should describe it.

---

[35] Parfit, *Reasons and Persons*, p. 210.   [36] Parfit, *Reasons and Persons*, p. 213.

In fact, most psychological continuity theories do render clear judgments about identity in each case, but this does not mean that the question of identity is not an empty one. Empty questions can be given definitive answers; their emptiness consists in the fact that that these answers are not dictated by facts about the world but rather by decisions about how to describe these facts. Since identity as a logical concept requires determinacy, psychological theorists produce a determinate answer by fiat. We see this in Parfit's use of strong connectedness and psychological continuity. Although psychological connectedness itself can hold to almost any degree, strong connectedness and psychological continuity are all-or-nothing. But this determinacy is achieved by setting a cut-off so that when there are 50% of the average number of connections (or overlapping chains of such) we have identity and where there is one fewer than 50% anywhere in the chain we do not. This means that in the middle ranges the difference between being the same person and not being the same person can turn on something extremely trivial.

Parfit is happy to acknowledge that this cut-off is arbitrary and that its arbitrariness, once recognized, will seem to most people a dire flaw in the psychological continuity theory. It is not plausible to most people that the existence of one psychological connection more or less could make the difference between identity and non-identity with some future person, which is, after all, the difference between life and death. To many, moreover, it seems almost incoherent to say that there are cases where there is no real fact of the matter about our identities. "When it is applied to ourselves," Parfit says, "this Reductionist claim is hard to believe.... most of us are inclined to believe that, in any conceivable case, the question 'Am I about to die?' must have an answer. And we are inclined to believe that this answer must be either, and quite simply, Yes or No."[37] He argues that it is, nevertheless, a consequence of reductionism, and so of the psychological continuity theory, that to the extent that we are able to give simple yes or no answers to questions about our identity in every case it is only because we have made arbitrary decisions about how to describe things, and this is a counterintuitive result we must just accept. He thinks, however, that the implausibility of a reductionist view of persons can be mitigated with the proper analysis.

One of the reasons that we find it so difficult to believe that there might not be a clear-cut answer to questions of our survival is because it is of the utmost importance to us. A great deal hangs on whether one will continue into the future or cease to exist, so it seems obviously false that this fact might be determined by one psychological connection more or less; one connection cannot carry all of that significance. Reductionism can be made more acceptable, Parfit suggests, if

---

[37] Parfit, *Reasons and Persons*, p. 214.

we come to recognize that our thinking about the importance of identity is misguided. Perhaps identity is important to us, he says, but not because it is *identity*; it is important because it is a species of psychological connectedness and continuity (relation R). If anything is important to us (and the need for this qualification will be clear in a moment) it is R. Since identity always entails a relatively high amount of R, it is important, but the importance of identity derives completely or almost completely from the fact that it is a species of relation R. In mid-range cases of psychological connectedness we have a certain amount of the relation that carries this significance, and one connection more or less is a small increment that does not, in the ordinary course of events, make much of a difference in what matters to us about our continued existence. So, although according to psychological continuity theorists the increment of one connection can make the difference between identity and non-identity, since this difference is not in itself the one that really matters to us, this fact is not problematic. A threshold is crossed at the 50% mark, but it is a threshold that determines nothing more than what name we give to a specific degree of the relation we care about. Identity, Parfit famously says, is not "what matters in survival."

He makes this same case very forcefully, and to great effect, in his analysis of a fission case, which he calls "My Division." Parfit imagines a brain with complete redundancy in the hemispheres being split and transplanted into two empty skulls, resulting in two people, each of whom is psychologically continuous with the original person. If just one of the people resulting from this surgery existed we would say (assuming a commitment to the psychological continuity theory) that the original person survived in him, since there would be complete psychological continuity caused by continued functioning of the same brain. But, Parfit argues, the existence of a second such person, as happens in fission, can hardly result in the death of the first. If everything we are looking for in survival would hold between a unique survivor and the original person (if, e.g., we transplanted only one hemisphere and let the other rot) adding a second person cannot undo this. The survivors might not even know of one another's existence or interact in any way, and it seems absurd to say that the existence of a second survivor half a world away, with whom I never interact, could make the difference between my surviving an operation and failing to survive it. Obviously, Parfit says, in the case as described each fission descendant possesses what we are hoping for in survival.[38]

It is problematic, however, to say that both of these descendants are *identical* to the original person, since it is highly implausible to claim that they are identical

---

[38] Although he does allow that it would be a minor inconvenience; Parfit, *Reasons and Persons*, p. 263. We will discuss the fission case and this aspect of Parfit's analysis of it in greater detail in Chapter 6.

to one another. It is equally problematic to say that either descendant is uniquely identical to the original person, since they bear exactly the same relation to him. Parfit thus says that *identity* is present only when psychological continuity holds uniquely between a person at one time and a person at another (this is the reason for the uniqueness clause in his criterion). He argues, however, that while uniqueness may have some small amount of practical importance it does not contribute significantly to the fundamental practical relations that we believe hold throughout the life of a single person. This significance can, after all, be doubly present in the fission case. Once again, then, we have the conclusion that identity itself is not what is really important; the practical significance we attribute to identity inheres instead in the psychological relations in terms of which identity is defined, which are present in each of the fission descendants even though neither is identical to the original person.

While the claim that identity is not what matters in survival is by no means uncontroversial, it has been very widely accepted and the focus of those giving psychological accounts of identity has tended more toward a general discussion of what matters. It may seem as if this trend speaks against my suggestion that psychological accounts run together considerations concerning the identity of the forensic unit and the identity of the moral self. Here a very explicit and clean division is made between facts about identity and the practical considerations that are connected with resolving specific practical questions. The distinction drawn here, however, does not actually separate the forensic unit from the moral self, but collapses them even further into one another. Talk of "identity" on this analysis is nothing other than shorthand for describing a particular configuration of individual psychological connections (where there are sufficient numbers, or overlapping chains of sufficient numbers, and this holds uniquely). There is no separate relation of identity which defines a more basic unity about which practical questions are raised. The identity of an individual person is made up of exactly the same relations we look to to answer specific practical questions. The very idea of a real unity is undermined by reductionism. On a reductionist account there can be no deep, metaphysical fact about whether someone is or is not the same person, all the facts that matter are determined by the individual connections. It is, as I will now argue, this very feature of the psychological continuity theory that leaves it open to what has been one of the most serious objections it has faced.

1.2.3 The extreme claim

Perhaps the most persistent and intractable objection raised against psychological continuity theories is the complaint that they cannot explain the practical

importance we attribute to personal identity.[39] If identity is defined as these theorists define it, the objection goes, it does not make sense to hold people responsible for their past actions, and there is no reason for a person to care about her
own future well-being in a different way than she cares about the well-being of
others. It is surprising that this, of all objections, should be the one that plagues
these theories. I have been arguing that they run together considerations relevant
to questions about the identity of the moral self and those relevant to the identity
of the forensic unit. It would thus seem as if these views should be especially well
placed to capture a connection between personal identity and particular practical
judgments, and yet this is arguably what causes them the most trouble. My claim is
that this happens because, as my reading of Locke suggests, individual judgments
about responsibility and like concerns depend upon the existence of a more basic
forensic unit for their legitimacy. Reductionist psychological continuity theories
do away with any kind of meaningful forensic unit, and so cannot provide that
legitimacy. Relations that would justify the ascription of moral responsibility if
they held within a forensic unit are not by themselves enough for such an ascription if the existence of such a unit is not presupposed. To see that this is so we need
to look in more detail at this objection, which Parfit has called "the extreme claim."

It is important first of all to be clear that the content of this claim is not the same
as the content of the claim that what matters in survival is not identity. This latter
claim, as described in the previous section, says that identity *per se* is not what matters; rather it is psychological continuity and connectedness. Those who accept
this slogan can still explain why judgments of personal identity carry practical significance; they do so because identity necessarily involves relation R and relation
R carries this significance. The extreme claim rejects the last part of this reasoning,
denying that psychological continuity and connectedness as defined in these theories are important in the way that personal identity is important. Since personal
identity *is* important, the argument for the extreme claim goes, something must be
wrong with the way psychological continuity theorists define it.

The argument that relation R does not carry the requisite significance rests on
the observation that all it provides is formal relations between different moments
of consciousness that amount roughly to a requirement of similarity of psychological makeup. Although we have a detailed version of the psychological continuity
theory in hand, for these purposes it is helpful to recall the more impressionistic
notion of psychological continuity that stands behind this approach. This is nicely

---

[39] In fact, this argument is also raised against Locke's view when it is read as a straight memory
theory. It does not, however, apply to the reading of Locke I have given. I will return to this point in a
moment (see note 42).

expressed by David Lewis when he says the intuition that he wants to capture in his psychological view is the following: "I find what I mostly want in wanting survival is that my mental life should flow on. My present experiences, thoughts, beliefs, desires, and traits of character should have appropriate future successors.... These successive states should be interconnected in two ways. First, by bonds of similarity. Second, by bonds of lawful causal dependence."[40] What this describes is a kind of stability in the contents of consciousness together with a mechanism of transition from one moment to the next. The moments of consciousness themselves, however, remain distinct from one another, and what he describes is more like a Humean bundle than a real unity. Those who argue against the psychological approach via the extreme claim argue that such formal relations between distinct moments of consciousness cannot provide the right kind of connection to make sense of our forensic practices. My relation to my future self, on this view, is like my relation to someone very like me psychologically, a kind of super psychological twin. Just as my psychological likeness to a twin does not make it legitimate to hold me responsible for her actions, the argument goes, psychological continuity and connectedness does not make it legitimate to hold me responsible for the actions of my past self if that is all that her being me amounts to.

Once again Parfit is keenly aware of this worry and addresses it at great length. He crystallizes the intuition behind it by offering a scenario he calls the "Branch Line Case." In this case someone walks into the Teletransporter to travel to Mars and, seemingly, nothing happens. The protagonist learns that this is a new machine which has built a replica on Mars as usual, but without destroying the original body. Alas, it turns out that the kinks are not worked out and the original body has been mortally damaged. The person on Earth has only a few days to live. This person is able to speak to the replica on Mars, and is assured that there are an overwhelming number of psychological connections, and so that there will be plenty of psychological continuity between himself now and the Mars replica in the future. Parfit acknowledges that this is not going to seem like survival to the dying individual on Earth.[41] This suggests that there is a deep connection between the person who steps into the Teletransportation booth on Earth and the dying Earthling that does not exist between that person and the replica on Mars, and that absent this deeper connection there does not seem to be a basis for the person on Earth to feel egoistic concern for the future of the replica, nor for the replica to be held responsible for what the original traveler has done.

---

[40] Lewis, *Philosophical Papers*, p. 17.   [41] Parfit, *Reasons and Persons*, p. 201.

It might seem that what is missing is physical continuity between the two—in particular sameness of brain—and so that the Branch Line Case simply shows that psychological continuity theories do need to insist that psychological continuity be caused by the continued functioning of the same brain if they are to be viable. As I mentioned earlier, there is far more consensus that brain transplants preserve identity than that teleportation does, and many psychological continuity theories do include this requirement. It is not clear, however, that this will really do the trick. Psychological theories get their main support, after all, from the kinds of intuitions generated in Locke's arguments, and these suggest that sameness of substance is not only insufficient for supporting the forensic practices associated with personhood but is in itself irrelevant. There must thus be a phenomenological difference between ordinary psychological continuity and one's relation to a replica if we are to explain why one is important and the other not—the mere presence of the same grey matter (which is itself changing over time) does not explain why someone is rightly held accountable for past actions or is rational to experience egoistic care about the future in the one case but not in the other.

It might, of course, be that psychological continuity generated by the same brain is in fact phenomenologically different from that which is not, and so that there really is a deep unity of consciousness in cases involving the same brain that is not present in cases of replication. I suspect that some presumption that this is so is what drives the intuitive response to these cases. But psychological continuity theorists who require the normal physiological cause of that continuity do not tell us what that phenomenological difference amounts to, or provide any argument that it will necessarily be absent in replication. Absent such an argument we still have no real answer to the objection from the extreme claim. When we are asking why it is just to hold someone now responsible for some past action Locke has a response: it is because there is a single experiencing subject who is involved in the execution of the action and will experience its consequences.[42] It is not evident, however, that this either requires or is guaranteed by sameness of brain. If, for instance, a vicious criminal were able to get a perfectly-functioning prosthetic cerebrum to replace the diseased one he possessed when planning his crimes (if we are willing to imagine teletransportation why not?) we would not be inclined to let him off the hook just because silicon chips rather than neurons are involved in generating the experienced pain of punishment.

Those who think a requirement of sameness of brain will resolve these difficulties can, of course, respond to these observations in many ways. I will not pursue

---

[42] It is for this reason that I think Locke avoids the argument from the extreme claim on my reading (see note 39 above).

these arguments any further here, as they will take us too far afield. I hope at least to have shown, however, that this strategy for resolving the problems of the extreme claim gets quickly into complicated and speculative waters, and that while it may seem that a requirement of sameness of brain will provide a tidy resolution to this problem it is far from obvious that it actually does. In fact, this strategy seems only to erode the original appeal of a psychological approach still further by relying on sameness of substance to do work that it is inherently unsuited to do according to the motivating arguments for the view.

There are, of course, ways in which psychological continuity theorists can and do respond to the argument from the extreme claim that do not rely on sameness of substance. One involves an argument that psychological continuity as defined in these theories in fact does provide a basis for practical judgments even though it is just a matter of formal relations between distinct moments of conscious-ness. Most versions of this strategy focus on prudential concern. John Perry, for instance, argues that what we are most immediately concerned about are our pro-jects, and that because our future selves are so much like us, they are more likely than anyone else to carry out those projects.[43] Parfit describes a similar possibility, which he calls the "moderate claim."[44] Ever the radical, however, Parfit also offers, and arguably favors, a more drastic solution, which is to take the extreme claim not as a *reductio* of the psychological approach, but as an interesting, if counter-intuitive, result. This is an extremely clear-headed and fruitful reply, and so worth discussing in some detail.

The practical importance of identity, Parfit suggests, may be not nearly as great as we think it is. In the end there is no plausible alternative to a reductionist view of personal identity, and such a view does in fact imply that the unity within a single life is not all that significant and that we are not connected to other times in our own lives in any more profound way than we are connected to the lives of others. The right response to the extreme claim is thus not to argue that psychological relations are capable of producing the deep connection within our lives that we assume is implied by identity; it is rather to accept that the shallow relation found in psychological continuity is what there really is. Parfit allows that the relation a person would have to her teleported replica does not bear the practical signifi-cance we take identity to carry in our own lives, but argues that this is not because the connection is relevantly different in the two cases; it is rather because we are mistaken about the strength of the ordinary connection. On this view it is not that

43 John Perry, "The Importance of Being Identical."
44 Parfit, *Reasons and Persons*, pp. 311–12.

having a replica is as good as ordinary survival, but that *"ordinary survival is about as bad as being destroyed and having a Replica."*[45]

Parfit finds this realization liberating, mitigating his fear of death and future suffering,[46] although he knows many will find it repellent and verging on incoherence. Although I disagree with Parfit's conclusion (and will explain later why I think we may safely reject it), my immediate interest is in understanding what the argument from the extreme claim reveals about the picture of the relation between personal identity and practical concerns found in the psychological continuity theory. While his arguments are not conclusive, I think there is something importantly right in Parfit's acceptance of the fact that the relations of psychological continuity and connectedness cannot on their own legitimate our forensic practices. What Parfit sees is the need to have an idea of the identity of a forensic unit which is distinct from the moral self if we are to explain the legitimacy of practices like that of assigning moral responsibility, and that the reductionist psychological continuity theory offers no such thing.

Parfit seems to assume further that any account of identity that could potentially explain its forensic significance will need to be reductionist in nature, and so that there simply is no way to provide an account that can make identity the deep fact that we take it to be. My alternate reading of Locke challenges this assumption. The relation that defines a forensic unit on this reading of Locke is not defined as something made up of individual psychological connections but as a prior and more fundamental unity. On this reading the relation of sameness of consciousness must conform to the logical structure of an identity relation in a way that relation R does not. A given experience either is or is not part of a particular consciousness.[47] A consciousness is thus a unit just as much as an organism or soul is a unit, and of these three types of units, Locke argues, it is the only one which is an appropriate target for particular forensic questions and concerns.

A definition of personal identity in terms of individual connections (even if we add further constraints about the number and uniqueness and cause of those connections) is necessarily reductionist, and can provide a determinate unity only artificially through the use of devices like strong connectedness and

---

[45]   Parfit, *Reasons and Persons*, p. 280.

[46]   Parfit, *Reasons and Persons*, p. 281–2.

[47]   In earlier work (Schechtman, *The Constitution of Selves*), I actually claim that appropriation into a consciousness can be a matter of degree. In some sense I think this is compatible with what I say here, but the explanation is a complicated one. I will return to this issue in Chapter 4, where I will explain in more detail how and why I deviate from some of my earlier views.

non-branching clauses. When we are addressing more metaphorical questions of personal identity, such as questions about the identity of the moral self, a reductionist approach seems well-suited to the task at hand. It may be that there are degrees of individual responsibility for an action or degrees to which we want to say that it is truly my own, and that we can accept that there will be circumstances in which questions of this sort will have no determinate answer. Kate's transformation may be an example of such a case. As we struggle to say whether the violent crimes are truly hers we may be tempted to say that to some degree they are and to some degree they are not. The question of who is the subject of these qualified attributions seems, however, to require a more determinate kind of answer, and so the Lockean view as I have described it is not a reductionist view and does not require us to give up on the importance of identity.

For this way of resisting Parfit's analysis to work, however, we need Locke's non-reductionist account of the forensic locus to be viable. Parfit's acceptance of the extreme claim is, I think, based on the conclusion that in fact it is not. The forensic unit is to be defined on this view in terms of a deep unity of consciousness which is all-or-nothing and supports our forensic practices. To make this view work we thus need to say what constitutes this unity of consciousness. This is where psychological continuity theories came in. Parfit's argument is that although we may pre-reflectively assume that there is such a thing as a deeply unified consciousness, on closer inspection this certainty dissolves and what we assumed is revealed to be incoherent. If "sameness of consciousness" is not to be defined in terms of certain kinds and numbers of psychological relations from moment to moment, Parfit asks, how can it be defined? And if we cannot define a deep unity of consciousness then we will need to admit that there is nothing like a forensic unit and all that ever holds us together are the relatively shallow relations of psychological connectedness and continuity.

This is a very serious challenge. In the end I do not think that a purely Lockean account of personal identity can work, and this is in part because I do not think that this challenge can be met within the framework Locke offers. I will return to discuss this challenge at various points throughout the book, including briefly in the next chapter. For the moment, however, the point I want to make is this. Whether it is possible in the end to adequately define the identity of a forensic unit or not, the existence of such a unit seems necessary to explain our forensic practices. Because Locke's view makes room for a distinction between the forensic unit and the moral self, it has room to provide an account of personal identity that legitimates these practices (assuming that a coherent understanding of sameness of consciousness can be provided). Psychological continuity theories cannot make this distinction, however, and as a result they are vulnerable to the extreme claim.

1.3 Summing Up

I have used a reading of Locke on personal identity to distinguish between two different ways of thinking about the relation between personal identity and practical considerations. On one understanding, the understanding implicitly presupposed in much of the discussion of personal identity, the limits of the person must coincide with the limits of particular practical judgments—if I am the person who took action A then I am responsible for A, and vice versa. We can call this the "coincidence model" of the relation between personal identity and practical considerations, since on it identity and practical concerns coincide. The second understanding sees a person as an appropriate target of practical questions and concerns, and says that an account of personal identity must individuate such a target. We can call this the "dependence" model of the relation between personal identity and practical concerns since it sees a relation of mutual dependence between the two. On this view an account of personal identity is conceptually dependent upon practical considerations because the relation which constitutes identity must by necessity be one which makes a person an intrinsically appropriate unit about which to raise particular practical questions. Practical concerns are dependent on facts about personal identity in the sense that identity must be in place before particular practical judgments can be appropriately made—identity is a necessary but not sufficient condition for these judgments.

While I am not certain my reading of Locke's view captures his intentions—textual evidence is, I think, inconclusive—his account at least leaves room for a distinction between questions about the identity of a forensic locus and questions about the identity of a moral self in a way that psychological continuity theories do not. Contrasting these two views thus provides valuable resources for formulating an understanding of how to think about what it means for an account of identity to be inherently connected to practical concerns. The susceptibility of psychological continuity theorists to the extreme claim reveals that if we are trying to provide an account of personal identity that does justice to the significance these facts have for us we will do far better to employ a dependence model than a coincidence model. The question of what constitutes the identity of a forensic locus is, moreover, both formally and intuitively better suited to serving as an account of literal identity than is the question of what constitutes the identity of the moral self. For a variety of reasons, some of which I have already mentioned, I think that the Lockean picture will need to be altered significantly to provide a satisfying practically-based account of personal identity. Nevertheless we have made good progress on understanding one of our key terms, and can now gloss the notion of an "inherent connection" between personal identity and practical concerns using a dependence model rather than a coincidence model.

2

Division of Labor

In the previous chapter we saw that the dependence model of the relation between personal identity and practical concerns is much better suited to providing an account of literal identity than is the coincidence model, and so that it is this model we should use in developing an account of our identity that is inherently linked to practical considerations. One might ask, however, why we should endeavor to offer a practically-based account of literal identity in the first place. Once we have the distinction between metaphorical and literal questions of identity clear in our heads we might be led to consider the possibility that literal questions about our identity need not be tied to practical considerations in any way, including that described in the dependence model.

This chapter considers that possibility, which I will call the "strong independence model." To investigate this model I will look at two philosophers who argue from very different viewpoints that a sharp division should be drawn between metaphysical and practical considerations in the investigation of personal identity. Christine Korsgaard makes this case from the perspective of value theory, arguing that our unity as agents does not depend upon any kind of prior metaphysical unity. Eric Olson makes the corresponding claim from the metaphysical point of view, suggesting that the assumption that a metaphysical account of our identity must justify practical judgments is mistaken and has obscured the debate.

The strong independence model has many attractions, not the least of which is simplicity. In the end, however, I believe that the dependence model provides a more accurate way of thinking about the relationship between our literal identity and practical considerations. I will not be able to offer a detailed defense of this claim until much later. In this chapter I undertake the more circumscribed aim of showing that even proponents of the strong independence model cannot do without the notion of something like a forensic unit, and that Korsgaard and Olson each need to presuppose the existence of such a unit to make sense of our person-related practices. This result does not in itself undermine the strong independence model's assumption that an investigation of metaphysical questions about literal identity should make no reference to practical considerations. Defenders of this model need only to say that questions about the identity of the forensic unit, no matter how different they may be from questions about the identity of the moral self, are still practical and not metaphysical. What we learn here does, however, help to clarify and cement the idea that a full understanding of our person-related practices requires the assumption of a more basic practical unit and hence of an inherently practical question about how such units are to be individuated. Later, after I have developed a fuller understanding of the nature of this unit, I will be in a position to explain why I think that an account of its identity conditions is rightly described as an account of our literal identity. An important first step in this development is the one I take here, showing that such a unit is required.

I begin the discussion with a selective overview of Korsgaard's and Olson's positions. Next I show that they each need to make room for a forensic unit. I conclude with a brief discussion of the implications of this fact, reviewing what my argument does (and does not yet) show about the value of offering a practically-based account of our literal identity.

2.1 Korsgaard: Autonomy and a Response to Parfit

Much of Christine Korsgaard's work on personal identity focuses on what I have been calling the identity of the moral self. She is interested in the constitution of autonomous agents and seeks to explain why some of our motivations are taken to legitimately represent the desires of the person while others are seen as impulses or pulls that move her without her consent.[1] Her question is what underlies our ability to say that a particular action or motivation is *truly* attributable to a person, and thereby determine when judgments of responsibility and commitment are warranted. For the most part she pursues these questions without reference to debates about the metaphysics of personal identity. In an early paper, however, "Personal Identity and the Unity of Agency: a Kantian Response to Parfit," Korsgaard describes the ways in which her understanding of the constitution of the moral self is connected to the issues raised in metaphysical debates, offering her analysis of the unity of an agent as a direct reply to Parfit's argument that there is no deep unity within the life of a person.[2] The discussion in that paper speaks explicitly to the relation between identity and practical concerns.

---

[1] This is very similar to the distinction drawn by Frankfurt and discussed in the previous chapter.

[2] "Personal Identity and the Unity of Agency: A Kantian Response to Parfit," *Philosophy and Public Affairs*, 18(2), Spring 1989, pp. 101–32.

Korsgaard argues that Parfit cannot find deep unity in the life of an individual person because he is looking in the wrong place. She invokes the Kantian observation that we can look at ourselves from either a theoretical or a practical perspective, and thus view persons either as subjects or as agents. Parfit's mistake, according to Korsgaard, is to assume that the deep unity of a life is to be discovered from the theoretical viewpoint, which focuses on the unity of a subject of experience. Our practical unity is, she says, a unity of agency.[3] She accepts Parfit's argument that there is no deep unity of consciousness of the sort we tend to assume there is and acknowledges that if we are looking for a significant unity within the life of a person we will not find it by looking for a unified subject of experiences. She allows that if we assume that there can be no moral self without a prior unity of self-conscious subject, as Locke suggests, the extreme claim is indeed inevitable. If, however, we think about persons as agents, a meaningful, non-arbitrary unity is easy to find. "Suppose," Korsgaard says, "Parfit has established that there is no deep sense in which I am identical to the subject of experiences who will occupy my body in the future.... I will argue that I nevertheless have reasons for regarding myself as the same rational agent as the one who will occupy my body in the future." She goes on to clarify that "these reasons are not metaphysical, but practical."[4]

When we start out by thinking of persons as agents, we will immediately come upon the obvious fact that as agents, we must act, and that means we must decide what to do (or not do, as the case may be). Once we concentrate on this aspect of human existence, Korsgaard says, it will be easy to see that in order to act we must conceive of ourselves as unified agents. To show this, she asks us first to consider what underlies our sense that we are unified *at* a time and says that there are two elements of this unity. First, the need for unity is forced upon us by the fact that, at least in our world, we control one and only one body. If we are divided about what to do, we need to overcome our division in order to act coherently and effectively. "You are a unified person at any given time because you must act, and you have

---

[3] Another philosopher who draws a similar point of contact is Carol Rovane. She offers a rare agential account of personal identity coming out of the discussion of the metaphysics of identity rather than value theory. Rovane describes her account as revisionary, suggesting that no account can capture all of our intuitions about personal identity and so that any will be revisionary to some extent. Her proposal is that we define personal identity not in terms of a single phenomenological point of view but rather in terms of a single rational point of view. There are many interesting points of overlap between Korsgaard and Rovane, and also many deep differences. For our purposes the differences are not important. I take Korsgaard's view rather than Rovane's as my example for a variety of reasons, not least of which is that coming out of value theory it helps highlight relevant distinctions more clearly. For Rovane's account see Carol Rovane, *The Bounds of Agency: An Essay in Revisionary Metaphysics*, Princeton: Princeton University Press, 1997.

[4] Korsgaard, "Identity and Agency," p. 109.

only one body with which to act."[5] The second element is the "unity implicit in the *standpoint* from which you deliberate and choose." She says that "it may be that what actually happens when you make a choice is that the strongest of your conflicting desires wins. But that is not the way you think of it when you deliberate. When you deliberate it is as if there were something over and above all of your desires, something that is *you*, and that *chooses* which one to act on."[6] It is for these reasons that "your conception of yourself as a unified agent is not based on a metaphysical theory, nor on a unity of which you are conscious. Its grounds are practical..."[7]

Korsgaard goes on to argue that *this* unity, unlike unity of consciousness, can easily be seen as stretching over time as well as holding at a time. A person needs to coordinate actions and motives diachronically as well as synchronically, since almost anything we want to do will take at least a bit of time to execute. Imagine, she says, that my body really is occupied by a series of subjects, changing from moment to moment. It is clear that they had better learn to cooperate if together we are going to have any kind of a *life*.[8] But more than this, the need to think of ourselves as unified agents acting from reasons means that we must identify ourselves with those reasons, and these reasons may, and probably will, "automatically carry us into the future."[9] If you understand yourself as an agent "implementing something like a particular plan of life," she says, "you need to identify with your future in order to be *what you are even now*."[10] The basis for our unity over time is thus the necessity of acting once we are thrust on the scene, and not some metaphysical fact. As Korsgaard sums it up, "You normally think you lead one continuing life because you are one person, but according to this argument the truth is the reverse. You are one continuing person because you have one life to lead."[11]

Everything said so far is still compatible with taking Korsgaard's practical/ ethical question about identity as ultimately dependent on a more fundamental metaphysical unity. Her concern, it might be thought, is really with the constitution of the moral, agential self. Her disagreement with Parfit, and by extension with Locke, might therefore be seen as directed not at the idea that the moral self depends upon the prior existence of some more basic entity, but rather at the Lockean claim about the *kind* of entity on which it depends. Parfit's embrace of the

---

[5] "Identity and Agency," p. 111.   [6] "Identity and Agency," p. 111.
[7] "Identity and Agency," p. 110.   [8] "Identity and Agency," p. 113.
[9] "Identity and Agency," p. 113.   [10] "Identity and Agency," pp. 113–14.
[11] "Identity and Agency," p. 113.

extreme claim stems from two factors: first, an acceptance of Locke's argument that only a unified self-conscious subject could serve as the right kind of unit to support a moral self and, second, a belief that no deep unity of self-consciousness is possible. Korsgaard's argument might then be understood as claiming that if we take the practical viewpoint we can deny the first of these assumptions—that the forensic unit must be a self-conscious subject. Since it is being embodied in a single human body that forces us to unify as agents, she might be taken to say, biological continuity does, in the end, define the conditions of the identity of the forensic unit.

Whatever the attractions of such a view (and we will discuss some of these later), the details of Korsgaard's response to Parfit make it clear that it is not hers. The human body does not fulfill the function in Korsgaard's view that the self-conscious subject did in Locke's; nothing does, and her point is that we do not need anything to fill this role. The unity of will that defines the identity of the moral self does not, for her, depend upon a more fundamental unity, but is basic in its own right. She tells us, for instance, that the practical and theoretical perspectives on our actions are "equally legitimate, inescapable, and governed by reason"[12] and, in a particularly unambiguous passage, that seeing ourselves as the causes of what we do is a "fundamental" attitude that "is forced upon us by the necessity of making choices, *regardless of the theoretical or metaphysical facts.*"[13]

It is important to be clear that the claim here is *not* that we cannot help but think of ourselves as unified agents even though in truth we are not. Rather, Korsgaard is claiming that there are two equally basic ways to think about ourselves, and that the view necessitated by the practical stance yields a picture of what we are actually like that is distinct from but as legitimate as the view necessitated by the theoretical stance. Parfit, she says, gives us only half the picture. From the theoretical viewpoint reductionism is perhaps an inescapable conclusion, but from the practical viewpoint unity is equally inescapable. For the question at hand, moreover, the practical stance is arguably more appropriate than the theoretical stance, and so provides superior insight if our goal is to understand the nature of personal identity. "[I]t is from the standpoint of practical reason," she tells us, "that moral thought and moral concepts—including the concept of the person—are generated."[14] Questions about persons are not natural to the theoretical standpoint and so it is no wonder that they are difficult to answer from that point of view. If it is

---

[12] "Identity and Agency," p. 120.
[13] "Identity and Agency," p. 120; emphasis added.
[14] "Identity and Agency," p. 132.

persons we are interested in, Korsgaard argues, the more basic standpoint is the pragmatic one.

Korsgaard does, as already noted, see the fact of our embodiment in a single body as fueling the practical necessity to unify our lives in the way we do. She is careful, however, to make it clear that the sense in which a single biological life sets the boundaries within which a moral self is forged is a *contingent* one. She emphasizes this contingency in two ways. First, she considers science fiction scenarios of the sort offered by psychological continuity theorists in which a single body might no longer play the role in forming our agency that it currently does. She tells us that "as things stand, [the human body] is the basic kind of agent"[15] and that "the basic leader of a life is a human being, and this is what makes the human being the unit of deliberation."[16] She adds, however, that "if our technology were different, individual human bodies might not be the basic kind of agents. My argument supports a physical criterion of personal identity, but only a conditional one. *Given the technology we have now*, the unit of action is a human body."[17] To show a scenario in which the human body might not play this role, she offers Thomas Nagel's concept of "series-persons" who exist in a society where, after reaching a certain age, persons are replicated once a year to prevent degeneration and disease, essentially having their psychological lives continued in a brand new body each year. Since series persons could coordinate plans and activities over the existence of many different bodies, she says, a single agent would span many bodies in the world of series persons.

To underscore that the contingency of the human body as basic unit of agency is not dependent on far-fetched cases Korsgaard also points to circumstances in actual life where agency seems to bleed out beyond the limits of a single body. Responding to Parfit's discussion of the extreme claim she acknowledges that the considerations against a deep metaphysical separateness of persons that can be found in both her view and Parfit's do have some implications for the structure of prudential concern, but denies that they are the implications Parfit draws. Although the human body is the basic unit of action, we can and do form agential units with others (e.g., families, political entities, sports teams, symphony orchestras), she says,[18] and to the extent that we do so our self-interested concern can move beyond the limits of a single body:

---

[15] "Identity and Agency," p. 115.
[16] "Identity and Agency," p. 129.
[17] "Identity and Agency," p. 115.
[18] It is in this discussion that the overlap between Korsgaard's view and Rovane's is most evident.

The territory of practical reasons is not split into two domains—self-interested rationality concerned with the occupant of this particular body on the one hand, and reasons of impartial morality on the other. Instead, the personal concern which begins with one's life in a particular body finds its place in ever-widening spheres of agency and enterprise, developing finally into a *personal* concern for the impersonal—a concern, that is to say, for the fate of one's fellow creatures, considered merely as such.[19]

This is not, of course, the utilitarian emphasis on the impersonally described quality of experience that Parfit is after, but rather a Kantian respect for all agents.

Korsgaard's view of the relation between personal identity and practical concerns thus departs quite radically from the dependence model described in the last chapter. That model assumes that the possibility of moral agency depends upon the existence of a more basic unit—on Locke's view a self-conscious subject. It is only if the same subject who undertakes an action experiences its consequences, he says, that our moral practices are justified. Korsgaard's position is that the unity of the agent is a basic unity of its own that does not depend on the unity of self-conscious subject or any other kind of unity. The distinction Korsgaard draws between the practical and theoretical viewpoints thus implies that the question of the boundaries of the moral self can and should be pursued independently of questions about the individuation of any entity and, presumably, that metaphysical questions about the identity of the entities (contingently) involved in our actions can and should be pursued independently of any practical considerations.

In the next section we will look at another view that makes a similar claim from a very different angle before discussing the strong independence model more generally.

2.2 Olson's Animalism

Eric Olson defends a biological account of personal identity, or animalism. This is the view that each of us (each human person) is identical to a human animal and persists for the duration of a single biological life. Olson offers an extended defense of this position, arguing for its superiority over the "psychological approach," which for him means roughly what I have been calling the psychological continuity theory.[20] Employing a broadly Lockean conception of personhood, he argues that the question of personal identity as it is usually phrased—"What are the necessary and sufficient conditions for a person at time t_2 to be the same person as a person at time t_1?"—is ambiguous. When disambiguated, he says, it is either trivial or question-begging.

Olson explains this ambiguity by making use of a distinction between substance concepts and phase sortals.[21] An entity's substance concept is the concept that it cannot cease to fall under without ceasing to exist altogether. A phase sortal, on the other hand, is a concept that something falls under during some or all of its existence, but which could cease to apply without anything going out of existence. In fifteen years my adorable new puppy may be a crotchety old dog. There is no mystery about her ceasing to be a puppy as she ages, because *puppy* is a phase sortal. It is difficult to imagine how she could remain alive and cease to be a dog, however. This would make *dog* her substance concept.

When we ask what is required for a person to persist, we might be asking one of two questions. On the one hand, we might be asking what is required for something which is a person to continue to be a person, just as we might ask, for instance, what is required for an athlete to continue being an athlete or a puppy to continue being a puppy. On the other hand, we might be asking what is required for something which is a person to continue to exist at all. Unless *person* is our substance concept these are different questions. The question of what is required for my puppy to continue to exist is different from the question of what is required for her to remain a puppy because she can outgrow the stage of puppyhood and still be a happy member of the household who needs to be walked every morning. The question of personal identity as it is usually phrased might be either the first sort of question, which sees *person* as a phase sortal, or the second, which sees *person* as our substance concept. Most of those working on the metaphysical problem of personal identity, Olson points out, seem to assume that it is the latter question (or to ignore the distinction altogether). They are not asking merely what is required for something which is a person to continue being a person, but rather what is required for something which is a person to continue to exist at all. Phrasing *this* question as the question of what is required for a person at one time to be the same person as someone at another time assumes—or at least implies—that *person* is our substance concept and that determining what is required for someone to continue as the same *person* will automatically settle the question of what is required for someone to continue at all. Olson rightly complains that this is a substantive philosophical thesis and it is question-begging simply to assume it.

---

[21] Olson has abandoned talk of substance concepts and phase sortals in making the argument for animalism in his later work. Nonetheless, these later arguments continue to depend upon this distinction or something very close to it.

The question of personal identity is, by Olson's lights, only a truly metaphysical question when it is understood as asking what is required for that thing which is a person to continue to exist. To avoid ambiguity he thus suggests that we rephrase the relevant question as the question of what is required for something which is a person at t_1 to be identical to *anything* at t_2. If we open up the possibility of our surviving as non-persons by formulating the question this way, he says, it will be easy to see that, at least in the case of human persons,[22] what is required is the continued existence of a living human organism. His argument for this position is premised on the assumption that each concrete particular has one and only one substance concept; each thing, that is, belongs essentially to exactly one kind. Psychological theorists imply that our substance concept is *person*. Olson's argument for animalism is based on considerations that are meant to show that it is instead *human animal*, and that *person* should be viewed as a phase sortal, albeit one that is extremely important to us.

A significant part of Olson's defense of this position involves explaining away the appeal of the psychological approach. This is important to do for two reasons, he says. "First, any difficulties that a theory faces will be seen as little more than research projects and opportunities for further refinement if there are believed to be compelling arguments in favor of that theory." The problems he finds with the psychological approach to personal identity are thus not conclusive unless he shows that there is no good reason to try to save that approach. "Second, a great many thoughtful and intelligent philosophers have accepted the Psychological Approach, and if it turns out they were mistaken, it would be gratifying if we were able to say something about what led them astray."[23] It is in the attempts to diffuse the initial attractions of the psychological view that Olson's project intersects most directly with our present concerns. His diagnosis is that the pull of the psychological approach depends upon an unjustified mixing of metaphysical and practical questions. "The Psychological Approach," he argues, "is based largely on practical considerations that do not provide clear support for that view, and that may well be compatible with the Biological approach."[24]

To make this case Olson notes, as we have also, that hypothetical cases in which a psychological life continues in a body other than the one in which it started (cases like Locke's prince and cobbler or our case of Jack and Ben) provide the basic intuitive support for the psychological approach. This support rests on the

---

[22] He acknowledges there might be other kinds.

[23] Eric Olson, *The Human Animal: Personal Identity without Psychology*, Oxford: Oxford University Press, 1997, p. 42.

[24] Olson, *The Human Animal*, p. 42.

presumption that in these cases we will have strong intuitions that moral responsibility and similar practical relations will follow psychological rather than biological continuity. Olson does not dispute this presumption. He acknowledges the strength of our intuitions about the connection between psychological continuity and practical judgments, and is willing to stipulate to their force. What he denies, however, is that these intuitions, when properly analyzed, tell us anything important about the conditions of our persistence.

What our responses to these cases actually show us, Olson suggests, is that moral responsibility and other practical relations track psychological rather than biological continuity. But this only shows that *identity* tracks psychological continuity if we assume that the practical judgments *typically* associated with identity *must* be associated with identity and, he argues, there is no reason to assume any such necessity. The hypothetical cases that are used to show that personal identity tracks psychological continuity can just as reasonably be taken to show instead that when biological and psychological continuity diverge the correspondence that usually holds between practical relations and identity does not hold any longer. Here Olson uses Parfit's argument that identity is not what matters in survival to lend plausibility to the idea that these practical responses might not track identity per se, but only psychological continuity. The judgment that when Ben's psychology enters Jack's body the resulting person is responsible for Ben's actions does not automatically imply that that person is Ben. It might just as well show us that Jack can become responsible for Ben's actions by being infused with Ben's psychological life (while Ben, meanwhile, can be absolved of responsibility for his actions by transferring his psychology to Jack). So long as it is allowed that in unusual circumstances these practical relations might not presuppose identity, the biological approach can fully accommodate the intuitions that support the psychological approach by allowing that practical relations go where psychology goes.

In assuming that reflection on our practical judgments will yield an account of our identity, Olson says, psychological theorists conflate ethical and metaphysical questions. There is no prima facie reason to suppose that our ethical judgments have anything to say about the metaphysical facts of our persistence. "Ultimately," Olson says, "it is for ethicists to tell us when prudential concern is rational, when someone can be held accountable for which past actions, and who deserves to be treated as whom. These are not metaphysical questions because, *being the same person*, as we might say, is not a metaphysical relation."[25] Once we distinguish these questions, Olson continues, the intuitions generated by the puzzle cases can be dealt with in the context of ethical inquiry, and the impetus to give a psychological

---

[25] *The Human Animal*, p. 69.

account of identity itself is dissolved. We can even call the relation that underlies these practical judgments "personal identity" if we wish, he says, and claim that, e.g., after the transfer J.B. is the "same person" as Ben. We need to be perfectly clear, however, that in using these phrases we are not talking about the actual identity of any entity. We can "define a sense of 'being a particular person' as a sort of role or office that a human organism (or any other appropriate object) might fill at a particular time."[26] J.B. (or, as Olson would have it, Jack) can, post-transplant, be the same *person* as Ben before the transplant in the same way that Reagan and Clinton were the same *elected official*, even though there is no sense in which they are numerically identical to one another.

This analysis, Olson says, shows that we need not take the intuitions that seem to pull us toward the psychological approach to be intuitions about identity at all. And once we direct our focus to the strictly metaphysical question of our numerical identity we can see that the biological approach offers a far superior answer to *this* question than does the psychological approach. The main thrust of the many arguments he gives for this claim is that *person* makes for an extremely awkward substance concept. Although the details of these arguments are not terribly important for our present discussion, they will become so later on, so I will take a moment to give an overview of the kinds of considerations he raises.

Olson outlines several problems with the assertion that our persistence conditions are those of Lockean persons, among them the "fetus problem," the "vegetable problem," and the "thinking animal problem."[27] The fetus problem comes from the observation that the claim that we are fundamentally persons commits us to the counterintuitive claim that none of us was ever a fetus. This is because fetuses do not have the kind of psychological life that would make it possible for any one of us to be psychologically continuous with any fetus. Yet, Olson says, it seems like a complete truism that each of us was indeed once a fetus who grew into an infant, and eventually an adult. The vegetable problem is similar in form. Someone who falls into a permanent vegetative state (PVS) is presumed to have no consciousness, and so no ongoing psychological life. This means that it can never be true to say of someone that she might one day, through tragic misfortune, become a human vegetable. But we must recognize that this possibility is all too real.

The depth of the problem can be seen if we try to describe the trajectory of a life that includes a vegetative state at the end. First there is a human fetus that turns into an infant and eventually acquires the psychological capacities that make it a person. When the person comes into existence what can the psychological approach

[26] *The Human Animal*, p. 66.   [27] *The Human Animal*, pp. 73–123.

say about what happens to the fetus? Does it cease to exist by gaining new capacities? Later, when this individual suffers a stroke and falls into a vegetative state, the person ceases to exist. Does this mean that a new entity, a vegetative human that is spatiotemporally continuous with the unfortunate person, pops suddenly into existence? The entity in the vegetative state is a human animal. Is it the same human animal as the fetus that popped out of existence when the person came into being? It seems it must be. But then where was it in between?

Perhaps the claim is that there is an animal that remains throughout these vicissitudes. But if psychological theorists say this they are forced also to say that during the time at which the capacities of personhood are in place there are two distinct entities, the person and the human animal, who are completely coincident but have different persistence conditions. Not only is this claim counterintuitive, Olson says, it leads to what he calls the "thinking animal" problem. If the person and the animal are completely coincident, and the person is thinking, then it seems that the animal must also be thinking—there is no obvious basis on which this could be denied since, being entirely materially coincident with the person, it must be doing exactly what the person is doing. On this view there are thus two thinkers of each of my thoughts, and when I think "I am a person, not a human animal" it is not clear how I can know whether I am the person thinking a true thought, or the animal thinking a false thought. These consequences seem absurdly unacceptable.

The simplest and most commonsensical way of avoiding these infelicities, Olson argues, is to accept the biological approach. The animalist can describe the life trajectory from infant to vegetable very easily. According to this view there is one thing, a human animal, that starts as a non-person when it is a fetus and infant, becomes a person for much of its life, and ceases to be a person after suffering a stroke. During the time that the animal is a person, according to the animalist view, there is one thinker, the animal, which is able to (correctly) think thoughts like "I am a person" because it is in a phase of personhood. All of the problems of taking *person* as our substance concept can be avoided by animalism, and once we distinguish between ethical and metaphysical questions we can do so, Olson argues, without giving up the most compelling insights of the psychological approach.

Finally, there are some general theoretical considerations that suggest that *human animal* is a more suitable substance concept than "person." One is that *person* as understood here is a functional concept. Personhood is defined in terms of capacities rather than in terms of structure, and so it seems to be the kind of relation that needs an underlying substance to have the capacities or carry out the functions. "To say that something is a person," Olson says, "is to tell us something about what it can do, but not to say what it is. To say that something is a person is to say that it can think in a certain way—that it is rational, that it is ordinarily conscious and aware of itself as tracing a path through time and space, that it is morally accountable for its actions, or the like. But it doesn't tell us *what* it is that can think in that way."[28]

He likens the concept *person* to the concept *locomotor*. Many things can move—ships, crabs, cars, wagons—but we are not tempted to think that any of these things is essentially a locomotor, that they are all the same kind of thing, or that any of them would cease to exist if it became unable to move. When you point to a crab and say "what is that?," "a crab" is a much more natural answer than "a locomotor." Part of the reason for this, Olson says, "is that locomotion is a dispositional or functional property that can be realized in a wide variety of intrinsic structures. Different locomotors may have little in common besides the fact that they are locomotors—besides their ability to perform a certain kind of task."[29] Personhood is also a dispositional or functional property, and so suspect as a substance concept in just the way *locomotor* is.

An additional and related advantage of taking *human animal* rather than *person* as our substance concept, he says, is that this makes our persistence conditions of a piece with those of other living things. Dogs, cats, horses, crabs, bacteria, and trees all cease to exist when their basic metabolic functions cease. Olson finds it incredible that our persistence conditions should be wildly different from those of all other animals. We *are* human animals whether we are essentially or only contingently so. It thus seems highly anomalous that we, among all of the animal kingdom, have psychological rather than biological persistence conditions. He concludes that it is much more plausible to say that our metaphysical persistence conditions are biological and that we care deeply about our ability to function psychologically than to say that we, unlike any other kind of animal, have psychological persistence conditions.

Animalism thus holds that we are, as a matter of metaphysical fact, human animals throughout our entire existence and that we typically develop psychological capacities that are of immense practical significance to us. This view can, Olson argues, easily accommodate the intuitions that pull us toward the psychological approach while at the same time avoiding the metaphysical difficulties that arise from taking *person* as our substance concept. In later chapters we will revisit these arguments at length. For the moment, however, our main concern is with the strong and very explicit claim that practical concerns have no role whatsoever to play in the investigation of metaphysical identity questions. This claim is, in

---

[28] Olson, *The Human Animal*, p. 34   [29] *The Human Animal*, p. 34.

important ways, complementary to Korsgaard's. We will explore the points of contact further in the next section.

2.3   The Strong Independence Model and the Forensic Unit

Korsgaard and Olson differ greatly in basic sensibility and in their ultimate aims. Nevertheless, when it comes to the question of the relation between personal identity and practical concerns they can be seen as representing different sides of the same coin. Both argue that there should be no expectation that practical judgments either follow from or determine the answer to metaphysical questions about the identities of persons. There are, they both point out, two different kinds of questions that are typically referred to as questions of personal identity. One is a question about what underlies attributions of responsibility and like concerns and is *not* a metaphysical question about the identity of an object (this is what I have called the question of the identity of the moral self). The other is a question about the identity conditions for individuals who are (for at least part of their existence) persons. Both Olson and Korsgaard suggest that the powerful intuitive pull of the psychological approach comes from a conflation of these two questions. Once we see that there are two independent questions that are described as questions of "personal identity," each of which must be considered in its own terms, they argue, the idea that practical and metaphysical considerations must be woven together in a single account will dissipate. This is the position I am calling the *strong independence model* of the relation between personal identity and practical concerns.

There is something very compelling about this analysis, and we saw in Chapter 1 that the conflation of different questions can lead to difficulties if it takes the form of a coincidence model. The charge of conflation leveled by the arguments for the strong independence model do not apply directly to the dependence model, which does not assume that a single relation underlies both facts about identity and facts about particular forensic judgments, but draws a distinction between them. There is, however, still a challenge to the dependence model implicit in these arguments. According to the dependence model, the identity of the forensic unit (and hence the identity of beings like us) must be defined in such a way that it is, by its very nature, an appropriate locus about which to raise specific practical questions. This model assumes that affirmative answers to particular questions about responsibility and prudential concern presuppose a more basic identity that necessarily makes reference to practical considerations, albeit less direct reference than in the coincidence model. For adult Kate to be responsible for the actions of teenaged Kate it is a necessary, but not sufficient, condition that she be the same forensic unit.

The strong independence model does not directly consider the existence of forensic units, but Korsgaard and Olson both suggest that we can raise and answer questions about moral responsibility and like relations without reference to any more basic unity and this seems to imply that everything we want to know about the moral self can be known without making reference to a forensic unit. My goal in this chapter is the relatively modest one of showing that this is not so, and that on both views something like a forensic unit is required to serve as a precondition for coherently raising questions about moral responsibility and related concerns. This means that if there is a sharp distinction between the metaphysical and practical it is not quite between free-floating questions about responsibility on the one hand and literal questions on the other; forensic units must also play a role. This leaves us with questions about how to categorize the question about the identity of the forensic unit and where it stands with relation to metaphysical questions of personal identity. We will return to these issues later. For the moment our task is only to show that we need a forensic unit for a complete understanding of our practices.

2.3.1 Korsgaard

Korsgaard argues that practical issues of personal identity must be addressed from the practical perspective and that this must be distinguished sharply from the theoretical perspective. It is natural to think that questions about the unity of individual entities is a theoretical concern, and foreign to the practical standpoint. To address practical concerns, Korsgaard suggests, we do not need to make reference to the unity of any kind of entity beyond the agent in the act of choosing, and so it seems as if on her picture there would be no need for anything like a specifically forensic locus that is inherently connected to practical considerations. On closer inspection, however, it is not entirely evident that we do not have a need for a locus which presents a point of contact between practical and metaphysical questions even in this picture.

Korsgaard's story involves some set of impulses and pulls that are, as it were, ours to unify, and that we must unify if we are to constitute ourselves as agents or, in my terminology, "moral selves." The set of impulses and drives out of which the moral self is formed needs to be delimited somehow. If Kate is feeling rage and I am feeling calm I am not the one who needs to decide whether I endorse the expression of this rage or repudiate it, or whether I take this rage as a reason for action; Kate is the one who must do so. She might decide that she does not want to live like this anymore and so we may, as Korsgaard suggests, conclude that this rage is not part of her true self and that when she acts on it she is not really acting and so cannot be held fully responsible; she is overcome by her passion. Be this as it may, the rage is, to begin with, Kate's practical problem to solve because she is the one who is being pulled by it. The good impulses that counter the rage are also part of Kate's overall profile, and she can turn to them to help her fight against the rage she experiences. Kate is stepping back and asking which of her impulse to seek vengeance and her impulse to move on she appropriates as her own and which has the authority to represent her in action, and so there must be some prior sense in which both are hers.[30]

The need for something like a forensic unit becomes clear when we think about the way in which the identity of the agent can come apart from the identity of the human body. Reconsider, for instance, the case of Kate and K.J. Kate, we can imagine, decides in prison that when she gets out she is going to change her life, and work to make the world a better place. She still sometimes feels murderous rage toward all of those she believes were complicit in her abuse but she wholeheartedly repudiates the drive for revenge and makes plans to better herself. She gets a steady job, signs up for therapy and volunteer work, arranges to live in a supportive group-living situation, and so on. These are the kinds of actions and commitments that Korsgaard describes as carrying us beyond the present into the future. If Kate is going to execute these actions and live the life she has planned she therefore needs to commit herself to these steps not just for now, but into the future (she must coordinate with later Kate if together they are to have any kind of a life). If this body in the future decides to stop therapy and go on a rampage or just to be careless about supporting her commitment to a new life, Kate cannot enact her will or "be what she is even now." So far so good. But things become more complicated when we bring in the transfer case. Now imagine that Kate's cerebrum is going to be transplanted into Juliet's body, resulting in K.J., who has Kate's psychological life and Juliet's body. Since Kate is looking ahead, she knows that she needs to make choices not just for what to do now, but also for what to do in the future; she must coordinate actions with her future self. But which is the future self with whom she needs to coordinate? For Kate to carry out her life plan it is not enough

---

[30] In principle, of course, we could say that a person should step back and consider which of all possible actions she should take and which of all possible motivations she should follow. In practice, however, this is not possible for us. The demands of considering all possible courses of action and adjudicating among them would leave us unable ever to do anything. Korsgaard's Kantianism sometimes does seem to demand that we do what we feel is better than any other possible course of action, but in laying out her view she acknowledges that many of our motivations and commitments come from contingencies of our histories. See, for instance, *The Sources of Normativity*, Cambridge: Cambridge University Press, 1996, pp. 238–42.

that *someone* in *some* body goes to therapy and to the group home; *she* has to do it. But who is the relevant "she" in this case and how is that determined?

Korsgaard's discussion of series people and related topics seems to commit her to the claim that in the transfer case it is K.J. who must carry out Kate's plan, and this is, as we have already discussed, an intuitively plausible position. But why does Korsgaard conclude that it must be K.J.? Kate controls a single body when she is in prison planning her life and must choose between competing impulses to take any action at all (e.g., she must either sign up for therapy or not sign up for therapy but cannot do both), and K.J. controls a single body after she gets out of prison and must make a choice between competing actions (e.g., she can either go to the therapy session or skip it, but cannot do both), but why must Kate and K.J. coordinate their actions? Or, put differently, why must K.J. rather than anyone else be the one with whom Kate must coordinate action if she is to carry out her life plan?

The answer seems fairly straightforward. It is because after the cerebrum transplant K.J. and no one else will have Kate's psychological make-up, and the carrying out of plans requires a certain amount of psychological continuity. It is K.J. who will remember signing up for therapy and why she did so. It is also K.J. who will need the therapy because it is she who will experience rages and have trouble controlling them, and who will also remember those horrible nights in prison and her vow to get her life straightened out. The relevant feature for the point I am making here is not that K.J. is the same moral self as Kate, or that she has the same values, commitments, and traits that defined Kate's true self. It is rather that she has the same conflicts, temptations, strengths, and weaknesses that Kate had.[31] The psychological context out of which Kate builds her moral self, making choices to endorse some of her impulses and repudiate others, is transferred from Kate's body to K.J.'s. Earlier I said that it is presupposed in Korsgaard's view that there is some set of impulses and motivations which it is mine to coordinate if I hope to constitute myself as an agent. Reflections on diachronic coordination in the transfer case help to highlight the fact that what delimits which impulses and motivations these are is something like the relations that define personal identity according to psychological continuity theorists. It is because K.J. will experience the same set of conflicting impulses that Kate did that hers is the future body with which Kate must try to coordinate action. It is because she has Kate's psychological life—not just the

---

[31] Of course, the same point holds even if we are talking about someone who is not deeply conflicted or has not undergone a radical change. The use of a case like Kate's is helpful for highlighting the difference between individual judgments and the unit about which the judgment is made and for showing that this unit need not coincide with the limits of a human life, but the conclusions drawn apply more generally.

parts she endorses but also those she repudiates—that K.J. is the person who can, in the relevant sense, complete or fail to complete the life plan Kate started.

Since I have said that psychological continuity theories do not provide a viable forensic unit it may sound strange that I am here claiming that Korsgaard's need to presuppose the existence of psychological connectedness and continuity amounts to an assumption of a forensic unit. The dynamics here are complicated, however. Korsgaard is in fact trying to answer the extreme claim here, and in doing so urges a very different view of the unity of consciousness than is found in Locke. Her analysis in fact goes a long way to demystify this problematic notion, and so within the context of Korsgaard's views these relations look more plausible as the basis for defining the unity conditions of a forensic locus than they did in the psychological continuity theory. More specifically, Korsgaard rejects a standard picture according to which "the sphere of consciousness presents itself as something like a room, a place, a lit-up area, within which we do our thinking, imagining, remembering, and planning, and from out of which we observe the world, the passing scene." This idea of the unity of consciousness, she says, "supports the idea that consciousness requires a persisting psychological subject." Against this view she urges the idea that consciousness "is a feature of certain activities which percipient animals can perform." It is not that our experiences are *in* our consciousness but rather that we can engage in activities like thinking, planning, and remembering *consciously*. The unity of consciousness, on this view, "consists in one's ability to coordinate and integrate conscious activities."[32] Split brain patients, she points out, cannot easily coordinate or integrate conscious activities between the two hemispheres of the brain, and this is why they seem to be two people with two consciousnesses. This same model applies over time. It is K.J. who can either execute or fail to execute Kate's plans because it is with K.J. in the future that Kate has the ability to coordinate and integrate conscious activities; K.J. is the one who has the cognitive information required to make this possible.

The kinds of connections psychological continuity theorists use to define identity thus have an important role to play in Korsgaard's view as well. Her point is that if we want to see why these connections are important to the unity of the person we must take the practical stance rather than the theoretical stance. We can only see the depth of these connections when we think about agency and recognize that they are necessary to allow the agent to coordinate and integrate conscious activity. What is important for our purposes is that to have the kinds of psychological connections required to be in a position to integrate and coordinate conscious action is not the same as already to have integrated and coordinated that action.

---

[32] Korsgaard, "Identity and Agency," pp. 117–18.

One can be in a cognitive position to do so but remain so hopelessly ambivalent and conflicted that agency is undermined. It is essential for my purposes also to appreciate that although the more basic unity I see as essential on Korsgaard's view is constituted out of roughly the same connections psychological continuity theorists use to define identity, hers is not a reductionist view. The difference comes from the switch to the practical viewpoint, which requires that there be a single, unified agent. In this way her conception of this basic unity is structurally more like that in my reading of Locke than that found in standard psychological continuity theories.

Korsgaard's view thus involves two important and importantly different types of unity in understanding the basis for moral responsibility. First, there is the varied set of impulses and motivations that I am in a position to coordinate and integrate and which must be coordinated and integrated before I can take autonomous action, and then there is the subset of such impulses and motivations that I have endorsed and given the authority to represent me in action. It is for this reason that I claim that Korsgaard's view includes something like the forensic unit, whose identity must be presupposed to make sense of our forensic practices.

The point I have tried to make about Korsgaard's work is much more straightforward in Olson's, so before taking stock of just what follows from my discussion of Korsgaard I will demonstrate the role of the forensic unit in Olson's animalism.

2.3.2 Olson

On the surface, it is not evident that there is any need for a forensic locus within Olson's view. Questions about moral responsibility, the appropriateness of moral concern, and who should be treated as a particular person, he seems to say, can be asked directly, and the answers to these questions can apply across different basic units. Olson thinks this happens, for instance, in the case of the prince and the cobbler, where the entity which is Cobbler can be held responsible for actions of the entity which is Prince if Cobbler is now psychologically connected to Prince at the time of the action. In such a case, Olson says, there will be no single entity that contains both Prince's action and Cobbler's just punishment; the relevant relations hold across entities. He does allow however that we can, if we wish, define a relation of *being the same person as* in the following way:

X is at time t the same person as y is at a later time t^* if and only if x ought to be prudentially concerned, at t, for y's well-being at t^*; and y is responsible at t^*, for what x does at t; and it is natural and right at t^* to treat y as if she were x.[33]

---

[33] Olson, *The Human Animal*, p. 66.

We just need to be clear, however, that this relation of "same person" does not define the identity of an entity but is instead a kind of shorthand for the holding of certain practical relations.

In fact, Olson expresses some skepticism about whether we can really provide a unified definition of "same person" even in this weaker sense. While his reasons for saying so do not play a key role in his own view, they will be important for us and so it is worth lingering on them for a moment. It is somewhat implausible, Olson suggests, to think that the different practical judgments that are meant to be part of what constitutes the "same person" are all grounded in a single relation. What makes it right for someone to be prudentially concerned about a future experience may well be different from what makes it appropriate to hold her responsible for a past action, which may in turn be different from what makes it appropriate for her intimates to treat her the way they treated someone in the past (which, for that matter, is probably yet different from what makes it appropriate for casual acquaintances to treat her as some past person).[34]

This skepticism seems well founded, and it is something I think any account of the relation between personal identity and the practical must address. In the next chapter we will discuss a way in which the multiplicity of our different practical concerns about persons makes trouble for the dependence model (and, in Chapters 4 and 5, how that difficulty can be overcome). For the moment I want to concentrate on the implication of this fact for Olson's claim that animalism can capture the intuitions evoked by the transfer case. If indeed these different practical judgments are connected to different relations, the view that the practical questions can be addressed in their own terms, and possibly apply across entities, implies that a single individual at time t_1 might bear individual practical relations to several different entities at time t_2. By transplanting selectively, in other words, we should at least in theory be able to bring about a situation where Kate at t_1 can rationally have prudential concern for Juliet at t_2, while Shannon at t_2 is rightly held responsible for the actions of Kate at t_1 and the intimates of Kate at t_1 would be right to treat Claire at t_2 as they treated Kate at t_1.

This is hardly coherent, however, and has little claim to capture the intuition behind the transfer case. It certainly can happen that *within* a single life sometimes one of these relations will hold but not the others—Jane at age six may be right to take a prudential interest in what will happen to a particular human at age forty, even if we think it is a mistake to hold the forty-year-old human morally responsible for what six-year-old Jane did. The idea that these relations might hold individually between six-year-old Jane and several different forty-year-old women

---

[34]   David Shoemaker develops this point in great detail, as we will discuss in the next chapter.

is hard to make sense of, however (i.e., that Jane at six is right to take prudential concern for Sally's wellbeing at forty but that Mary at forty is responsible for Jane's actions at six). There is a fairly straightforward reason for this. Although these are distinct judgments they are not completely unrelated. The fact that questions of responsibility and prudential concern are intertwined in complicated ways is, after all, the basis for Locke's argument that personal identity must be defined in terms of sameness of consciousness. Moral responsibility, he says, requires legitimate reward and punishment, which in turn requires prudential concern. And it is fairly easy to see that the question of who to treat as whom is also bound up with these relations. Surely whether I am to treat Claire as my friend Kate is not entirely independent of whether she is rightly considered responsible for the actions Kate took toward me in the past (her kindness and generosity, for instance), or whether her experiences are the fulfillment of Kate's prudential reasoning. (Should I celebrate with her when Kate's hard work comes to fruition? Commiserate with her when the very thing Kate feared comes to pass?)

Although these practical relations do not always occur together in specific instances they are nevertheless interdependent in various general ways. Rather than a collection of different relations that happen to be co-present in a single individual our practical relations and capacities are part of a single nexus that potentially (but not inevitably) gives rise to them all. In the classic Lockean transfer case we are asked to imagine that the whole network of relations is transferred all at once (this is, recall, an important distinction from the more piecemeal transformation cases that test for the identity of the moral self). When Kate's psychology is transferred to Juliet's body our intuition is that the whole constellation of practical considerations and concerns that were directed at Kate's body before (whatever those may be) are now rightly directed at Juliet's body. It is this which gives the impression that an entity—the person—has switched from one location to another, and this is the intuition that must be accounted for or explained away by the strong independence model if it is to capture what is legitimate in the intuitions behind the Lockean view.

If we are to acknowledge the fact that different practical relations do not always occur together but also accept that they are not entirely independent of one another we seem to need something like a forensic unit which provides a unified target of our various practical questions and considerations but within which not all of the particular practical relations need apply simultaneously. Animalism thus cannot capture our deepest intuitions about the practical nature of personal identity merely by allowing that specific practical relations may sometimes hold between different human animals. It needs further to make sense of the idea that a unified locus of all of our practical concerns can be transferred from one body to another. Olson in fact does allow for such a possibility when he says that we can understand sameness of person by thinking of being a particular person as a kind of office or role, like President of the United States. We might imagine that there is a constellation of practical judgments that go together in something like the way the rights and responsibilities of the President do, and that these get transferred with psychological life. The office of Katehood, for instance, might be taken on by two different individuals at different times just as the office of U.S. President can during a transfer of power, even if the presidency as an office could not survive the distribution of the rights and responsibilities that define it into several different individuals.

This analogy is worth considering in somewhat more detail. Olson has told us earlier that the concept *person* is like the concept *locomotor*, but there is a big difference between concepts like *president* and concepts like *locomotor*, and this difference has important implications for our project. More specifically, thinking about locomotors and offices together reminds us that there are two different kinds of phase sortals. Some, like *parent, student*, or *locomotor*, are necessarily confined to a single substance. I can be a particular parent, student, or locomotor for part of my existence and so can you, but (making the fairly safe assumption that Olson is not a Platonist in this sense) I cannot be *the same* parent or same student or same locomotor as you. My locomotive capacities are a phase of my substantial existence and yours are a phase of yours, and they cannot be transferred from one substance to another; the individuation of a locomotor must be achieved by the individuation of the substance locomoting. An office like U.S. President is quite different in this respect, since the very same office can be a phase sortal of more than one substance. If Bush is U.S. President for part of his life, and then Obama for part of his, the same office has been transferred from one human to another. This means that there must be a set of conditions for individuating the office of U.S. President that are distinct from the conditions for individuating the substances that happen to be filling this office at any given time. We can talk about the U.S. Presidency from the founding of the nation to the present day, and name the various humans who have revolved through it, in a way in which it does not make sense to talk about Studentdom and all of the humans who have revolved through it, or Locomotorhood and all the substances that have passed through it (again, assuming that we are not Platonists).

It seems clear that being a particular person, like Kate, is more like being U.S. President than it is like being a locomotor, and Olson seems amenable to this idea. This has implications for how we should think about what a criterion of personal identity (in the sense that Olson allows) would look like. A criterion of identity for the office of U.S. President must not rely on the same relations that constitute the identities of the substances that fill that office, and should tell us which substance to look to at a given time in order to answer questions about the actions of the President (i.e., it should tell us who the President is). This means that if we are to provide a criterion of "personal identity" in Olson's sense we will need an account that individuates persons without reference to the identity of the animals (or other substances) that fill the office of a particular person and tells us which substance to look to when we have questions about that person (i.e., if I have a question about Kate the person post-transplant which human animal should I look at to address it?). This means that in addition to Olson's answer to the question of what constitutes the purely metaphysical identity of beings like us (the biological account) and the answers ethicists offer to the question of what makes someone responsible for a given action or right to be prudentially concerned about a particular future event, or whom to treat as some particular earlier person, we will *also* need an account of what constitutes the integrity of the "office" of being a particular person, possibly through change of substance. We will need, that is, an account of the identity of the forensic unit if we are to explain our person-related practices.[35]

2.4 Summing Up

I have argued that both Korsgaard and Olson ultimately need to make room for something like a forensic unit in their views and so for a question about the identity of the forensic unit. In the end, the arguments for this claim are very much like those offered in the previous chapter, and once again depend upon the insight that is generated by considering the transfer and transformation cases side-by-side. Particular practical judgments presuppose an appropriate unit about which they can be made, and in the end we cannot understand our forensic practices without assuming that there is such a locus. We are thus left with a question about what constitutes this more basic unity, and it is a question whose answer is inherently connected to practical considerations.

This result does not in itself indict Korsgaard's or Olson's view, or the strong independence model, because although they do sometimes imply that particular practical questions can be addressed without reference to a more basic unity they never explicitly deny the existence of a forensic unit and they do not need to do so. Their claim is only that we should distinguish sharply between the practical

---

[35] Providing such an explanation is not, of course, the goal of Olson himself. He does, however, offer the ability to capture the intuitions behind the psychological approach as part of his defense of animalism, and to the extent that capturing these intuitions requires an account of the identity of the forensic unit, Olson's defense also rests on an account of this unity.

and theoretical viewpoints when asking questions about personal identity. If we in fact do need a forensic locus, from their perspective this just means that the structure of the practical viewpoint is somewhat more complicated than we may have thought. So long as the question about the identity of the forensic unit is understood as a practical question, it is still possible to insist that there is a separate, purely metaphysical, question of identity that is distinct from both the question of the identity of the moral self and that of the identity of the forensic unit. This result does not indict the strong independence model because this model equates literal questions of personal identity with entirely theoretical, metaphysical questions. If a sharp distinction between practical and theoretical questions can be maintained, with questions about the identity of the forensic locus on the practical side, questions about our literal identity can still be seen as completely independent of practical considerations.

The conclusions drawn in this chapter thus do not so much resolve the issues we are considering as focus them. Having established the necessity of something like a forensic unit I need to show that an account of what constitutes the identity of this unit can and should be seen as a metaphysical account of the conditions of our literal identity. In order to make that case it will be necessary first to expand the set of practical considerations associated with personal identity. For these first two chapters I have operated with a basically Lockean conception of personhood in order to get the structure of the dependence model clearly on the table. Now that this has been accomplished it is time to assess this conception more critically. When we do so we will find, in the end, that it is too narrow to serve as the basis for a plausible account of our literal identity. This, I think, is one of the things that animalism gets very right. As important as the sophisticated psychological capacities associated with Lockean personhood are to us, we do not really take their presence or absence to make the difference between continuing to exist and ceasing to exist. When Grandmother succumbs to dementia we do not think that she literally disappears and is replaced by something else, and when a child develops reflective self-consciousness and other sophisticated psychological capacities we do not think that something totally new comes into existence.

I disagree with the animalist analysis of these observations, however. The problem with the Lockean approach is not that the considerations linked to literal identity are practical rather than theoretical, it is instead that the conception of the practical employed is too limited and too higher-order to tell the whole story of what we are and what is required for our continuation. There is an enormous number of practical questions and concerns that are associated with personal identity. If we are interested in providing an account of literal identity we should not limit ourselves to looking for an appropriate target of forensic concerns alone, but look instead for a target of all of these myriad concerns and practices—not a forensic unit, but a more basic practical unit. It is an account of this basic practical unit that I will urge as an account of our literal identity. The next chapter describes in more detail the motivation for this expanded view of the practical as well as considering some of the challenges it brings.

3

The Expanded Practical and the Problem of Multiplicity

The first two chapters provided insight into how best to think about what it means for facts about personal identity to be "inherently connected" to practical concerns given our goal of providing a practically-based account of literal identity. More specifically we have seen that theorizing this connection according to a dependence model is a far more promising approach than using a coincidence model. The next step is to get clearer on just which practical considerations should play a role in understanding our identity. At the end of the previous chapter I indicated that we will need to expand our conception of the practical concerns associated with personal identity beyond the forensic picture inherited from Locke. As I observed at the outset, the people in our lives are practically significant to us in all kinds of ways, many of which have little to do with assessments of moral responsibility or prudential rationality. These more basic kinds of significance have received little attention in the literature on personal identity, but on reflection there is no reason to think that they are not as closely related to facts about personal identity as are the interests and practices that have stood at the center of this discussion.

In this chapter I will argue for attending to the full range of our person-related practices and concerns in developing an account of literal identity. Since we have decided to offer a view with the structure of a dependence model, this means that we are looking for an account of personal identity which makes a person an appropriate unit of all of these practices and concerns—instead of a *forensic* unit we are looking more broadly for a unit of all of the different interests, judgments, and practices involved in our interactions with other people, forensic judgments included. To explore the wide range of practical concerns that can be linked to questions of personal identity I will look at work by Hilde Lindemann. Lindemann's discussion is a particularly helpful vehicle for exploring these matters, not only because of the clarity with which she lays out the issues that concern us here, but also because it contains elements that will be important in developing my positive account of personal identity later on. This expanded notion of the practical leads immediately to the *problem of multiplicity* described in the introduction. It seems that the conditions for being an appropriate target for particular practical concerns will be different depending on which practical concern we have in mind. This makes it difficult to see how we could provide a single account that defines an entity which is an inherently appropriate locus of the full range of our practical concerns; different concerns require different loci. In this chapter we will explicate the problem of multiplicity and gain an understanding of its depth and implications. The next two chapters will offer solutions.

3.1 Lindemann and the Range of the Practical

Hilde Lindemann writes about identity in a variety of contexts, but her focus is always broadly ethical, and questions about the moral significance of personhood and personal identity are never far from her discussion. In some respects, then, her work can be seen as directed at questions about the identity of the moral self rather than the underlying locus or unit of moral concern. Her conception of the moral self is, however, much broader than what we have seen, and a close look at this conception will be very useful for our purposes.

3.1.1 Lindemann on the identity of the moral self

In an early book, *Damaged Identities, Narrative Repair*, Lindemann addresses a question that looks very much like the question of the identity of the moral self as we have been understanding it so far. Here her main concern is the relation between identity, oppression, and autonomy, which she believes can be usefully unpacked through the concept of narrative. She investigates the ways in which oppressive narratives can damage our identities, and describes how the construction of alternative narratives can help to repair that damage. Lindemann glosses the sense of "identity" at issue in *Damaged Identities* as "the interaction of a person's self-conception with how others conceive her: identities are the understandings we have of ourselves and others."[1] Elsewhere she defines the concept this way:

an identity is a representation of a self: it's a narrative understanding of who someone is. It is generated from both an internal and an external perspective, and consists of the tissue of stories and story fragments that are woven around the acts, experiences, personal

---

[1] Hilde Lindemann, *Damaged Identities, Narrative Repair*, Ithaca: Cornell University Press, 2001, p. 6 (published as Hilde Lindemann Nelson).

characteristics, roles, relationships, and commitments that matter most about a person—either to her or to others around her.[2]

Because our identities are generated from both inside and outside, the stories others tell about us can oppress us when they overpower or distort the stories we would tell about ourselves. Our social world, Lindemann says, is shaped by *master narratives*—"the stories found lying about in our culture that serve as summaries of socially shared understandings."[3] These master narratives can act as oppressors insofar as they preconfigure the ways in which individuals and members of groups are understood by others and limit the tools members of those groups are given to think about themselves. Like Korsgaard, Lindemann draws a close link between agency and identity. Oppressive narratives interfere with agency both by depriving those who are their subjects of opportunities and, more insidiously, through "infiltrated consciousness," in which someone comes to see herself through the lens of the pernicious narrative. The remedy for this kind of damaged identity is a *counterstory*, a more advantageous depiction of who one is. Of course, the extent to which a counterstory can repair a damaged identity will depend upon how fully it is recognized by oneself and others but "if the retelling is successful, the group members will stand revealed as respectworthy moral agents. Since a powerful group's misperception of an oppressed group results in disrespectful treatment that can impede group members in carrying out their responsibilities, the counterstory also opens up the possibility that group members can enjoy greater freedom to do what they ought."[4]

To introduce the central ideas and provide an example of this basic dynamic Lindemann tells the story of a group of nurses who, in the course of meeting to plan a Nurse's Recognition Day, begin to discuss some of the frustrations they experience in their daily work. It emerges that many of these are related to a particular narrative about what nurses are like—"touch-feely Earth Mothers" with minimal technical medical knowledge—a narrative accepted by the doctors, the medical community at large, and to one extent or another by many of the nurses themselves. Through discussion consensus emerges that this narrative is badly out of date and interferes with the nurses' ability to express their opinions and treat their patients as they think best. There is some disagreement about exactly how far the master narrative goes wrong and in what ways, but over time even those

---

[2] Hilde Lindemann, "Holding on to Edmund: The Relational Work of Identity," in Hilde Lindemann, Marian Verkerk, and Margaret Urban Walker, eds., *Naturalized Bioethics: Toward Responsible Knowing and Practice*, New York: Cambridge University Press, 2009.

[3] *Damaged Identities*, p. 6.

[4] Lindemann, *Damaged Identities*, p. 7.

among the nurses who had largely accepted the standard narrative come to see the ways in which the judgments and experiences of the other nurses resonate with their own and with the patterns that they had found in their own lives. In the end, the nurses begin to reinterpret the anecdotes they had recounted in a way that yields a new narrative about nurses and their relation to doctors, patients, and the life of the hospital. This is their *counterstory*.

The narrative account of identity and autonomy offered in the book is complex and subtle, and there is a great deal more to it than I have described, but what we have here will be enough to get us started. So far what Lindemann has offered is an account of the identity of the moral self traditionally conceived. Like Korsgaard, she sees the constitution of this kind of identity as intimately connected to the conditions of agency, although her conception of what unifies the agent is quite different from Korsgaard's. For Korsgaard, the constitution of an agent is something that happens in the privacy of one's own will. There are, naturally, many ways in which the actions of others might make it easier or harder to gain a stable agential unity, but the task of unification is a task that sits in the hands of the individual. For Lindemann, by contrast, recognition by others is part of what *constitutes* the identity of the moral self. "It's my contention," she says, "that freedom of agency requires not only certain capacities, competencies, and intentions that lie within the individual, but also recognition on the part of others of who one *is*, morally speaking."[5] Agency is not, for her, an internal act of will, but a relationship with others, and one cannot be fully an agent without being recognized as such.

Since agency is crucial to the identity of the moral self, recognition is, for Lindemann, also partially constitutive of identity. The identity of the moral self is negotiated through interactions with others, and the concept of such a self is a relational concept that necessarily makes reference to one's place in a social world. This difference is connected to a much larger difference that emerges in the context of Lindemann's work in bioethics, and it is here that the possibility of expanding our notion of the practical concerns relevant to identity arises.

3.1.2 *The expanded practical*

In addition to the questions of autonomy, agency, and oppression that occupy *Damaged Identities*, Lindemann spends a great deal of time discussing the status of humans who lack the capacity for autonomous agency—the very young, for instance, or those with severe dementia or other cognitive deficits. Her position is that these humans are also persons with personal identities, and this is because she sees the practical implications of personhood as going beyond the sophisticated

---

[5] Lindemann, *Damaged Identities*, p. 24.

forensic concerns that are usually the focus of practically-oriented discussions of personal identity. For Lindemann the practical implications of personhood involve not only what someone is able to do, but how she should be treated. This is not in itself a unique position. Korsgaard would of course claim that persons must be treated with respect, and Locke sees persons as those who can be rightly praised or blamed. Lindemann's conception of the relevant kind of treatment is, however, much broader than Korsgaard's or Locke's. For her, treating someone as a person does not only involve treating her as a moral or rational agent, but includes the full range of everyday behaviors that make up the lives of human persons.

To see someone as a person, Lindemann says, is indeed to recognize her as the bearer of certain rights and the object of certain moral duties, "but it is more than that. It includes taking for granted that persons wear clothes and are given names rather than numbers, or that they are to be referred to as 'who' instead of 'what.' "[6] The social recognition that constitutes our identities on her view goes far beyond the acknowledgement of rights and responsibilities. She follows Carl Elliott in thinking about personhood as a "form of life" in Wittgenstein's sense. To recognize someone as a person is not to make one particular kind of judgment about her, but rather to treat her in the myriad ways that this form of life entails, those that involve moral responsibility and autonomous agency and those that do not. Social recognition is not necessary for and constitutive of agency alone on her view; it plays this role for the whole range of practical interactions that make us persons and create our narrative identities.

What this means, among other things, is that being taken up into the form of life that is definitive of persons can confer personhood even on individuals who do not possess the capacities required for this designation in most of the views that define personhood in practical or psychological terms. There are many aspects of this form of life, and someone need not engage in all of them to count as a person or to have a personal identity. Most important for the contrast with Korsgaard and Locke I am drawing here, none of the elements that have received the most attention or been regularly suggested as the defining features of personhood (i.e., the capacity for reflective self-consciousness, autonomous agency, prudential reasoning, language use, self-narration) is in and of itself essential to personhood according to Lindemann. Even those who lack these capacities (e.g., very young children, the demented, and those with significant cognitive deficits) can be treated as, and so constituted as, persons with personal identities.

---

[6]   Hilde Lindemann Nelson, "What Child is This?," *Hastings Center Report*, November–December 2002 (published as Hilde Lindemann Nelson), p. 33.

The way in which this happens is movingly and effectively depicted in her reflections on her sister Carla, who was born with hydrocephaly in the 1950s and lived
only eighteen months. Because of her illness and her extreme youth, the "narrative
tissue that constituted her personal identity... contained no stories from her own,
first-person perspective. It was constructed entirely from the third-person point of
view."[7] From that third-person point of view, however, Carla received an identity,
constituted through the many person-specific interactions her family and others
had with her. The stories that make up Carla's identity, says Lindemann, are "stories of her birth and her repeated hospitalizations, of the day my sister bathed her
under close maternal supervision, of the time when my father took her outside to
show her our tree fort..."[8] Although no judgments were made concerning Carla's
moral responsibility for particular actions and no questions raised about her true
beliefs or commitments, she was nevertheless recognized and treated in ways that
characterize the form of life peculiar to persons. It is, moreover, not only family
members and intimates who played a role in constituting an identity for Carla,
but her doctors, the neighbors, people they met on the street, and others encountered in her short life. Despite the lack of reflective self-consciousness, language, or
story-making capacities, Carla had a personal identity because of the recognition
she received from others.

Lindemann is sensitive to the worry that the role she gives to third-person
narration in the constitution of personhood and personal identity may raise the
specter of uncontrolled constructivism. It is important to her that third-person
identity construction manages to "confer actual rather than merely honorific
personhood,"[9] and that some account must be given of the circumstances under
which this can happen. Otherwise her account of personhood will be too promis-
cuous. She believes that such an account is possible, however, and that she can
provide non-arbitrary grounds for saying that the fact that it is genuinely possible
to constitute someone like Carla as a person with a personal identity in the way she
describes does not imply that it is possible to make *anything* into a person just by
treating it as such. Despite the socially constitutive aspects of identity on her view
she maintains that a meaningful distinction between something's actually being a
person and our merely acting as if it is can still be drawn.

Lindemann demonstrates the basis for this distinction by considering the cat
that lived in her household at the same time as Carla. The family cat, she says,
could not be and was not constituted as a person with a personal identity despite

---

[7] Lindemann, "What Child is This?," p. 32.   [8] "What Child is This?," p. 31.
[9] "What Child is This?," p. 33.

the fact that he was treated in many of the same ways Carla was ("we considered him a member of the household, we fed him and met his physical needs, we played with him, we had a narrative understanding of who he was, and when he was sick we took him to the vet's"), and this is so even though "the cat's capacities and capabilities outstripped Carla's by a long chalk."[10] There seem, for Lindemann, to be two basic requirements for being the kind of creature that can be brought into the form of life that is personhood and so be socially constituted as a person. One is sentience, and the other is (visible) humanness. I will ultimately disagree with Lindemann on the details of these constraints, but discussing why she endorses them will nevertheless provide a useful picture of a general strategy for avoiding conventionalism in a socially-based view of identity, which we will develop in a somewhat different direction later on.

Both of Lindemann's requirements are connected to the idea expressed in Wittgenstein's remark that "The human body is the best picture of the human soul." Sentience is required because the interactions that make up the form of life which constitutes personhood involve reading and recognizing the meanings of others' bodily attitudes, and this requires that "there is something here to be recognized. There is something to get right or wrong, something we can see or misperceive, something to which we can respond well or badly."[11] The meanings of bodily attitudes are socially mediated, but this does not mean that they do not have their own reality. She thus holds that "our psychological states, their bodily representations, others' uptake of these representations, and the treatment based on that uptake all play a part in the formation and maintenance of personhood." She sees personhood as the "bodily expression of the feelings, thoughts, desires, and intentions that constitute a human personality, as recognized by others, who then respond in certain ways to what they see."[12] For this reason, a human in a persistent vegetative state (PVS) or an anencephalic human infant cannot be constituted as a person on her view, no matter what our attitudes toward them. Of course, we may (and do) still have reason to treat such humans with a kind of respect, but "where there are no mental states there is nothing for the body to express, no picture for others to recognize."[13] Carla, because she had experiences and sentience, was able to fix attention and to be distressed or comforted. She thus had enough of an underlying inner life to be brought into the practices of social recognition that are constitutive of personhood, while permanently non-sentient humans do not.

---

[10] "What Child is This?," p. 35.   [11] "What Child is This?," p. 34.
[12] "What Child is This?," p. 34.   [13] "What Child is This?," p. 35.

The requirement of *humanness* comes from the fact that our ability to read and recognize the inner lives of others, and to bring them into our form of life more generally, depends upon their being embodied as we are. The mode of being which is supported by the embodiment of cats or other nonhumans is, to Lindemann's mind, too different from ours for us to draw them into our form of life. There are, of course, many ways in which we can value nonhuman animals and interact with them, "but we cannot occupy their life-world, nor can we fully bring them into ours. Humans, it seems, can confer personhood only on other humans."[14] Lindemann also holds that a fetus cannot yet be brought into our form of life, since its body is hidden from view and so cannot serve as the basis for the kinds of mutual recognition that make up persons' lives (hence the requirement of "visible" humanness). She does allow that there might be other creatures with a social structure enough like ours to have their own practices of personhood depending on their own specific form of embodiment, but doubts that we could interact with them as persons.[15] They could confer something like personhood on one another, but we cannot confer personhood on them or hold them in personhood.

While there is, of course, a great deal more that could be said about the details of Lindemann's view, I will leave my exposition here. What I have said so far lays out three main components of the view, each of which will eventually be relevant to our project. The first is the expanded conception of the practical interactions associated with personhood which holds that they include not only sophisticated assessments of moral responsibility or prudential rationality but also much more fundamental practices. The second is the constitutive role of social recognition in agency and in identity more generally, and the third is her analysis of the role of being human in personhood and personal identity. The second and third elements will reappear later. For now let us turn our attention to the implications of the first.

3.2 What Kind of Practical Unit?

Whether or not one agrees with the whole of Lindemann's analysis (and as the discussion goes on I will note some ways in which I do not) it brings to the forefront the question of just which practical concerns we are talking about when we say that personal identity is inherently connected to practical considerations. The view of personhood taken from Locke links identity to those sophisticated forensic practices which rely on higher-order psychological capacities (especially those practices surrounding moral agency and practical

---

[14] "What Child is This?," p. 35.   [15] "What Child is This?," p. 36.

rationality). Lindemann reminds us that there are a host of different kinds of practical elements that are characteristic of the lives of persons, and many of these have little to do with assessing moral responsibility or taking an attitude of prudential concern toward the future. Our whole way of life expresses our personhood. If our goal is to develop an account of a person as the unit of the practical questions and concerns associated with persons and their identities, we thus need to get clear on whether we are looking specifically for a target of the forensic concerns on which Locke focuses or for a target of the full range of person-related practices.

There are some considerations to be offered in favor of the Lockean approach. The driving idea behind this conception of personhood is that it is precisely these higher-order psychological capacities and the new kinds of practical abilities that rest upon them that most clearly and significantly distinguish persons from other kinds of beings. One of the most distinctive features of persons is that we can reflect on ourselves as continuing beings, think abstractly, and therefore grasp the concept of contingency. This allows us to step back from the flow of experience and from the pull of our various motivations and ask what we ought to do, introducing normative possibilities that are not there for beings that do not have reflective capacities and opening up new dimensions of experience and interaction. Call these abilities the "forensic capacities." The standard understanding of personhood sees possession of these game-changing capacities as the defining characteristic of persons. We may indeed have all kinds of other practical concerns about and relations to persons according to this perspective, but these are not distinctively *personal* concerns and relations. Following this logic, an account of personal identity that is going to capture the intuition that practical considerations are inherent to personhood should look specifically for an account of the identity of a forensic locus.

I certainly do not want to deny that the Lockean conception of personhood is an important one, nor that questions about the identity of the forensic unit are interesting and significant in their own right. I also do not want to suggest that a practically-based account of our literal identity could be complete without seeing us as, among other things, forensic units. The claim is rather that it is not enough to define identity in a way that makes persons exclusively forensic units. An adequate account should be such that on it persons are appropriate units of forensic concern as well as of the other kinds of concerns and practices associated with personal identity. The forensic capacities will, in fact, play a very central and special role in the account of personal identity I offer, but before we can understand the exact nature of that role it is important to appreciate the significance of practical considerations that have been given less attention in discussions of personal identity.

There are all kinds of ways in which we interact with others that are person-specific but not directly forensic. Singing duets, dancing a tango, picnicking in the park, playing tag, racing to the deep end, watching the big game together, telling ghost stories by the campfire, and sharing popcorn at the movies are all forms of interaction that are unique to persons even though they may involve no direct judgments of moral responsibility or assessments of prudential concern. In many ways these activities depend upon the forensic capacities and are shot through with forensic significance. For one thing they all involve a certain amount of planning, the marshalling of necessary resources, and some thought about the consequences of the course of action undertaken. They will also usually involve some moral dimension (e.g., you shouldn't picnic where the "keep off the grass" sign is; you shouldn't cheat at tag; you shouldn't hog all the popcorn). Forensic practices may thus be implicated in these kinds of uniquely personal interactions, but the interactions themselves are not, most immediately, forensic practices.

Lindemann's work points out that one implication of this fact is that those who do not themselves possess the forensic capacities can be included in these other kinds of person-related practices and interactions so long as there is someone with the forensic capacities to initiate or facilitate them. It is possible to sing duets with Grandfather who is suffering from severe dementia even if he no longer has the capacity for moral agency or prudential planning; Carla can be brought out to picnic in the tree fort; children who are too young to count as Lockean persons (or to fully understand the game) can be brought to sporting events, dressed in jerseys, and join in the cheering and general excitement; baby sister can be included in a game of tag or go to a movie. These activities would not exist at all unless it were characteristic of persons to possess the forensic capacities. Since persons do typically possess these capacities, however, their form of life includes many activities which can include those who do not possess them, and many distinctively personal practical questions and concerns of which someone without the forensic capacities can serve as the target.

In fact, I would argue for an understanding of personhood even more inclusive than Lindemann's. Arguably, those who lack sentience can be (and are) included, albeit minimally, in person-specific activities. Someone in a persistent vegetative state (PVS) is typically dressed in clothes, lies in a bed with sheets, and is referred to by name. They are the recipients of person-specific attentions even if they cannot actively reciprocate. Loved ones may come to visit regularly and decorate the room, mark anniversaries, talk to the vegetative individual and play her favorite music; she may be covered by health insurance and receive disability checks. All of these are part of a form of life that is distinctive of persons, even if the individual in a PVS is included in that life in a purely passive way. Lindemann's constraints make sense given her project, which is to look directly at the practical issues rather than seeking to define the identity conditions of the locus to which they are directed. For our purposes, however, increasing the boundaries of person-related practices even further makes sense.

I realize that to many the inclusion of someone in a PVS within the scope of personhood will seem a stretch. We will return to these issues later as well as to a far more in-depth discussion of the form of life that defines personhood, and when we do I will say more about why I think that an individual in this state should be included. In any event PVS is at best a degenerate form of personhood, and I do not want to deny that. For the moment, however, our interest is in the question of whether we should think of persons specifically as forensic units or rather as units of the full range of person-specific practical questions and concerns. The recognition that distinctively personal forms of interaction go well beyond forensic interactions gives us reason to think that a practically-based account of literal identity should include all of these concerns.

Let me reiterate that there is certainly a use for a purely forensic notion of personhood, and the traditional concept of the moral self is an important one; if our goal is to give a literal account of the identity of persons, however, we would do well to focus on the full range of considerations that express our interests in our children, parents, colleagues, and friends. And if we look at our lives it becomes evident that we do view others who lack the forensic capacities as persons, and interact with them in decidedly interpersonal ways. Think, for instance, of the aftermath of a disaster like a major earthquake or explosion in which people are frantically searching for their loved ones. When family members are interviewed it is usually clear that *everything* of practical importance turns on whether their son, or mother, or brother is found alive and whole. At that moment these worries seem to have nothing directly to do with questions of moral responsibility or prudential concern, but more to do with the continued existence of someone to talk to and laugh with and love and care for. We can see that this is so by recognizing that we would expect the worry expressed by those seeking missing family to be at least as intense, maybe more so, if the missing individual is very young or cognitively impaired. The idea that one's toddler or demented parent might be wandering lost, confused, and frightened is especially horrifying. It seems evident, moreover, that the missing loved one is not being viewed solely as an organism, but as *someone* with whom one has a personal relationship—"my baby" or "my mother."[16]

---

[16] Of course, finding a lost loved one who had been in perfect health and discovering that she has suffered a severe brain injury and lost cognitive function or fallen into a PVS would be considered a grievous loss, and one might even say something like "we lost Mother the day she was hit in the head by that beam." The relationship with Mother will, nevertheless, continue, even if it is very different. There is thus evidence that we do not believe in such a case that the locus of our concern is actually gone, just altered.

This point becomes even clearer when we think not about traumatic or unusual cases, but about the standard relation between parents and children. The forensic capacities do not come into existence all at once, but develop over time. The caregiver of a young child would almost certainly deny that a whole new being comes into existence when these capacities come online. This is not, or at least not only, because there is a single human organism throughout but also, and likely more importantly, because of an experience of practical continuity. Well before the capacities of forensic personhood emerge there is a relationship between the caregiver and child that involves singing to, bathing, playing peekaboo with, reading to, teaching, feeding, and a variety of other interactions. When the child develops forensic abilities and becomes capable of moral responsibility and prudential reasoning these other kinds of interactions do not suddenly disappear. The newly formed agent remains the child with whom one sings songs, for whom one cooks favorite dishes, with whom one shares a joke and plays board games; the repertoire of interactions merely becomes increasingly complex and varied.

Not only are interpersonal interactions in place before the forensic capacities are developed, there is, moreover, good reason to believe that these interactions are an essential precursor to becoming a Lockean person. Psychologist Katherine Nelson, who has extensively investigated the development of human self-consciousness, suggests "the hypothesis of a new level of consciousness that emerges in early childhood together with a new sense of self situated in time and in multiple social realities."[17] She describes the increasingly complex kinds of self-awareness that can be identified during the normal development of a human infant and sees the emergence of a "new subjective level of conscious awareness, with a sense of a specific past and awareness of a possible future, as well as with new insight into the consciousness of other people" that develops in the late preschool years.[18] This level of consciousness is linked to the development of the ability to tell simple narratives about one's life, and so she finds a "close connection between narrative and the emergence of a specifically human level of consciousness."[19]

Nelson's idea is that as children enter into language they learn, with the help of their caregivers, to narrate the events in their lives. At first this involves nothing much more than describing things that happened to them in sequence and

---

[17] Katherine Nelson, "Narrative and the Emergence of a Consciousness of Self," in Gary D. Fireman, Ted E. McVay, jr., and Owen J. Flanagan, eds., *Narrative and Consciousness*, New York: Oxford University Press, 2003, p. 17.

[18] Nelson, "Narrative and the Emergence of a Consciousness of Self," p. 33.

[19] Nelson, "Narrative and the Emergence of a Consciousness of Self," p. 22.

offering rudimentary evaluations (e.g., "We went with Mommy to see Daddy at work in a big building. There was a high window. We had fun.") In the beginning even these very basic narrations require a great deal of prompting and reminding from adults. Gradually, however, children learn to do this work themselves, and when they do they enjoy qualitatively new kinds of experiences and are able to participate in new forms of social interaction. Nelson describes the transformation this brings about: "This level of self understanding integrates action and consciousness into a whole self, and establishes a self-history as unique to the self, differentiated from others' experiential histories.... [I]t adds... a new awareness of self in past and future experiences and the contrast of that self to others' narratives of their past and future experiences"[20]

Children thus become Lockean selves gradually, precisely because they *already* have relationships with mature persons, interactions with whom provide the scaffolding that allows the child to develop the full range of practical capacities associated with mature personhood. While the nature of interpersonal relationships obviously changes greatly as children mature, forensic interactions do not completely overwrite what came before, and persons continue to have a wide range of different kinds of practical interests in, concerns about, and relations to others. It thus seems arbitrary and unnecessarily restrictive to think of persons as loci only of the capacity to engage in forensic relations; at least if we are looking for a practically-based account of our *literal* identity. If we wish to capture fully the practical significance facts about personal identity have for us we will need to include the practical significance of the fact that the toddler I pick up at daycare is my son, or that the individual I am backpacking with is the friend I've known since we were in preschool (and with whom I still sing "the sharing song" as we hike along the trail), as well as of the fact that the person from whom I am going to collect the money is the one who promised to pay it back or that the person who will experience the ill-effects of my failure to keep my dental appointment will be me.

3.3 The Problem of Multiplicity

When we were assuming the Lockean conception of personhood and the corresponding conception of a person as a forensic unit, the idea that personal identity should be defined in terms of sameness of consciousness was compelling. However difficult it might be to say precisely what this relation amounts to, and

---

[20] Nelson, "Narrative and the Emergence of a Consciousness of Self," p. 7. For an important philosophical treatment of related issues see Tamar Schapiro, "What is a Child?," *Ethics*, 109(4), July 1999, pp. 715–38.

whether in the end it actually is the best account of the identity of the forensic unit, it at least has plausibility as the basis of such an account. If, however, we are seeking to individuate a broader practical unit that is an appropriate target of *all* of our person-related practices and concerns a sameness of consciousness view is not a viable option, nor is anything like the relation of psychological continuity as defined by psychological continuity theorists. Some of our person-related practices and concerns apply to individuals who are not Lockean persons (e.g., infants and the demented), and the relation which constitutes a unit of these practices and concerns cannot be one that requires the cognitive machinery necessary for Lockean personhood.

In contemplating what relation might constitute a basic practical unit of the sort we are seeking, we instantly hit a rather solid-looking brick wall. Precisely because there are so many different kinds of practical considerations that apply in a person's life it is by no means obvious that we will be able to find a single relation that defines an appropriate target for them all. In looking for targets of forensic judgments and maternal ministrations alone we are pulled in two different directions. If we include all of the other practical relations that make up our form of life, the project of finding a single relation that defines the appropriate locus for our practical concerns appears, at least initially, hopeless. This is the *problem of multiplicity*.

We might be tempted to think that this problem could be addressed by simply concatenating all of the relations necessary for each of the kinds of concern we are talking about and defining personal identity in terms of that conjunction. In that way we would be guaranteed to define a unit to which all of our concerns appropriately apply. But clearly this will not accomplish what we are trying to accomplish. For one thing, a concatenation is not in itself a unit. More to the point, the motivation for the more inclusive conception of personhood was precisely to acknowledge that individuals like Carla, infants, and those with dementia *are* persons, and requiring that a person have the features necessary to be a unit of each of the different types of concern would exclude these individuals from personhood. Once the problem is laid out this way, however, our stated goal does seem truly incoherent. If the aim is to define a locus which is the appropriate target of *all* of our person-related practices (including forensic judgments) *and* to define personhood in such a way that those who are not appropriate targets of forensic judgments are persons, it is going to be a pretty hard aim to meet. We thus need to consider how we might respond to this difficulty.

One obvious possibility is to just embrace the multiplicity of personhood and give up altogether on the goal of defining a unified locus that is an appropriate target for all of our practical questions and concerns about persons. We do, in fact, use the terms "person" and "personal identity" in many different ways, some of which seem to have little to do with one another. Perhaps we can just accept that there is a wide range of different practical concerns that we have about "persons" and that these different concerns rely on different relations. This possibility is considered in depth by David Shoemaker, who provides an extremely insightful discussion of these issues. Shoemaker identifies four methodological assumptions about the relation between personal identity and practical concerns that stand behind much of the discussion in the philosophy of personal identity, and shows that each faces a serious challenge. These challenges can be met, he says, but only by revising our understanding of the project we are undertaking.

The most important revision for present purposes comes from the realization that neither our practical concerns nor our conceptions of identity are monolithic. This means that "finding *the* relation between personal identity and our practices and concerns may be a fool's errand; instead, there may be many such relations, depending on which practice or concern is in question."[21] We have many different practical concerns that we associate with personal identity, and there is no reason to think they are all connected to the same kind of identity (e.g., some might be connected to the identity of the moral self and others to numerical identity; some may be tied to biological continuity and others to psychological continuity), or that they are all connected in the same ways to the notion of identity to which they *are* connected (e.g., moral responsibility might be coincident with the identity of the moral self but dependent on sameness of consciousness). Shoemaker suggests that rather than trying to find *an* account of the relation between personal identity and practical concerns we dedicate our efforts instead to developing a better understanding of the nature of the individual concerns and the ways in which they are connected to different notions of identity.[22] There are so many different kinds of practical relations associated with persons, he concludes, and they are connected to so many different notions of identity in so many different ways, that there is no reason to suppose that we can find *a* practically-based account of personal identity.

Shoemaker's suggestion amounts to a more inclusive and somewhat softened version of the strong independence model defined in the previous chapter. The question about numerical identity is seen as one question among many, and it is not assumed that it is connected in any particular way with any of the practical concerns we have about persons. This approach is more inclusive than the strong independence model as we originally described it because the original version gave us the Lockean conception of *person* on one side and the question

---

[21]   Shoemaker, "Personal Identity and Practical Concerns," *Mind* 116(462), April 2007, p. 339.
[22]   Shoemaker, "Personal Identity," p. 354.

of metaphysical identity on the other whereas Shoemaker fractures our original question not only into two, but into an indefinite number of different inquiries. It is softened because the original strong independence model insisted that the two sets of questions were fully distinct[23] while Shoemaker leaves open the possibility that the metaphysical question of numerical identity could be connected to some practical concerns and insists only that we should not presume that it is. What Shoemaker's approach shares with the strong independence model are the claim that we do not need to assume that there is any single, unified target for all of our practical questions and concerns about persons and the suggestion that we can pursue the practical questions on their own without looking for such a locus.

There is much that is attractive in this solution, and Shoemaker is undoubtedly right that we need to understand and accept the diversity of the different kinds of questions of personal identity that we ask; the distinction between the question of the identity of the moral self and that of the forensic unit is a case in point. These are important and interesting questions in their own right, and there is no doubt that we can learn a great deal by addressing each individually in its own terms. The claim that we do not need to conceive of an ultimate locus to which the full range of our questions and concerns about a person are addressed, however, does not ring true to the experience of how we relate to the people who make up our social world. We know others as unified (albeit ridiculously complex and multi-faceted) individuals. This is most evident when we think of the people with whom we are most intimate and therefore engage along many practical dimensions. The son I feed and clothe and comfort is the same person I chastise for behaving badly to his sister and the same person to whom I try to teach the value of hard work and explain the benefit of making small sacrifices now for larger benefits later. He is also the same person whose straight As bring me pride and whose disappointments are a cause for my sadness, and the person whose health I am concerned to safeguard. I do not have a moral son and an animal son and a psychological son—I have a single son who has all of these aspects and is important to me in all of these ways. Similarly, it would be absurd for a doctor to tell a worried husband that his animal wife survived the stroke, and perhaps his sentient wife, but probably not his moral or rational agent wife.

---

[23] This is not entirely accurate since Korsgaard does think that the unity of the organism constrains the unity of the agent in the ways we have described in the previous chapter, and Olson also sees connections between the identity of the organism and some minimal kinds of practical concerns. For our purposes, however, these inaccuracies make no real difference and they can be safely ignored in the present context. What they suggest is that perhaps neither Korsgaard nor Olson is offering a pure version of a strong independence model.

This is not to deny, of course, that in many cases our interactions with others are limited to a small range of practical considerations. A surgeon may see some-one only as a patient with a biological problem to be solved; a judge may see the accused only as a being whose moral responsibility is to be assessed; and a finan-cial planner may see her client as someone whose future financial wellbeing must be optimized. This narrowing of perspective does not actually fracture the person, however, and we tend to think that a broader view might serve better (that, as it is often put, these professionals should address the "whole person"). Moreover, those who take this kind of limited viewpoint on an individual undoubtedly presuppose, if only implicitly, that there are more dimensions to the individual with whom they are interacting and that these are expressed elsewhere in their lives. However much complexity there is to our practical lives each of us is, in the end, a single thing with many facets and that is why we have a further question about *what* it is that possesses self-conscious reflection, rationality, and the ability to act as a moral agent. Olson rightly points out that this is something an account of personal iden-tity must provide and that psychological continuity theories do not do it very well. Our practical concerns are directed at *someone*, and in the end we want an answer to the question of what constitutes the integrity of that someone. Shoemaker is absolutely right that if we are to understand the nature of human identity fully we will need to recognize the extreme complexity and diversity of our practical con-cerns. But we also need to understand how, in the end, they are all concerns about a single individual.

If we must have a single unified entity that is the target of the full range of person-related practices, and if no single relation can carve out an *appropriate* tar-get of these different practices, perhaps we need to give up on the idea that the target of our practical interactions and judgments must be intrinsically suited to being so. Perhaps all we need is *an* entity that we are able to individuate and track over time, and which can be designated as the individual about which we ask prac-tical questions, make practical judgments, and otherwise engage in person-related interactions. Of course we have such an entity ready to hand in the form of the human organism.

No one I know of denies that in daily life we do, as a matter of fact, individuate persons by individuating human animals, or that human animals are in fact the loci of the myriad practical concerns we have for others. Caregivers bond with human infants and have the kinds of interactions appropriate to infants. As human children develop and gain more capacities they interact with a wider range of peo-ple in the greater variety of ways these capacities allow. If an adult human loses some of these capacities we once again revise the types of interactions in which we engage with that individual. What stays the same throughout, at least in the cases we actually encounter, is the fact that there is a single human animal involved. If we are looking for a single, unified target of all of the questions, concerns, and attitudes directed at a particular person it may thus seem as if the simplest strategy, and the one most consonant with what we actually do, is to look to the identity of the human animal.

This strategy, it should be noted, does not have quite the form of a strong independence model. The position just described, unlike that model, draws a connection (albeit a pretty weak one) between the identity of the objects that are persons (here understood in biological terms) and practical concerns. The connection is that on this view the animal represents the locus within which practical questions must be raised. This means that there can be no person-related practices that transcend the limits of a single animal; sameness of organism is necessary to being a unit of practical concern in a way it is not for the strong independence model.[24]

There is no denying that this view has a certain commonsense appeal. Furthermore, the main considerations we have seen pulling against this approach so far have come from reflection on the transfer case. The use of fantastic scenarios as a means of discovering facts about personal identity is, as I have mentioned, one that has been the subject of much suspicion, and there is good reason for this. It is not always clear that we can truly imagine what we think we are imagining, that we are not implicitly relying on illegitimate assumptions, or that we are not being manipulated by the way the tale is told. Even if we do have clear intuitions about what would happen in a world where psychological lives could change bodies, moreover, it is not clear that these would tell us anything important about our lives. Such a world might be so different from ours that it would not contain persons as we know them.[25] We should also recall that our intuitions that a locus of practical concern could be transplanted were generated when we were focusing exclusively on the forensic concerns. Perhaps this limited set of concerns moves all together, but there may be less reason to think that the full range of our practical concerns must be transferred, if at all, as a group. Our intuitions about which

---

[24] A position roughly like this has been defended by David DeGrazia, among others. See, e.g., David DeGrazia, *Human Identity and Bioethics*, Cambridge: Cambridge University Press, 2005, especially chapters 2 and 3.

[25] See, e.g., Kathleen Wilkes, *Real People: Personal Identity without Thought Experiments*, Oxford: Clarendon Press, 1988, p. 11; Peter Unger, *Identity, Consciousness and Value*, Oxford: Oxford University Press, 1990; Paul Snowdon, "Personal Identity and Brain Transplants," in D. Cockburn, ed., *Human Beings* (Royal Institute of Philosophy Supplements 29), New York: Cambridge University Press, 1991; Roy Sorensen, *Thought Experiments*, Oxford: Oxford University Press, 1992; Sören Häggqvist, *Thought Experiments in Philosophy*, Stockholm: Almqvist and Wiksell International, 1996; Tamar Gendler, *Thought Experiment: On the Powers and Limits of Imaginary Cases*, New York: Garland Pub., 2000.

concerns are to be directed where are, for instance, probably somewhat murkier when the cerebrum that is transplanted is that of an infant or someone with severe dementia.

The worries about fantastic hypothetical scenarios must be taken seriously and I will return to discuss them in Chapter 6. But we must take no less seriously the fact that discussion of the possibility that the *person* that we care about and interact with might be able to come apart from a particular human organism has been a ubiquitous part of virtually every human culture throughout history, expressed not only in philosophy, but in religion, literature, film, science fiction, folktales, and a wide variety of other forms. This does not guarantee, of course, that those who believe we can coherently imagine such a possibility are correct to do so, but it does show something about a natural and persistent part of our experience of persons. When we are not doing metaphysics at least, we in fact do perceive others as something "more than" human organisms. We do not see others (or ourselves) only as animals with particular capacities, but as beings somehow essentially connected to the capacities that are displayed by the animal.

Admittedly, this proves very little by itself. Defenders of the view that the locus of our concerns is a human animal can reject this widespread sense of persons as a muddled artifact of pre-scientific thought or wishful thinking. That we see it that way does not make it so. This is a powerful position, and I will not be able to explain fully why I reject it until the very end of the book. For now I will merely invoke Olson's observation that unless the intuitions pulling us toward a position are dispelled what we have is a research project rather than grounds for rejection. The intuition which I am relying on now is not, I should make it clear, necessarily the intuition that a person can continue separately from the human organism it now inhabits—this is a somewhat stronger claim to which we will return later. For now, I am focusing only on the somewhat weaker idea that to define the identity of a person in terms of biological facts alone somehow fails to capture not only what is important to us about persons, but what persons fundamentally are. The research project this idea inspires is the project of providing the alternative definition of "person" that will capture what is lost in the biological approach.

In order to pursue this project, however, we will need somehow to get over or around the brick wall we have encountered. We are looking to define persons as unified targets of all of our person-related practical concerns and have rejected a definition of persons in biological terms because a human organism as such is not an inherently *appropriate* locus for these concerns. We have also seen, however, that there is reason to expect that no single relation can define a locus that will be by its nature appropriate to all of these different practical considerations, at least not one that will also allow us to count infants and those with cognitive deficits as persons. We thus need a response to the problem of multiplicity.

There are, in fact, a few slightly different kinds of challenges that arise from the problem of multiplicity. One might be called the "challenge of individual unity." The challenge here is to explain how an *individual* person, defined as the appropriate target of the range of person-related practices and concerns, can be a single entity given that the appropriate loci of the various concerns and practices are defined in terms of different relations. This challenge has both a synchronic and diachronic dimension. The synchronic challenge asks how we prevent the individual from splintering into a moral person, and a prudential person, and a playmate person, and an object-of-maternal-care person, etc. in the way Shoemaker's analysis suggests. Why isn't a mature adult person, in other words, actually a concatenation of several different loci rather than a single locus? The diachronic challenge asks how an infant and the mature adult she becomes can be the same person on this view given that the adult is an appropriate locus of particular practical concerns that the infant is not.

The other challenge is what might be called the "challenge of definitional unity." This is the challenge of explaining how we can offer a unified and meaningful definition of what it is to be a person in terms of being the locus of person-related practices and concerns when different individuals are appropriate loci of different ranges of such practices and concerns, as must be the case if we are to claim that individuals like Carla are persons. The worry can be put this way: forensic judgments are among our person-related practices; an individual either is or is not an appropriate target of such judgments; those with severe cognitive deficits are not appropriate targets of forensic judgments; therefore either persons are not necessarily appropriate targets of all of our person-related practices or the severely cognitively impaired are not persons.

This reasoning appears sound and so seems to present a challenge to our project that is insurmountable. There is, however, a way to resist the argument made here, and hence ways of meeting the implied challenge. To do so, however, we will need to tweak our understanding of what it means to be an "appropriate" target of a particular practical concern. So far we have not given this question much explicit attention. We have been implicitly assuming something like the following understanding: In order for someone to be an appropriate target of, for instance, moral judgments, it must be the case that a question about whether she is responsible for some action might coherently be answered "yes." If I ask whether K.J. is responsible for Kate's earlier crimes the answer might conceivably have been answered "yes" (since K.J. is the right kind of thing about which to ask questions about moral responsibility) even if it turns out that the answer is in fact "no." If I ask whether a two-day-old infant or a severely demented octogenarian is responsible for what they have just done there is, in at least one sense, no meaningful way to give an affirmative answer and a clear way in which they are the wrong kind of thing about which to ask such a question. We can call this understanding of what it is to be an appropriate target of a particular practical concern "strong appropriateness" and say that someone is a "strongly appropriate" target of a particular concern when this condition holds with respect to it.

If this is our conception of appropriateness, it does indeed seem impossible to find a relation that defines a single unified locus which is the (strongly) appropriate target for all of our practical questions and concerns. The question of appropriateness, however, turns out to be somewhat more complicated than that, and I will argue that there is a weaker understanding of this idea that allows us to see infants and the demented as (in this attenuated sense) appropriate targets of forensic judgments without (as it may be feared) robbing the notion of appropriateness of any content. To get to this understanding of "appropriateness" and the practically-based account of personal identity it entails we can start by looking more closely at the challenge of individual unity, which we will consider in the next chapter. The challenge of definitional unity will be addressed in Chapter 5.

4

Complexity and Individual Unity

In this chapter we will find important resources for meeting the challenges of individual unity by looking at two different accounts of personal identity. The first is Jeff McMahan's Embodied Mind Account; the second is the Narrative Self-Constitution View, an account that I developed earlier in *The Constitution of Selves*.[1] Neither view has the exact question we are addressing here as its target, and neither provides a direct response to the challenge of individual unity. Each, however, provides a new perspective on the structural features of the unity of the self which can be extracted from the context in which it appears and adapted to our current aims.

I will begin with McMahan's account, which is especially helpful in answering the synchronic challenge of individual unity, and then move on to the Narrative Self-Constitution View, which provides tools that can be used to address the diachronic challenge. The key move in each case is the description of a kind of holism (synchronic in McMahan's cases and diachronic in the case of the Narrative Self-Constitution View) which allows us to attribute characteristics to wholes that do not apply to each of their parts. Not only do these views give us insights that allow us to answer the challenges of individual unity, they also point the way to a strategy for addressing the challenge of definitional unity.

4.1 McMahan's Embodied Mind Account

In *The Ethics of Killing: Problems at the Margins of Life* Jeff McMahan addresses difficult questions about the permissibility of killing in cases where "the metaphysical or moral status of the individual killed is uncertain or controversial"[2] or where

---

[1] Marya Schechtman, *The Constitution of Selves*, Ithaca: Cornell University Press, 1996, pp. 93–135.
[2] Jeff McMahan, *The Ethics of Killing: Problems at the Margins of Life*, Oxford: Oxford University Press, 2002, p. vii.

death would be a benefit rather than a harm to the individual killed. Such questions arise with respect to abortion, the removal of life support from the terminally ill, and the harvesting of organs for transplantation from comatose patients, to name just a few examples. Intuitively, McMahan says, these questions are inextricably bound up with questions of personal identity. To know what kind of harm we are doing to a person who suffers some kind of vicissitude we need to know whether the person has survived that vicissitude, and so whether she is still there to be harmed or benefitted. We also need to know about the limits of a being's egoistic concern—her stake in having a future and in that future's having a certain character. He thus begins his investigation with a theoretical discussion of personal identity, and develops an account which he calls the "Embodied Mind Account." The part of McMahan's work that is most relevant to us is his discussion of how the intuitions behind psychological continuity theory fit into the Embodied Mind Account. Before we can get to this material, however, we need a relatively detailed overview of the account and his main arguments for it.

4.1.1 An overview

Because of the nature of his overall project, McMahan's search for an account of identity focuses on those who do not have the full complement of capacities typical of mature adult persons and emphasizes the connection between personal identity and egoistic concern. It is, for him, a basic methodological principle that we should look for an account of identity where the limits of the person coincide with the limits of this concern since there is, he says, "a strong *presumption* that personal identity is a sufficient basis for egoistic concern," and this alone "would support the requirement that, in developing an account of personal identity, we should seek to achieve maximum congruence between personal identity and the reach of egoistic concern."[3] His principle is thus to give precedence to any view that makes egoistic concern and personal identity coincide "where it is logically possible to do so." [4]

McMahan uses this principle to argue against the major accounts of personal identity, including sameness of soul views, psychological continuity theories, and animalism. For our purposes, what is most important is the way in which this

---

[3] McMahan, *The Ethics of Killing*, p. 52.

[4] McMahan, *The Ethics of Killing*, p. 54. This caveat is required because he believes that the fission case *as originally described by Parfit* (the importance of this qualification will be explained later) represents a situation in which the two cannot be made to coincide. In this case, McMahan says, the original person does have a true egoistic interest in the two fission products, even though he is identical to neither. Aside from this case, however, or any other where it can be shown to be logically impossible to make personal identity and egoistic concern coincide, he takes it as a strong count against an account of personal identity if it fails to do so.

COMPLEXITY AND INDIVIDUAL UNITY 91

method works against psychological continuity theories. McMahan charges these accounts with defining identity in a way that allows for an unnecessary divergence between personal identity and egoistic concern. Using the definition found in psychological continuity theories, he says, it is possible to generate cases in which intuitively there is a basis for egoistic concern but identity does not hold and cases where the view says there is identity but intuitively there is no basis for egoistic concern.

As an example of the first kind of situation he offers the all-too-real case of Alzheimer's disease. It is a consequence of the psychological account that in late-enough stages of Alzheimer's-related dementia, the conscious being who will come to inhabit one's body will no longer be oneself, but rather a "post-person" that is left when the person has ceased. This, says McMahan, is extremely counterintuitive. "If, for example, one were to imagine oneself in the early stages of Alzheimer's disease," he argues, "one would fear any suffering attendant upon the final stages of the condition in a self-interested or egoistic way."[5]

McMahan allows that a reductionist psychological theorist like Parfit might well acknowledge the likelihood of such an attitude and attempt to capture it by distinguishing between the psychological account *of identity* (which he refers to just as the "psychological account") and the psychological account *of egoistic concern*; in other words, distinguishing between personal identity and what matters in survival. A psychological account of egoistic concern proposes psychological continuity as an account not of identity itself but of the "prudential unity relations"—the relations that support egoistic concern. Egoistic concern, unlike identity, can admit of degree. Since identity is determinate[6] Parfit's psychological account defines it in terms of overlapping chains of *strong* connectedness. As we have seen, this provides a "yes" or "no" answer about identity in every case at the cost of some arbitrariness. Parfit could then say that there are some grounds for egoistic concern even where there are only overlapping chains of *weak* psychological connectedness (which holds where there are some psychological connections, but fewer than half the number of connections that hold every day in the lives of typical people) even though identity does not hold. This move does capture our intuitions about egoistic concern in the Alzheimer's case, McMahan allows, but only at the cost of unnecessarily severing the conditions of identity from the conditions of egoistic concern. If our best account of the prudential unity relations

---

[5] McMahan, *The Ethics of Killing*, p. 47.
[6] That is, the logical relation of identity must be determinate, so if we wish to give an *identity* criterion we must make the criterion determinate by fiat, even if the question of identity is ultimately empty in the sense discussed in Chapter 1.

puts the threshold for egoistic concern well below where the psychological account of identity places the threshold for personal identity, McMahan argues, we should revise the account of identity so that where the threshold for concern is met (as in late-stage Alzheimer's) so is the threshold for identity.

An example of the second kind of case—where the psychological account says there is identity but intuitively there is no basis for egoistic concern—is found in Parfit's Teletransportation case. I have already alluded to this response to Teletransportation in the context of discussing the justification for and nature of the psychological continuity theory's requirement that psychological continuity be "appropriately caused." While many people have a strong intuition that the transplantation of one's brain into a different body would involve the transfer of *oneself* into a new body, McMahan argues, considerably fewer feel confident that the destruction of one's brain and the construction of a replica on Mars or anywhere else would count as one's survival. Nor is it evident to such people that one should have *egoistic* concern for the replica's experiences in such a case. [7]

Taking his reflections on the cases of Alzheimer's and Teletransportation together, McMahan says, suggests two changes that should be made to the psychological account of both egoistic concern and personal identity. First, the bounds of both identity and egoistic concern should be defined in terms of "broad psychological continuity" (i.e., the weaker kind that meets the minimum threshold for egoistic concern) instead of "strong psychological continuity" (i.e., overlapping chains of strong connectedness); second, it should be required that this broad psychological continuity be caused by the continued functioning of the same brain. Recognition of the need for these revisions, together with the tying up of a few loose ends, leads to a new account of both egoistic concern and identity—the Embodied Mind Account. The Embodied Mind Account of egoistic concern defines the limits of that concern in terms of the "physical and functional continuity of enough of those areas of the individual's brain in which consciousness is realized to preserve the capacity to support consciousness

[7] It is here that the qualifier that the fission case *as described by Parfit* shows a legitimate disconnect between identity and what matters becomes important (see note 4). In Parfit's case, as you will recall, a brain with complete redundancy in the two hemispheres is bisected and transplanted into two waiting skulls. While Parfit's case is compelling, McMahan says, the parallel case of "Double Replication" in which two replicas are created by teletransportation-like scanners is not. My discussion of the extreme claim in Chapter 1 raises a question about how seriously we should really take these intuitions, since I suggested there that Parfit is right that on reflection they are suspect. Since all I am trying to do here is give an outline of McMahan's view which will allow me to describe in detail the part that will help with the problem of multiplicity, I will ignore that complication here. Even if we reject McMahan's claim about egoistic concern in cases of replication, the part of the view that matters for my purposes stands.

or mental activity."[8] Since McMahan follows the methodological rule that an account of personal identity should coincide with an account of egoistic concern as far as possible, he proposes that "the corresponding criterion of personal identity is the continued functioning, in nonbranching form, of enough of the same brain to be capable of generating consciousness or mental activity."[9] This view, he claims, captures the intuitions that the psychological account could not, providing a closer congruence between the absolute limits of egoistic concern and the absolute limits of the person.

There is a great deal of interesting and important analysis in McMahan's discussion which I have omitted here, but this overview will suffice for a general background picture of the view. It should be evident that my approach to the question of personal identity is somewhat different from McMahan's. I would link identity to a broader range of practical concerns than he does and, as I mentioned in the last chapter, I would also argue that personhood and personal identity can extend beyond the bounds of sentience.[10] Moreover, his account operates with a coincidence model of the relation between personal identity and what he takes to be the relevant practical consideration (egoistic concern), while I endorse a dependence model. What I hope to take from his view is an insight about a possible *structure* for an account of personal identity rather than details about the specific relation in terms of which identity is to be defined. This structural insight is found in an element of his account that we have not yet discussed, the theory of time-relative interests.

4.1.2 The theory of time-relative interests

While McMahan rejects the Lockean claim that higher-order psychological connections are necessary for personal identity, he does see a grain of truth in this assertion, and he makes room for the intuitive pull of the view within the Embodied Mind Account. All that is required for identity on this account is egoistic concern, and egoistic concern can be in place without complex psychological connections. His concession to the Lockean intuition is to allow that there are significant differences between the grounds for egoistic concern in creatures with the forensic capacities and creatures who are minimally sentient. McMahan develops this idea in his innovative theory of time-relative interests. The basic idea behind this theory is that egoistic concern can be a matter of degree, and that psychological unity

---

[8] McMahan, *The Ethics of Killing*, pp. 67–8. Peter Unger develops an account of our identity that has interesting points of convergence with McMahan's but is nevertheless quite different in *Identity, Consciousness and Value*, Oxford: Oxford University Press, 1990.
[9] McMahan, *The Ethics of Killing*, p. 68.
[10] Although these are admittedly degenerate cases, and I have not yet provided a full account of why I think this. I will discuss some of these reasons later in this chapter.

of the sort psychological continuity theorists use to define identity can provide the basis for a higher degree of concern than is strictly necessary for personal continuation. He thus argues that "the rational degree of egoistic concern about one's own future varies with the degree of *psychological unity* between oneself now and oneself in the future,"[11] where psychological unity is understood as "a complex notion, encompassing both psychological connectedness and continuity."[12] The degree of psychological unity within a life, according to McMahan, is "a function of the richness, complexity, and coherence of the psychological architecture that is carried forward through time."[13]

The kind of psychological unity found in the lives of typical adult human beings is responsible for the especially strong kind of egoistic interest we have in our own continuation. Consider, he says, a sentient animal with a very simple psychological life and contents of consciousness limited to the specious present—one with no "memory or foresight" and "no psychological architecture to carry forward: no structure of beliefs, desires, attitudes, dispositions, or traits of character."[14] All such a creature has is its experiences. Since those experiences might be pleasant or unpleasant, the animal has grounds for some egoistic concern for the future, "but," McMahan adds, "our intuitive sense is that the reason to care *for its sake* is absolutely minimal."[15] The difference between that creature continuing and its being replaced by another with a similarly pleasant life becomes very thin. This reflection leads to the insight that "psychological unity within the lives of persons such as ourselves gives our lives as wholes a moral and prudential significance that the mere sum of our experience lacks—or to put it differently, that makes our lives as wholes significant *units* for moral and prudential evaluation."[16]

He thus offers a theory where the degree to which a conscious being has an interest in (in the sense of a stake in) the nature of its future depends upon the degree of psychological unity in its life and its psychological connection to its future. The grain of truth in the psychological account's suggestion that psychological unity is required for egoistic concern, according to McMahan, is that without such unity the degree of justified egoistic concern is very small. Most of what we think of when we think of our egoistic interests does, in fact, depend upon the kinds of higher-order connections and capacities psychological continuity theories require. This view can thus acknowledge that the continuity of a single brain

[11] *The Ethics of Killing*, p. 74. [12] *The Ethics of Killing*, p. 74.
[13] *The Ethics of Killing*, p. 75. [14] *The Ethics of Killing*, p. 75.
[15] *The Ethics of Killing*, pp. 75–6. [16] *The Ethics of Killing*, p. 76.

with the capacity for bare sentience is indeed a very thin relation that does not give us much reason to care about the future, while still insisting that it provides some basis for egoistic concern.

McMahan uses this analysis to set up arguments for his ethical claims about the margins of life; specifically that in marginal cases the morality of killing should be evaluated primarily by the impact it would have on the victim at the time instead of in terms of the value of the life as a whole. Given the purposes to which he is putting it, McMahan offers the theory of time-relative interests as a theory of ego-istic concern and not of personal identity. In light of his methodological princi-ple, however, we can ask exactly how this part of the view fits with his account of identity. It is here that we find ideas useful for developing our response to the synchronic challenge of individual unity. It is clear, of course, that on McMahan's view sophisticated psychological relations and strong psychological unity are not required for identity or survival. As soon as the threshold for minimal egoistic concern is met the threshold for the continued existence of the person is also met. But where these more powerful connections *do* exist, we might ask, do they play any role in constituting identity at all?

One natural reading says that they do not. They are icing on the cake, a psycho-logical relation that occurs within the already fully-defined confines of a single life. These relations may give that life a significance it otherwise would not have had, but they in no way contribute directly to its continuation. There is, however, another way of thinking about the connection between the theory of egoistic concern McMahan offers and his account of personal identity. According to this second reading the psychological unity relations that support the sophisticated prudential concern that typical adult humans have for their futures are not *added on* to the basic continuity of consciousness that supports this egoistic concern, but are instead the *form* our continuity of consciousness takes. This means that in the lives of typical adult humans there are not two distinct sets of relations—a con-tinuity of the capacity to support minimal consciousness or mental activity that defines our identity, and some other relations which, when they occur together with this minimal sameness of sentience, make our futures matter to us in the spe-cial ways that they do. Instead, the single relation that in fact defines our identity (and grounds our egoistic concern for the future) takes a form that is particularly strong, stronger than it needs to be for our continuation—and when it takes this form it generates an especially powerful kind of concern for our own futures, one that is unique to beings like us, while also supporting more basic prudential rela-tions at the same time.

The difference between these two readings is fairly subtle, but it is important. On the first reading continuity of bare sentience establishes the threshold for minimal concern and this very relation must hold throughout a single life. Other kinds of connections can come and go, as it were, on top of this identity-establishing relation, but if the person is to continue, the continuity of bare sentience must continue in its original form no matter what other, more sophisticated, relations are added to it. On the second reading the relation that defines identity (continuity of consciousness) can take many different forms, some quite basic and others very sophisticated. On this reading the complex psychological relations are not simply present within an existing continuity of bare sentience as additional relations, but instead constitute the form that the capacity for sentience takes in this case.

Some analogies may help to make this difference clearer. To illustrate the first reading we can employ the common metaphor of consciousness as a room or place (the metaphor that, as we saw earlier, Korsgaard rejects). On this reading, the continuity of the capacity for bare sentience in terms of which the Embodied Mind Account defines identity is like the walls that literally delimit the space, and the rich psychological relations called for by psychological continuity theories are like furnishings which can make the room sumptuous and comfortable, or allow us to engage in new and different kinds of activities within it, but which do not alter its architecture or boundaries in any fundamental way. On the second reading the relation between minimal sentience and more complex psychological relations is more like the relation between a musical theme and complex variations upon it. Consider Mozart's *Ah Je Vous Dirai Maman*, which starts with the simple folk theme known broadly as *Twinkle, Twinkle Little Star* (among other things) and presents twelve variations, some of which are extremely complicated. Although each variation is a *version* of the simple theme, none is generated by the mere addition of other notes, and there is no note-for-note reproduction of the original in the sophisticated variations. The musical sophistication of the variations is not achieved by placing something else on top of the original melody, but rather by transforming and complexifying it. On the first understanding of McMahan's view adding sophisticated psychological capacities is like plunking out the simple theme with the right hand and then adding some sophisticated left hand pyrotechnics. On the second understanding it is more like replacing the simple plunking with one of the variations.

I am not sure if McMahan himself takes a position with respect to these two readings, and in any case I will, at this point, abandon McMahan's own exposition to reflect on the ways in which the ideas I have been focusing on can illuminate our own project. For a variety of reasons—including the fact that I believe it is the most intrinsically plausible and coheres the best with existing empirical evidence—I favor the second of the two readings of the theory of time-relative interests. The virtue of this second reading from our perspective is that it provides a compelling picture of how the identity of a person could be defined by a *single* relation that makes her an appropriate locus of the full range of person-related concerns even though these concerns can come apart. It shows us, in other words, a way of thinking about how a person at a time can be a genuinely unified target of a variety of different practical concerns.

To see this, let's restrict our attention for the moment to a segment of a life in which there is uncontroversially (or as uncontroversially as is possible) a single continuing person—the adulthood of a typical human in good health. According to the view we are describing, the relation that constitutes the identity of this person over time is a sophisticated form of sameness of consciousness that, by its very nature, defines an appropriate target of the range of practical considerations we associate with full-blown personhood, from the basic to the forensic. The person is, during this phase of life, a locus of all of these questions and judgments in virtue of a single complex relation (for McMahan, the strong continuity of consciousness), which makes the person at once an appropriate locus of the full set of person-related practices.

It is crucial to understand (and so I reiterate) that the situation described here is not the same as that in which a person is an appropriate locus of all of these concerns because in *addition* to the relation that defines his identity there are also other, distinct, relations that make the already-defined person more complicated, and so a target of additional practical judgments. The relation that makes a mature person an appropriate locus of forensic concern is, for a typical adult, the very same relation that makes him an appropriate unit of fundamental egoistic concern. Return to the analogy with *Ah Je Vous Dirai Maman*. One of the more sophisticated variations it contains may be an appropriate vehicle through which to display one's virtuosity in a way that the simple theme introduced at the beginning is not. This is undeniably in some sense because the complex variation contains *more* than the simple introduction of the theme, but it would be a mistake to say that the features that make this particular variation appropriate for a display of virtuosity are distinct from the features that make it a version of *Twinkle, Twinkle Little Star*. The virtuosic bits do not sit on top of the simple theme and cannot, in this particular variation, simply be separated off from them. This version of *Twinkle, Twinkle Little Star* is inherently an appropriate locus for displaying virtuosity, even if other versions are not. My suggestion is that the version of the relation that defines identity in typical adult human persons is, in a similar way, inherently a target of the full range of person-related concerns.

McMahan (like Lindemann) sees bare sentience as the minimum relation that must hold for basic prudential concern to apply, and if he endorsed my preferred reading of the theory of time-relative interests he would say (like Locke) that strong self-consciousness, a stronger version of the more basic relation, is the relation that underlies the full complement of person-related capacities, both basic and forensic. In order to meet other desiderata I will ultimately define personhood and personal identity in terms of different relations than he does, and so the solution to the problem of individual unity his view yields is not precisely the same answer I will use (I will describe the overlap and differences in more detail in the next chapter). The theory of time-relative interests does, however, provide a new way of thinking about what it means for an entity to be an appropriate target of multiple practical concerns at once which gives us a general structure for answering the synchronic challenge of individual unity.

The synchronic challenge arises because it seems as if the fact that different practical concerns (or interrelated sets of practical concerns) can hold independently in different loci implies that each must have an independent relation that defines its appropriate target. This is taken to further suggest that something which can be a target of all of these concerns must be so in virtue of having all of these different relations co-present within it—like a computer that is useful and important in several different ways because it happens to have many different kinds of software loaded on to it, each of which supports one function. Understanding the nature of the multiple practical concerns that apply to a person this way, it is unclear how we could get a single locus that is by its very nature an appropriate locus for the full range of practical concerns. Our reading of the theory of time-relative interests shows us where the reasoning that leads to this impasse breaks down.

Staying within McMahan's parameters, we see that the fact that a person on the margins can be an appropriate target of minimal egoistic concern without being an appropriate target of some of the more sophisticated types of moral and prudential considerations that apply to typical adult humans does *not* imply that in the adult human the relation that supports minimal concern is present in its original form within the adult but *conjoined* with other relations. Instead we have a different relation that by its nature supports the whole of the expanded set of concerns. More broadly, we do not need to move from the fact that we can have loci that are appropriate targets of some but not all of our person-related practices to the conclusion that something which is an appropriate target of more than one of these concerns is so because it contains each of the relations that independently defines an appropriate target of a particular concern. Instead, there can be individual relations, different from one another, that define appropriate loci which are inherently appropriate targets of sets of different concerns, just as the complex variations in *Ah Je Vous Dirai Maman* are simultaneously versions of the original theme and vehicles for displaying virtuosity without including the exposition of the theme in its original form at all.

This offers a rather tidy response to the synchronic challenge of individual unity, but it does not help much with the diachronic version of this challenge. In fact it makes it worse. Even if each is a strongly unified locus it remains the case that infants are defined in terms of one relation that makes them the appropriate target of one set of practical concerns and adults are defined in terms of a different relation that makes them the target of a different set of practical concerns (one that overlaps to some extent, but not entirely, with those related to the infant). We have a way of understanding how a mature person can be a truly unified locus, but if personhood requires being an appropriate target of forensic concerns, we do not have a way of understanding infants as persons, and so no way to see them as the same persons as adults. To respond to this challenge we will need some slightly different tools. These can be found by reflecting on the Narrative Self-Constitution View.

4.2 The Narrative Self-Constitution View

The Narrative Self-Constitution View was developed as an alternative to psychological continuity theories and devised to capture the original Lockean insight while avoiding the objection from the extreme claim. The view is thus broadly Lockean, understanding personhood primarily in terms of forensic capabilities, and this is an obvious limitation with respect to our current endeavor. Nevertheless, some of its key features speak directly to questions of how to build a strong diachronic unity, and so once again there are structural features of the view that can be expanded to help address the issues arising from the problem of multiplicity. As before I will begin with an overview of the account before focusing on the way in which it can be used for current purposes. To clarify my current position I should add that although I stand by a great deal of what I said in originally defending the view, I now believe that the Narrative Self-Constitution View is more limited in scope than I originally thought and is also guilty of conflating questions about the identity of the moral self with questions about the identity of the forensic unit. I will explain where I think these confusions arise over the course of the discussion.

4.2.1 An overview

The defense of the Narrative Self-Constitution View rests on the claim that psychological continuity theories are subject to the argument from the extreme claim because they have misrepresented what psychological continuity consists in. The argument is that they are forced to this misrepresentation because they frame the question of personal identity as a question about the reidentification of an object. This requires that they define identity in terms of relations between time-slices, which in turn requires thinking of our psychological lives as something that can intelligibly be described in terms of momentary units, distorting the very features that make the psychological approach appealing in the first place.

I thus suggested that we instead think of the problem of personal identity as one of *characterization*—the question of which actions, experiences, and traits are rightly attributable to a person. The answer to a question of personal identity can then take the form of a relation between persons and psychological elements or actions rather than of a relation between time-slices. Such an account, I argued, will be non-reductive but still informative. In particular I urged that rather than thinking of identity-constituting psychological continuity in terms of overlapping chains of psychological connections properly caused, we should instead understand it in narrative terms, a revision made possible by framing the question as one of characterization. We constitute ourselves as persons, on this view, by developing and operating with a (mostly implicit) autobiographical narrative which acts as the lens through which we experience the world. Persons experience their present as flowing from a particular past and flowing toward a particular future, and this way of relating to the present changes the character of experience altogether. The claim is that understanding psychological flow in narrative terms generates the deep diachronic unity of self-consciousness that is taken to underlie the capacity for forensic actions and which psychological continuity theories fail to adequately express (hence their susceptibility to the argument from the extreme claim).

The key move here is the claim that narratives have a kind of diachronic holism that psychological continuity as it is understood in psychological continuity theories does not. While psychological continuity is defined as a relation between independently definable time-slices, in a narrative the parts exist in the form they do only as abstractions from the whole, and so the whole is, in an important sense, prior to the parts. This is not to say, of course, that there are no individual moments of a life until the life is over, but it does imply that in constructing an account of personal identity this view does not start with person-parts that must somehow be brought together into a single entity. It begins instead with the ongoing narrative of a person's life from which individual moments can be abstracted. This allows the view to address the challenge from the extreme claim because being a person, on this view, involves conceiving of our lives in this holistic way, experiencing them at each moment as ongoing wholes. (Nelson's account of the development of self-consciousness concomitant with the development of self-narrative discussed in Chapter 3 lends further credence to this claim.)

The fact that persons experience their lives as unified wholes makes it rational for a person to have a special kind of concern for her own future. If, for instance, the hard work I do now will be rewarded in the future when I achieve my goal, the Narrative Self-Constitution View implies that I am, right now, experiencing hard-work-in-the-service-of-a-goal rather than hard-work-imposed-on-me-for-the-benefit-of-another, and these are different experiences. The anticipated future reward is already affecting the character of the hard work, just as anticipated trouble already tempers present joy. Of course, anticipations can be in error. My anticipated reward may make work light now, but in fact the reward may go to someone else when the time comes. If so, at that time I will experience not just a privation of reward, but a peculiar kind of disappointment that comes not just from being denied something I value, but from having worked so hard and expected so much only to have my expectations dashed. This experience, too, has the character it does because of its role in the narrative. The possibility of such an outcome will, moreover, already be part of the experience of the initial trying, even if my expectations are high, and so will condition and influence the experience of anticipation.

There are many features that must be added to this basic view to make it viable as a proposed account of personal identity. It is important, for one thing, to make clear that "having an autobiographical narrative" does not amount to consciously retelling one's life story always (or ever) to oneself or to anyone else. The sense in which we have autobiographical narratives on this account is cashed out mostly in terms of the way in which an implicit understanding of the ongoing course of our lives influences our experience and deliberation. It is also necessary to put constraints on what counts as an identity-constituting narrative. A view which had the implication that a person could make whatever attributes, experiences, or actions she chooses her own simply by thinking that they are is obviously a non-starter. The Narrative Self-Constitution View thus demands that a properly identity-constituting narrative meet what it calls the "reality constraint" and the "articulation constraint," constraints aimed roughly at ensuring that an individual is applying our shared conception of personhood to herself, and so is able to interact effectively with others along the forensic dimensions which are taken to define personhood in the Lockean tradition.

In its original form, the Narrative Self-Constitution View is, I now think, guilty of running together the questions that have been distinguished in the preceding chapters. It is an account of forensic personhood, but in retrospect, I think it wavers between offering an account of the identity of the moral self and an account of the identity of the forensic unit. For many, the switch from the reidentification to the characterization question automatically signals a switch to questions about the moral self. There are some good reasons for thinking so—my first move in introducing the view is to draw a distinction between the "Who am I?" question raised by a confused adolescent (which I link to the characterization question) and the "Who am I?" question asked by an amnesia victim (which I link to the rei-dentification question). At the same time, however, I meant for the characteriza-tion question also to answer questions about attribution at the most fundamental level—not only which beliefs and desires are *truly* mine in the sense of the moral self, but which are mine in the most basic and literal sense. The distinction here, which I now figure as one between the identity of the moral self and the iden-tity of the forensic unit, is described in the original discussion of the Narrative Self-Constitution View as one of degree. Those elements of my narrative that are especially central, I said, are truly mine, while those on the periphery are mine in only the most basic sense. I now think this is far too simple, but I do believe that when the appropriate distinctions and caveats are made and the scope of the view properly delimited, the Narrative Self-Constitution View can provide compelling answers to some questions about personal continuation and moral selves.[17]

For present purposes the important feature of the Narrative Self-Constitution View is that it sees persons as inherently diachronic entities. What makes someone the right kind of thing to be held responsible for at least some of her past actions and to have prudential concern for at least some of her future experiences is not simply some attribute that she possesses at the moment (e.g., self-consciousness or rationality), but the fact that past and future events are actively incorporated into present experience. It is the way in which experience is structured over time that generates the deep connections among different moments of a life that make a person a strongly appropriate target of forensic judgments, and so the attribute of being such a target should not be thought of as something that applies from moment to moment, but rather as something that inherently applies only over a stretch of time during which the structure of experience generates a diachronically as well as synchronically unified locus.

This feature does not yet, of course, provide a solution to the diachronic chal-lenge of individual unity as we have raised it. The Narrative Self-Constitution View is an account of Lockean persons and is meant to explain what makes persons suitable targets of forensic judgments. What is described is how first-personal experience can be unified over time in the way that seems neces-sary for there to be an appropriate target of the forensic capacities. This strong

---

[17] Much of my work on personal identity since *The Constitution of Selves* involves a similar confla-tion of questions, I now think. I do not disavow this work, but I see it as fleshing out various practical or metaphorical conceptions of identity rather than speaking to the literal question I am addressing here. Some examples include "Diversity in Unity: Practical Unity and Personal Boundaries," *Synthese*, 162(3), June 2008, pp. 405–23; "Personal Identity and the Past," *Philosophy, Psychiatry, and Psychology*, 12(1), March 2005, pp. 9–22 and 27–9; and "Empathic Access: The Missing Ingredient in Personal Identity," *Philosophical Explorations*, 4(2), 2001, pp. 94–110.

diachronic unification, although central to the lives of healthy adult persons, is not part of the psychology of infants and the demented, and explaining how it happens does not yet show us how to allow that an infant, a mature person, and her later demented self can all be persons, let alone the same person. In fact, the Narrative Self-Constitution View is explicitly committed to the fact that infants are not persons and that persons cannot survive severe dementia. I still believe that there is an important question about how the kind of unity that makes for an appropriate target of the forensic concerns is possible and that, properly delimited, the Narrative Self-Constitution View can provide a satisfying answer to that question. Because of the basic practical concerns discussed in the last chapter, however, I now also believe that a plausible account of *literal* identity will need to allow for the personhood of infants and the cognitively impaired, and so to explain how a Lockean person can be the same person as her earlier infant self and later demented self.

While the Narrative Self-Constitution View does not answer, or even ask that question, it does contain a feature that can be expanded to do so. Key to the diachronic unity defined by the Narrative Self-Constitution View is the idea that we should understand that unity not just in terms of relations between individual moments, but also in terms of the overall structure in which those moments play a role. A narrative is not merely certain kinds of connections between one event and the next; it is a structural whole that gives unity to the events within it in virtue of the fact that they together instantiate that structure. With the proper modifications this general idea can be applied beyond the confines of discussions of Lockean personhood and first-personal experience.

4.2.2 *Expanding the narrative self-constitution view—narratives and lives*

The Narrative Self-Constitution View, as we have just seen, is focused on the phenomenology of personhood, and so on the question of how unity of first-personal experience is formed. The narratives in terms of which it defines identity are thus self-narratives, generated from the first-person perspective. Since infants and those with dementia do not self-narrate, they are outside of the purview of the Narrative Self-Constitution View. To expand the account for present purposes, however, we can take the general ideas about narrative unity it employs and combine them with Lindemann's views about the role others play in constructing a person's narrative. This role is twofold: First, the recognition of one's narrative by others is an essential feature of identity for mature adults; an identity-constituting narrative is not just a story you have about yourself but also the stories others tell about you. Second, those without the wherewithal to narrate their own lives (e.g., infants and those with cognitive deficits) can be given an identity through narratives created by others.

These claims about the function of social narrations in a person's life suggest a way of expanding the basic concepts employed in the Narrative Self-Constitution View to allow for the inclusion of infants and the demented. What I propose is that we think of identity-constituting narratives not just as the narratives we create for ourselves, but the narratives of our lives that are created in conjunction with other people. Infants and the demented cannot self-narrate, but other people can and do form narrative conceptions of them. In keeping with present aims, the claim is not about the way in which others can form narrative conceptions of what infants and the demented are *like* (although of course they can do that as well) but rather about the way in which they can begin or continue an *individual* life narrative that anticipates or recalls the unfolding of that *individual* life, bringing past and future into the present, as it were, on behalf of the person who cannot do it herself.[18]

The interactions between infants and caregivers that we discussed in the previous chapter are an example of this. When parents, pediatricians, and other adults interact with an infant it is in anticipation that the infant will develop in ways that will be influenced by what happens now. Our interactions with young children who do not yet possess forensic capacities anticipate their development, and so we treat them as individuals who *will* possess these capacities. We talk to infants and very young children as if they have a level of self-consciousness or narrative skill that they do not yet have, and we treat them (in an attenuated way) as moral and prudential beings before they have become such. We do not treat them exactly like fully developed adults or have the expectations of them that we have of adult persons, but we play-act as if we have these expectations as a way of beginning their moral and rational development.[19] We may offer an eighteen-month-old a complicated justification for strapping him into his car seat or making him relinquish the keys he has latched on to, or subjecting him to a vaccination, even though we know full well that he cannot comprehend our arguments and wouldn't care if he could. Treating the toddler in this way prepares him for the give and take of reasons that will be an essential part of his interactions for years to come. When he is slightly older we will offer him simple forms of justification that he can comprehend, and will expect the same from him. Eventually, if all goes well, he will become a competent giver and receiver of justifications. We make two-year-olds apologize when

---

[18] My use of these concepts thus goes beyond Lindemann's insofar as it applies them to developing an account of the individuation and persistence conditions of persons, a question she does not directly address, at least not in this guise.

[19] For an insightful treatment of this see Tamar Schapiro, "What is a Child?", *Ethics*, 109(4), July 1999, pp. 715–38.

they have taken someone else's toy or hit someone not because we think they are fully developed moral agents who should be regretful for what they have done, but because we are trying to teach them to be such agents.

At the other end of life, the treatment of dementia patients acknowledges their current circumstances as the continuation of a particular narrative. Close friends and family who had relationships with the person usually continue their relationship with the patient even when he can no longer recognize them. This can happen in the ways discussed in conjunction with PVS patients in the previous chapter— e.g., coming to visit him, overseeing his care, playing him his favorite music, decorating his room with significant items from his past and worrying about whether to let him sit around in his robe since "Father was always a natty dresser and would be mortified." There are, of course, many different ways in which narrative continuity might be acknowledged, and these are just examples. Friends who refuse to visit a dementia patient because they cannot stand to see the once-brilliant mind reduced to *that* are recognizing the continuation of his narrative just as surely as those who visit regularly, and we can find this kind of socially-generated continuation of narrative even in cases where it might at first seem absent. When someone looks at the Alzheimer's patient and claims "Father is gone; that's not him," she does not, as we have said, truly see a brand new being, but rather the sad continuation of a once vigorous life—otherwise it would not be painful in just the way it is. Even in the case of someone with dementia who is warehoused in a state institution or found dying of hypothermia homeless and alone on the street we are inclined to muse that this was "someone's baby boy" and wonder how he came to this.

It is from this perspective and with respect to this question that I depart from Lindemann on the question of whether someone in a PVS might be a person. A PVS is the continuation of a life that can be narrated from the outside in much the same way dementia is; here is the ending of a particular life story, and there are implications of that fact. Think of the images of Terri Schiavo's parents tenderly brushing her hair and fighting to keep her on life support; and equally of her husband's fight to terminate support because of the implications for himself and, he argued, for Terri, of maintaining her in this condition.[20] In similar ways a fetus

---

[20] Although the attitudes here are admittedly complex. McMahan points to the tombstone of Nancy Cruzan, who suffered biological death in 1990 after eight years in a PVS. Her family had it inscribed "DEPARTED JAN 11, 1983 / AT PEACE DEC 26, 1990" (McMahan, *Ethics of Killing*, p. 423). This is difficult to parse. On the one hand there is the assertion that she is gone for those eight years and on the other an assertion that she is not at peace until 1990. The question is where she was when not at peace. There are many ways to read this, including some where she continues disembodied. But the fact that her parents were so desperate to terminate the life support of the being in a PVS indicates a certain kind of continued relationship. As I have already said, however, PVS is at best a degenerate case of survival and the kinds of relationships that are involved here are going to be just barely discernible as interpersonal relations.

might also be included in a life narrative. It is by no means uncommon to name a child before it is born. Fetuses are talked to; they have clothing and diapers purchased for their future needs and rooms prepared for their arrival; they may have Mozart played to them (perhaps even *Ah Je Vous Dirai Maman*) in order to make them smarter. In these and myriad other ways the fetal stage is seen as the beginning of a life narrative just as PVS is seen as the end stages of one.[21]

It is important to emphasize that in a typical case the narrative started or finished by others is intertwined with a person's first-personal self-narrative when she is able to produce one (cases like that of Lindemann's sister Carla, who never becomes a self-narrator, will be discussed in the next chapter). After mastering the narrative capacities described by Nelson, an individual comes to be a self-narrator in the ways the original version of the Narrative Self-Constitution View describes, and the first-personal experience this self-narration generates becomes a constitutive part of her life. The life narrative with which someone operates does not begin with self-consciousness and end with its dissolution, however, even when she is actively narrating it. We all know that we have pasts that go back to a time before we can remember and that what happened in that past is partially responsible for how things are for us now. Our understanding of where we were born, where we lived, who we lived with, and the basic circumstances of our youth all become part of our adult narratives, even if we do not remember them directly. People who do not have this information usually feel as if they are lacking something important and seek to fill in the blanks.[22] Similarly, we all know that we might end up with dementia or in a PVS and this, too, is a part of present experience. People express this knowledge in different ways—by saving money or buying insurance to make sure that they are cared for, by drawing up a living will, by living for the moment while they can still enjoy it—all of these common behaviors acknowledge a possible future in which self-narration is not possible.

---

[21] It is important to emphasize that no direct conclusions about the morality of abortion or termination of artificial life support can be drawn from these considerations. While this way of thinking about fetuses and those in a PVS may make them persons on my view, the view claims only that to be a person is to be an appropriate *target* of certain questions and maintains that answering these questions requires further investigation. If a human fetus or human in PVS is a person it means that it is appropriate to have the kinds of conversations we do about the morality of treatment at the margins, but it does not tell us how the questions raised in these conversations should be resolved. For this we need further reflection of the sort we find, for instance, in McMahan's application of the theory of time-relative interests to the morality of killing those at the margins. I will address these themes further in Chapter 5.

[22] Although, as Galen Strawson points out, it is dangerous to assume that everybody does or should feel that way. (See "Against Narrativity," *Ratio* 17(4), 2004, pp. 428–52.) For present purposes we can concede Strawson's point since I think he would allow that at least most people are aware that they have a past of this sort and that it plays some part in their current circumstances and since, as we will see, I am going to give up the word "narrative" in a moment.

This expansion of the notion of narrative identity points to a fairly straight-forward way of answering the diachronic challenge of individual unity. The key move is the recognition that the unity of a narrative (and so of a person) comes from its characteristic developmental structure. The chief difference between the narrative view and psychological continuity theories can be described in terms of this aspect of narrative. Whereas psychological continuity theories define conti-nuity in terms of gradual change, the Narrative Self-Constitution View looks at it in terms of organized development. What is story-like about lives is that they unfold according to a certain kind of trajectory. In the kind of extended narrative I have been describing the stages of infancy and dementia are part of the structure of a standard life story. Infancy happens at the beginning and dementia, when it occurs, mostly after maturity. A story is always something with a beginning, mid-dle, and end, whichever part of the story you happen to be at at any given moment. Similarly, a typical person is, at every moment in her life, something that was (or is) an infant and developed (or is expected to develop) in certain ways.

These claims can be clarified by once again using an analogy with music. This time, however, rather than the theme and variations that displayed the structure of synchronic unity let's consider a sonata—a piece of music with a standard form. A sonata may start by introducing a simple theme which then gets developed in a variety of ways, coming and going and changing keys before finally resolving. The fact that a sonata is a complicated piece of music with a defined form has, I argue, important implications for each note that occurs within it. It informs how the very first notes are played or heard, even in an unfamiliar piece of music. If we think about a highly complicated sonata, it is completely reasonable and natural to say that the piece is a difficult piece even if some passages are quite easy taken in isolation. In fact, the easy parts may themselves become more difficult because of the ways in which they need to interface with the difficult parts. If we want to say something about what kind of piece a given sonata is—whether, for instance, it is appropriate for a beginner or the right kind of piece to play at a recital or com-petition—we will make this judgment about the piece as a whole, and not about its various parts. Saying that it is too hard for beginners does not mean that every passage is too hard for beginners; there are attributes of the whole piece that do not apply to each of its individual parts.

A similar kind of claim can be made about a human life. It is a structural whole that has, by its very nature, attributes that apply to it as a whole which do not neces-sarily apply to each individual portion. We can thus say that the mature person is the same person as the infant or (in unlucky cases) dementia patient because there is a single life course that starts (roughly) with infancy, develops into maturity, and devolves (possibly) into dementia. The person is defined by the unfolding of the pattern in which these stages all play their part. The person as a whole can be an appropriate target of forensic judgments even if the infant and dementia patient she was and will be are not, in the same way a sonata can be devilishly difficult to play even if some passages are quite easy. It is not just the fact that the easy and difficult passages happen to be linked by some external relation (e.g., they happen to be played on the same keyboard in temporal succession) that makes for this connection; it is that the structure that makes the piece as a whole what it is depends upon the difficult passages being linked to the easy passages in just the way they are. Just as the difficult passages might be a dramatic development of the simple theme laid out in an easy bit, the forensic nature of the mature adult is inherently linked to the events of infancy and decline by the structure of a person's life.

One of the reasons I have been keen to use the musical analogy is to show that what is doing the real work in this current expression of the view (and perhaps even in the Narrative Self-Constitution View) is not so much the story-like nature of a life but rather the idea that it is a diachronically structured unit, something which is also true of sonatas, sonnets, and many things which are not narratives. The claim is that the lives of persons share this general structure. Of course, the structure of a person's life will not be the same as that of any of these art forms. For this reason, as well as for many others (including the role of social environment in creating this structure), it seems more accurate and less liable to generate misunderstanding to give up the locution of "narrative" in this context and to describe the type of unity that defines a person's identity not as a *narrative* unity but simply as the structural unity of a person's life. This, of course, sounds circular in a way that defining identity in terms of a narrative does not. I have not yet said what the structure of a person's life is, nor explained how the identity of a person can be non-circularly defined in terms of it. All I mean to be offering here, however, is a schema for a view to be developed in the chapters ahead, where these questions will be addressed.

Those who object to the narrative view of persons might object just as strenuously to the sonata view, since sonatas, like stories, are artifacts that are not subject to the contingencies of the natural world in the same ways that our lives are. While a sonata may demand recurring themes and resolutions, it would be a mistake to look for these, at least in the same way, in our lives.[23] This is a legitimate complaint,

---

[23] In addition to the Strawson piece mentioned earlier, examples of those who might take this view can be found, for instance, in Peter Goldie, "Narrative Thinking, Emotion, and Planning," *The Journal of Aesthetics and Art Criticism*, 67(1), 2009, pp. 97–106; and Peter Lamarque, "On the Distance between Literary Narratives and Real-Life Narratives," in Daniel Hutto, ed., *Narrative and Understanding Persons* (Royal Institute of Philosophy Supplements 60), Cambridge: Cambridge University Press, 2007, pp. 117–32.

but it should not be overstated. While our lives are certainly not tidy in the way that traditional narratives and sonatas are, there is reason to think that they do have a typical structure, albeit one markedly less rigid than most art forms. Just as we can tell when a story or sonata breaks off in the middle we know an unfinished life when we see one, despite the fact that a "finished life" does not consist in the tying up of all loose ends or the return to the original key signature. Moreover, as we will see in the discussion to come, there are other natural models for this kind of diachronic structure.

My proposed schema for avoiding the two challenges of individual unity is thus to define personal identity in terms of the unity of a person's life. By "life" here, however, I do not mean biological life.[24] The role of biological life in this picture is quite complicated and will be discussed at great length in the chapters to come. For now the crucial thing to recognize is that the kind of life I am describing is held together by the form of its unfolding rather than by its instantiation in a single human animal. This approach offers a promising strategy for defining the identity of persons in a way that draws an intrinsic and essential relation between personal identity and our person-related practices and concerns. To show that this strategy can deliver on its promise we will need to describe the form of a standard person life and show there is such a thing. There is also still the challenge of definitional unity to address; we have not yet shown how a definition that makes persons inherently appropriate targets of forensic judgments can include those like Carla who have no life stage at which they are such targets. An account of the role of human embodiment in a person life is also still needed. These and other challenges will be addressed in the remainder of the book, which will develop and defend the account of personal identity I call the "Person Life View."

---

[24] Another philosopher who has used a notion of a life that goes beyond the notion of biological life is Lynne Rudder Baker (see, e.g., *Persons and Bodies: A Constitution View*, Cambridge: Cambridge University Press, 2000, p. 18; "When Does a Person Begin," *Social Philosophy and Policy* 22(2), 2005, pp. 25–48; and *The Metaphysics of Everyday Life: An Essay in Practical Realism*, Cambridge: Cambridge University Press, 2007, pp. 82–5). My "person life," as I will develop it, is very different from Baker's "personal life." It starts earlier, can last later, and is far more grounded in social interactions (Baker allows that personhood can be relational, but still grounds it firmly in the Lockean forensic capacities). In spirit, however, my view is in many ways like Baker's and indebted to it. We will discuss Baker's view of personal identity in more detail in Chapter 7.

5

The Person Life View

The person life view (PLV) which I will be defending in the remainder of the book holds that persons are defined in terms of the characteristic lives they lead. To be a person is to live a "person life"; persons are individuated by individuating person lives; and the duration of a single person is determined by the duration of a single person life. Put so bluntly the view may seem to face a variety of serious challenges. There may, to begin with, be legitimate skepticism about the idea that there is such a thing as "the characteristic life of a person." Persons have lived, do live, and will continue to live in many different ways. There is divergence of lifestyle from era to era, culture to culture, and individual to individual—and this is just when we are thinking about human persons. Even if there is such a thing as a characteristic person life, moreover, it may seem questionable that a *life* could define an entity, since on the surface it seems there must be an entity already in existence to lead a life. These and other challenges will have to be answered as the details of the view are filled in.

In developing PLV there are two different (although obviously related) questions that need to be answered. First, we need a general account of what a person life is—its basic structure and what distinguishes it from other kinds of lives. This is the question of what it is to be a person according to PLV. In addition we need an account of what individuates particular person lives and gives them their unity over time. This is the question of what constitutes personal identity according to PLV. This chapter will address the first of these questions and in so doing will also provide a response to the last challenge of the problem of multiplicity, the challenge of definitional unity. The next chapter will take up questions of personal identity.

Before we begin, however, it is worth flagging one issue that otherwise might become distracting. As may already be evident, and will become even more so shortly, PLV's description of the nature and identity of human persons makes heavy use of facts about our embodiment and about human biology. These facts are so central that it may seem unclear why the view is not, in the end, really just a form of animalism. It isn't, but to be in a position to see clearly and decisively why it isn't we will need to have more of the details of the view in place. The relation between human persons as PLV defines them and human organisms will be the subject of extended discussion in Chapters 6 and 7.[1] Here I will just acknowledge that this relation stands in need of explanation and offer reassurances that some is forthcoming.

5.1 Characteristic Person Lives: an Overview

PLV says that to be a person is to live a person life. To understand the view's content we thus need to know what a person life is. The most direct description is that a person life is the characteristic kind of life lived by a person. This is not in itself very helpful, since if we need to have a full-fledged definition of personhood in order to define a person life the view is straightforwardly circular and therefore uninformative. Fortunately, things are not as bad for PLV as they initially sound. Ultimately, any account of personhood and personal identity will need to start with paradigmatic cases on which there is general agreement and move from there, seeking to determine the relevant factors in the standard cases and offering a principled way of determining how much deviation is possible before personhood and personal identity are undermined. PLV is no exception. Our paradigmatic examples of persons are typical encultured humans, and this is the starting point I will use in developing the view. I begin with beings like *us*—you who are reading a book and I who am writing it—and take our lives as the model for the standard person life. Once this kind of life has been characterized we will be in a position to raise questions about personhood in non-paradigmatic cases, e.g., humans with atypical lives or nonhumans whose lives are fundamentally like ours. As a starting point we thus take healthy, encultured humans as our paradigm of personhood. In this section my goal is only to get the basic structure of a person life on the table, and so I will seek only to characterize the most standard kind of (human) person life, returning to questions of deviations from the paradigm in subsequent sections. As one might imagine, the idea of a person life is a complicated one, and so the description I give in this initial section will be somewhat schematic. Over the rest of this chapter and the next, however, a more concrete picture will emerge.

---

[1] Later in the chapter I will show that PLV allows for nonhuman persons, but this is a somewhat different issue. Animalism also allows for nonhuman persons. It insists only that each human person is identical to a human animal. PLV will deny this and the basis for that denial will be explained over the next two chapters.

Many of the features of a person life have already been touched on in the previous chapters but it will be useful to bring together observations already made in a somewhat more systematic form before adding some new features. The typical (human) person life begins with a period of social dependence, and relatively basic cognitive capacities which develop over time into the full range of personal capacities and activities discussed in Chapter 3. The typical mature person is sentient, reflectively self-consciousness, a self-narrator in the sense described by the Narrative Self-Constitution View,[2] and a rational and moral agent—a "person" in all of the senses in which we use the term. The standard life trajectory also allows that after maturity some of the capacities of the mature person may be lost or attenuated as happens, for instance, in cases of dementia or at an extreme in a PVS. In addition to the psychological development described above a characteristic person life also involves an array of complex and sophisticated interactions with other persons which involve, among other elements, adherence to moral, cultural, or personal norms (although the details of these norms may differ from context to context). Person lives usually involve friendships and family, tribal, or community ties. There is a standard developmental trajectory for these relations and engagements that runs parallel to the individual's cognitive and affective development. Persons begin in a condition of relative (but usually not complete) passivity with respect to these social interactions, and as they mature they typically become more active participants.

The development on the one hand of cognitive and agential capacities and on the other of increasingly complex and self-directed interpersonal relationships and interactions should not be seen as distinct processes, but rather as two sides of a single coin. In order to develop psychologically and physically as human persons typically do, it is necessary to mature in an environment that provides the proper scaffolding and social support for such development. By the same token, there are particular psychological capacities that are required if one is to engage in the more sophisticated kinds of interpersonal interactions found in a standard person life. This is the insight behind, for instance, Locke's claim that the forensic nature of personhood requires sameness of self-consciousness. Without the ability to develop these internal resources active participation in a person life would be severely limited.

For expository purposes we can thus divide a person life into three main components (although as we will see in a moment, it is one of the central claims of the view that this division is artificial). First, there are the attributes of the individual—the physical and psychological capacities and internal structures that she

---

[2] See Chapter 4, section 2.

possesses. Second there are the kinds of activities and interactions that make up the individual's daily life. Any individual's life will, of course, involve particular relationships and activities. What is most important here, however, are not the specific and unique details of the life but the general kinds of activities and interactions of which they are examples. The relevant question is whether the day-to-day activities of the individual and the way she is treated by and interacts with others are part of the general form of life of typical encultured humans. These are elements of a person life that we have already discussed, but there is a third crucial element as well. This is what might be called the social and cultural infrastructure of personhood—the set of practices and institutions that provides the backdrop within which the kinds of activities that make up the form of life of personhood become possible.

The concept of the infrastructure of personhood is new here and requires a bit more explanation, as it plays a key role in PLV. The idea is that to truly understand a person life we need to look not only at individual social interactions and practical activities but at the stable background structures that make these possible. The standard person life is, I have said, the kind of life lived by an encultured human, and this kind of life requires background norms and practices within which individuals operate and which set the parameters of their interactions. This infrastructure will contain, among other things, presuppositions about what (who) gets brought into the form of life that is personhood. In the case of human persons, for instance, other humans play a particular prescribed role that is set by social and cultural institutions and not accorded on an individual basis. We do not, when we encounter animate things in daily life, make an assessment of their attributes and capabilities before deciding whether they should be viewed and treated as fellow persons. When we encounter other humans we automatically see them as persons and interact with them as such.[3]

It is not at all surprising that we treat our conspecifics this way—there are very good reasons that our evolutionary history would have selected us to do so. The points I want to emphasize here are first, that we do not typically *decide* on the basis of explicit reasons to take (or not to take) this attitude toward particular others,[4] and second, that taking this attitude toward particular kinds of others is not only

---

[3] This assertion may seem questionable since people often mistreat their conspecifics. Everything here depends on what it means to "see" or "treat" someone as a person. Over the rest of this chapter I will spell out an understanding of these terms on which my claim is not contradicted by practices of oppression and mistreatment.

[4] This observation has, of course, been made before. We have already seen it in Lindemann's work and she herself follows Carl Elliott in referring to Wittgenstein's famous remarks from the *Philosophical Investigations* II.iv: "My attitude towards him is an attitude towards a soul. I am not of the opinion that he has a soul," and "The Human body is the best picture of the human soul." P. F. Strawson (see, e.g., "Persons" in *Individuals: An Essay in Descriptive Metaphysics*, Routledge, 1959, pp. 87–116,

natural but also institutionalized as part of our social and cultural infrastructure. The attitude is therefore both automatic and subject to cultural norms. In present-day industrialized countries, for instance, it means all the things to which Lindemann points: that human infants are dressed in clothes and their births are recorded; that human children are generally exposed to certain kinds of education; that all humans are subject to the laws of the land and can potentially be arrested and brought to trial if there is reason to think they have willfully violated them; that they are eligible to qualify for social welfare programs; and so on.[5] The particular practices and institutions will of course vary from place to place and time to time. The claim is only that there will be some such practices and institutions and that it is necessary for there to be some if there are to be person lives at all. This infrastructure may be said to define a "person-space" by setting the broad parameters within which interpersonal interactions take place. Being brought into the form of life of personhood may be described as being accorded a place in person-space.

It will be necessary to say a bit about terminology here. Sometimes in what follows I will talk about "culture" and sometimes about "social infrastructure" and sometimes about "social/cultural infrastructure." "Culture" and "society" are contested terms, so it is important to clarify how I am using them.[6] When I speak of "culture" I am thinking, roughly, of a set of traditions, practices, and worldviews that are transmitted from generation to generation by some form of teaching. "Social infrastructure" is meant to capture the notion of a society as an organization in which humans (at least in this case) live together according to established rules involving institutions of support and authority (this can range from tribal or clan organizations to the modern state). The notions of culture and society are often distinguished. A multi-cultural liberal state, for instance, can be viewed as a social infrastructure which, as the name implies, includes many cultures (there is room for some disagreement here, however, as some will see liberalism as itself a culture which contains subcultures). By the same token, cultures may be seen as transcending social boundaries. I will not enter into these debates, since they do not really bear on my use of these concepts. Arguably, a culture could not exist without some set of social institutions (which may be seen as part of the culture) and social institutions could not arise without culture (since they are sophisticated social arrangements that involve traditions and teaching).

---

and "Freedom and Resentment," *Proceedings of the British Academy*, 48, 1962, pp. 1–25) has also made a similar point, as have others.

[5] As we discussed in the last chapter, these do not all apply at each life phase.
[6] I am grateful to Sam Fleischacker for reminding me of the need to discuss these issues.

Whatever the relation of culture to society, the kinds of organization they describe, interacting in whatever way they do, together make up what I am thinking of as person-space—the social and cultural infrastructure within which persons interact and which supports personhood. I will use "culture," "social infrastructure," "person-space," and like terms more or less interchangeably to refer to this constellation. The kinds of things that constitute social/cultural infrastructure might include religious traditions, institutions of punishment, codified systems of governance, economies, educational institutions, technologies, systems of symbolic representation through which information and knowledge are transmitted, means of transportation, and developed practices concerning arts, entertainment, and leisure. Of course, not every culture must contain all of these elements, and the details of such institutions will vary over time and place.

Although cultural infrastructure is a core part of what distinguishes persons from non-persons it is important to see that life within such an infrastructure is nevertheless continuous with the social organization of nonhuman animals. In the lives of human persons, however, these functions are mediated through and transformed by cultural institutions. We can see this in, for instance, our forms of mating (e.g., marriage ceremonies, *in vitro* fertilization, prenuptial agreements, the television show *The Bachelor*), the way we raise our young (e.g., Baby Einstein videos, nannies, educational toys, boarding school), the ways we procure and consume food (e.g., grocery stores, restaurants, potlatches, business lunches, Thanksgiving feasts), the ways we create and find shelter (e.g., mortgages, rents, housing projects, architectural bids for government buildings), and the ways we eliminate waste (e.g., sewer systems, signs saying "restrooms for customers only," toilet paper commercials involving animated bears, diapers), all of which are governed by traditions and structures that connect them to the forensic aspects of our live in complicated and variable ways.

We now have a general picture of the three elements that make up a person life—individual capacities, typical activities and interactions, and social infrastructure. I mentioned earlier that distinguishing among these three elements is in many ways artificial. This is because in actual lives they constrain and support one another. We have already seen the way in which infrastructure shapes the kinds of daily activities, relationships, and interactions a person engages in by setting the parameters within which these take place and providing the background institutions and practices they require. But the infrastructure is also constrained by the physical and psychological attributes of the individuals who reside in the person-space it defines. The infrastructure could not exist unless those who are part of person-space have the necessary capacities and attributes to create and maintain it. This means nothing more mysterious than that the development of institutions and norms of the sort that define person lives (e.g., prisons or systems of punishment, economies, theologies, art) requires beings who have certain kinds of memory systems, reflective self-consciousness, rationality, and related cognitive and affective abilities—i.e., the forensic capacities. The notion of personhood that is inscribed in these institutions and norms will thus be one that recognizes that persons must typically possess these capacities (for at least part of their lives) or they will lack stability and efficacy.

This analysis may naturally lead to the suggestion that the real definition of personhood should therefore rest in the capacities and attributes that produce the infrastructure that allows for individual person lives. The heavy lifting, it might be argued, is done by the fact that persons are individuals with the ability to develop norms and institutions, and not by the fact that we are individuals who lead the kinds of lives these norms and institutions define; the infrastructure itself, it might be claimed, is not constitutive of personhood but is rather a product of already-existing persons. This is, however, a misperception. Although it is true that PLV sees the existence of person-space and the activities that characterize a person life as growing out of and dependent upon the capacities and attributes of individual persons, it is also true that the capacities and attributes of individual persons (at least in the case of human persons, which we are taking as our paradigm) depend upon the existence of a social infrastructure and engagement in characteristic activities.

We have already seen the basic reasons this is so. Earlier we discussed the ways in which the sophisticated psychological and agential capacities of human persons depend upon social scaffolding to develop. Human infants who are not exposed to language or the appropriate kinds of developmental stimuli will not develop the kinds of cognitive, social, and affective capabilities that are found in mature persons. While being brought into person-space will not *always* generate sophisticated capacities in humans (the biological potential must be in place), these capacities do not develop without the interactions and activities that make up a human life. We have also seen, however, that these interactions and activities themselves depend upon an infrastructure of cultural institutions and practices—without these there is no person-space and if there is no person-space no one can be accorded a place within it. For beings with our capacities to exist there must thus be a certain kind of social infrastructure in place, and so the capacities depend upon the social infrastructure just as much as the social infrastructure depends upon the capacities.

This claim may seem to lead to a kind of paradox. If beings with our capacities must exist to create the infrastructure of person-space, and if there can be no beings with our capacities outside of such an infrastructure, it does not seem possible for the whole enterprise ever to get off the ground. This is, to be sure, a genuine puzzle, but not an unsolvable one. Worries about chickens and eggs notwithstanding, both exist, and the same is true of persons and cultures. While there may indeed be a fair amount of mystery and controversy surrounding the mechanism by which culture came into existence, the fact is that the kind of cultural infrastructure I have described does exist on a widespread scale and so must have developed somehow. Like the origins of chickens and eggs, moreover, this is a question that admits of study and about which we may hope to find some answers.

There are a great many different theories of how cultural organization arises out of the natural social organization of hominids. One of my favorites is that of Merlin Donald, who argues that "the present form of the human mind evolved over the past two and a half million years...during that time, hominid cognitive evolution was increasingly tethered to culture...and our brains went through a series of modifications that gave them this strong cultural orientation."[7] On Donald's view what happened, roughly, is that developments in the tertiary regions of the brain gave hominids greater domain-general capacities and brain plasticity than their forebears. Through a series of back-and-forth developments between brain and social environment, incremental changes in each leading to further incremental changes in the other, this biological plasticity led to the development of culture, which is able to act on the plastic brain, using knowledge gained over generations, to shape and direct it in ways that allow it to do more than such a brain could otherwise do on its own. In particular, the symbolic mode of representation, which is possible only in culture, allows for an intermediate-range memory that gives us our special kind of self-consciousness and all that follows from it in terms of the development of infrastructure, agency, and social organization.[8]

This account is not, of course, uncontroversial, and for our purposes can serve only to illustrate that there are coherent and informed ways of considering the question of how persons might have emerged despite the fact that personhood depends upon capacities and infrastructure that presuppose one another. Whatever may have happened in the misty reaches of time, it is fairly easy to see how this boot-strapping principle works today in the lives of typical human persons. Infants are born, in the standard case, with plastic brains and certain biological potentials.

---

[7] Merlin Donald, *A Mind so Rare: The Evolution of Human Consciousness*, New York: W.W. Norton, 2001, p. 259. This view has become increasingly popular. Another psychologist who makes a similar claim is Roy F. Baumeister, *The Cultural Animal: Human Nature, Meaning, and Social Life*, New York: Oxford University Press, 2005. Baumeister defends the view that "our psyches are innately programmed by nature specifically to enable us to participate in culture and society. Or, more precisely, the human psyche emerged because natural selection redesigned the primate psyche to make it more suitable for living in a cultural society." (p. 29).

[8] Donald, *A Mind so Rare*, p. 259.

Human infants are automatically accorded a place in person-space, and so are caught up immediately (often even before birth) in the kinds of interactions and activities typical to persons at the beginning of their existence. This allows for the development of the capacities of mature personhood, thus expanding the range of interactions and activities that ultimately make up that person's life in ways that perpetuate and constitute the infrastructure that allows for persons. Person-space is thus self-perpetuating in that it serves to develop beings who sustain it. This kind of self-perpetuation should not, however, be understood to be inherently conservative. A revolution that radically alters social organization would, for instance, perpetuate person-space in the sense at issue here. While such a radical break would change the details of the institutions and practices by which a group of persons lives, it would also substitute new ones and so maintain a background of interactions and practices which both express and develop the forensic and other capacities of mature persons. The crucial point is that it is not a specific social organization which is required, but only the general kind of complex, normative, symbolically mediated organization we find in human societies and cultures.

The view of person lives I am offering takes the paradigmatic person life to be that of a human in a culture. The social and cultural infrastructure that supports personhood is absolutely central to this understanding. There would be no persons without person-space, and to be living a person life is to be accorded a place in person-space, to live as and be treated as a unified locus of the sorts of practical concerns and interactions that typify the lives of those who generate and maintain the social/cultural infrastructure within which these lives take place. I have also said that all humans are automatically accorded a place within person-space. PLV is the view that a person is constituted by a person life, and it is this view that I am putting forth as a practically-based account of our literal identity.

In developing PLV I have incorporated the lessons learned in previous chapters, and we are now in a position to see how all of the pieces collected over the last four chapters fit together. PLV employs a *dependence model* of the relation between personal identity and practical concerns. To be a person on this view is to lead a person life and to occupy a place in person-space. A person life just is a life made up of the kinds of practical interactions peculiar to persons, and occupying a place in person-space just is to be a locus of the practical interests and concerns that apply to beings like us. This means that a person will necessarily be a target of our practical concerns and judgments but there is no presupposition that the limits of the person will correspond exactly to the limits of particular practical judgments (this aspect of the view will be developed further in the next chapter). Since all of the person-related interactions are part of a person life, the view uses the *expanded conception of the relevant practical concerns* argued for in Chapter 3.

To avoid the challenge of synchronic unity, PLV applies the strategy extracted from McMahan's discussion of different modes of sentience to different kinds of lives. A person life is not simply an animal life with some extra capacities or inter- actions added on. The forensic capacities permeate the whole of our lives, and ani- mal and forensic elements are part of a *single integrated whole*. This can be clearly seen, for instance, when we think of a wedding ceremony followed by a party with toasts, and fancy dresses, and an elaborate honeymoon. It is not that we eat and mate and also have traditions, rituals, and forensic interactions; the eating and mating and traditions and rituals are all mixed together in what we do. Finally, the *diachronic aspects* found in the Narrative Self-Constitution View are also incorpo- rated in PLV's definition of persons in terms of a typical developmental trajectory rather than in terms of the possession of particular attributes.

There is a great deal that remains to be explained about this view and there are some obvious worries that are likely to arise based on what I have said so far. Perhaps the most immediate of these is the threat of conventionalism. If an individ- ual becomes a person just on the basis of being accorded a place in person-space, it seems as if we could make anyone or anything a person (or exclude anyone or any- thing from personhood) just by adjusting our social institutions. The short answer to this worry lies in recognizing that our social/cultural infrastructure is not sim- ply something we choose or make up, but rather something that evolves with us and is responsive to and constrained by facts about us and about the world. One of the easiest ways to expand and defend this short answer is to consider a variety of non-paradigmatic cases in which concerns about conventionalism arise. Looking at the judgments PLV makes about personhood in each case, and the basis on which these judgments are made, will provide a more concrete understanding of the view and demonstrate how it can avoid an objectionably conventionalist understanding of persons.

5.2 Atypical Developmental Trajectory

The first type of non-paradigmatic case we will consider is that of humans with atypical developmental trajectory. According to the sketch I have just given a per- son life involves a particular kind of developmental trajectory which leads from an infancy with a relatively circumscribed set of interactive capacities, to a mature adulthood, which includes a wider range of such capacities, including those that support forensic relations, possibly followed by a decline in which some of these capacities are lost. Not every human follows this trajectory, however. In some cases humans never develop the full complement of capacities found in typical adults, and in many cases we are able to predict early on that they will not (I will say that such individuals have an "atypical developmental prognosis"). We have already considered such a case in our discussion of Lindemann's reflections on her sister Carla.

The question before us now is what PLV says about the personhood of such humans. Given the discussion in Chapter 3 it will be no surprise that according to PLV they are persons, living person lives. It is true that these are not paradigmatic person lives, but these individuals are clearly seen as persons and given a place in person-space even when it is evident that they will lack some of the standard capacities persons usually possess and will not be able to participate in the full range of person-related activities. My reasons for saying this are basically the same as those evinced in favor of expanding our conception of the practical in Chapter 3. First we must recall that for any human many of the elements of a person life are in place well before maturity and do not require mature capacities. Infants are named (often before they are born), and in many cultures dressed in clothes, talked to, sung to, given a dedicated place to sleep, often brought into a religious community through some kind of ritual (e.g., christening, baptism, akika, bris, namkaran san-skar),[9] have their births registered in official civic records, and so on. Many of the details of this treatment will differ among cultures, subcultures, and eras, but in one way or another, infants born into a culture at a time will, as a matter of default, be brought into the person-space defined by that culture.

Importantly, this is true also of infants who are not expected to develop the full complement of capacities associated with mature personhood. As the develop-mental challenges of these humans are understood, some forms of interaction will change to accommodate the capabilities of the particular child, but this does not amount to suddenly seeing her as a completely different kind of *thing* from chil-dren who have a typical developmental prognosis. Infants who face these develop-mental challenges remain individuals with names, who wear clothes, sleep in beds, have their births registered, are brought into religious communities via rituals, and so on. While it may be that these humans will predictably never engage in forensic interactions, or do many of the other things that mature persons do, they never-theless live as persons in myriad ways.

PLV's analysis of this kind of case may, as I have already mentioned, raise the specter of an objectionable conventionalism about persons. If the personhood of those with atypical developmental trajectories depends solely on facts about how

---

[9] This obviously is not meant to imply that a child must be brought into a religious community to count as a person. Dissenters who reject religious practice, for instance, are demonstrating that they see their children as persons by refusing these traditions, since refusal is necessary only where a prac-tice potentially applies. Believers horrified by the refusal, meanwhile, demonstrate that they see these children as persons through their horror.

we think about or treat beings that look like us, the difference between being a person and not being a person starts to look pretty thin. Echoing some of the concerns that we saw arise in response to Lindemann's view, we might wonder why we could not see and treat a family pet as a person and thereby make it one.[10] Arguably some pets are treated this way. There are pampered poodles, for instance, who wear sweaters and jewels, sleep in beds, have their births registered, go to doggie daycare and on playdates, are given therapy if they demonstrate anxiety, and eat "people food" off of plates. If being brought into person life in the way humans with atypical developmental prognosis are is sufficient to make these humans persons, we might wonder why similar treatment is not sufficient to make a poodle a person.

To answer this worry it is crucial to appreciate the fact that our automatically seeing other humans as persons is not a mere convention or a status we just happen to confer; it is a non-arbitrary designation that carries real significance and is based in facts about our nature. This claim needs both clarification and defense. As a first step we can look more closely at what is really involved in seeing a human with an atypical developmental prognosis as a person. Doing so will reveal that even the most pampered pet is not truly seen as a person in the relevant sense, or brought into person-space. Once we have articulated the difference between the ways in which the pampered poodle and the atypical human are seen and treated we will be in a position to discuss why this difference is not an arbitrary one based on mere convention.

The difference we are after is perhaps most easily seen if we contrast the case of a family who are informed that their human infant will never be able to talk or dress or feed herself with that of a family who are told that their beloved poodle puppy will never be able to talk or dress or feed herself. We would expect the first bit of news to cause a range of complicated and powerful emotions as the family comes to grips with the challenges before them. We would expect the second to cause some puzzlement about why such an obvious fact needs to be stated at all. Someone who devotes himself to raising money to research causes and cures in response to the news that his human child has a condition which prevents her from learning to speak or become independent may be considered heroic in turning challenge to triumph. Someone who responds to the news that his poodle will

---

[10] There is, obviously, a good deal of overlap between the discussion in this section and some of Lindemann's work as described in Chapter 3. PLV is, however, a different view answering a different question, and so although my response to these concerns owes a great deal to Lindemann, it is not quite the same as her response to the corresponding potential objection to her view.

never learn to talk or become independent by raising money to research causes and cures is, by contrast, deeply confused.

There is a fundamental difference between the role that human infants with an atypical developmental prognosis play in our lives and the role that household pets with a similar level of cognitive capacity play, no matter how loved and how well integrated into the family these pets may be. The basic expectations aimed at humans and at other animals are different, even when we know in advance that the capacities of the human will not develop beyond those of the pet. This is, as I have said, because someone's location in person-space is not only a function of the way those with whom she interacts treat her or think about her, but also of the social infrastructure within which these interactions take place. A human infant—including one with atypical developmental prognosis—occupies a very different place in the whole set of institutions and practices that structure our lives than does a nonhuman pet. This, in turn, has implications for how such infants live in the day-to-day, making their lives very different from those of nonhumans with whom we share our existence. It is not simply that there are some activities that humans will engage in that nonhuman animals will not. Being seen as a person suffuses the whole set of activities and interactions in which the human infant is involved. It is not merely, that is, that the human with atypical developmental trajectory goes to one location (e.g., the church for a baptism) while the puppy goes to a different location (e.g., to the groomer), but everything that is implied by the fact that it is coherent that believers take their infant to the one place and their puppy to the other, that makes the difference in their lives.

It is this difference that allows us, finally, to answer the challenge of definitional unity. There is, as we have already discussed, an obvious sense in which someone in Carla's condition is not an appropriate locus of forensic judgment (an accusation of willful misconduct leveled at such an individual is, for instance, misplaced), but we now have a richer sense of how someone in this situation is, in another significant sense, the right *kind* of entity to be the target of such judgments. It is a notable anomaly if a human is someone about whom we cannot make (age-appropriate) specific forensic judgments; but it is absolutely standard that we can never rightly make such judgments about a typical poodle. In the case of a human, some kind of explanation is needed to forestall the application of such judgments (e.g., "don't be angry with him for [hitting you, screaming, disrupting the funeral, throwing dishes at the wall, refusing to acknowledge your greeting] he [has a disability and does not understand what he's doing; is not capable of behaving as you are expecting him to behave]").

Let me try to unpack this a bit more. In making the distinction between the dependence and coincidence models in the first chapter we talked about the fact

that within the lives of persons there are frequently mitigating factors that neutral-
ize judgments of responsibility or prudential concern. We may, that is, decide that
Jane is the person who broke the lamp insofar as questions about responsibility
must be directed to Jane while still acknowledging that she cannot be held responsible for the breakage because she is too young to know better or was pushed.
Similarly we can say of an adult that he is not responsible for actions we judge to be
his in the most fundamental sense because he was under severe duress or had been
drugged against his will. When I say that humans with atypical developmental trajectories are seen as persons, part of what this implies is that excuses and mitigating factors are called for in their cases to prevent the assessment of responsibility.
The deficits that prevent such an individual from developing the forensic capacities provide such an excuse. It is a particular kind of excuse, one that applies to all
actions and not just to particular cases, but having this kind of blanket excuse is
different from being the kind of thing that needs no excuse at all.

This difference is admittedly a subtle one, but it is real and it is a difference that
makes a difference. We do not tend to worry about who stands as decision-making
proxy for dogs and cats who are not mentally competent to plan their own estates
because the life of a dog or cat does not typically require estate planning; and even
if it does, they never do it for themselves. Nor do we feel compelled to require
someone to stand as legal proxy to manage the money or make decisions about
medical care for dogs and cats who do not have the ability to do this for themselves.
Put somewhat differently, the idea here is that those with radically atypical developmental trajectory can be viewed as "appropriate loci" of forensic concern in the
sense that they are the kinds of entities about whom it is typically appropriate to
make these judgments (and so about whom it is an anomaly when we cannot). In
the end, then, PLV sees humans with atypical developmental prognosis as persons
for much the same reason that it sees human infants as persons—because there is
a default expectation that such infants will develop into beings with the full complement of forensic capacities; an expectation which is over-ridden in the atypical
cases but does not disappear or cease to do work even when we know that expectation will not be met.

The question that remains to be addressed is why it is not arbitrary to have these
expectations of a human with atypical developmental prognosis and not of a poodle with equal or greater capacities. This challenge is, at least in part, based on an
overly simple understanding of the role the forensic capacities play in a person life.
These capacities are not something entirely distinct from the rest of our lives and
added on. Our earlier discussion emphasized the way in which our animal functions become infused with forensic structure and significance through our social
infrastructure. To the extent that humans with atypical developmental trajectories

are biologically like us, they will participate in these distinctive activities. Our expectations with respect to other humans are therefore not best described as an expectation that they will exhibit the forensic capacities, but rather as an expectation that they will be capable of living person lives which are governed by forensic structure, and of which forensic interactions like the assessment of responsibility are only one part.

We do not grant other humans a place in person-space simply because they look like us, we do so because they are embodied like us and this has all kinds of implications for the sorts of interactions we can have with them. This is of a piece with Lindemann's point about embodiment and forms of life. Lindemann's focus is primarily on the way in which shared forms of embodiment allow us to read each other's inner lives, but it is easy to think of many other ways in which human embodiment makes a real and salient difference to how we live (and I think Lindemann probably also had these in mind). Human children are, to begin with, born from us (and later can reproduce with us). When they are born they are dependent, and require the kind of nourishment and temperature regulation that are optimally provided by a human mother. They have the same sleep cycles we do, are nourished by the same foods, rely on the same senses, are subject to the same illnesses, can move at roughly the same speed, and so on. These are all facts about our biology, but they are also facts with immediate and wide-reaching implications for how we can and do live together.[11]

There is, of course, a great deal of variation in our lives and we do not expect every human to be able to do everything that every other human can do. The important point for present purposes, however, is that the implicit assumption that a human is a person is not primarily an assumption specifically that this individual will develop the forensic capacities, but rather that this individual is "one of us," suited to living the kind of life we lead and being engaged in the kinds of interactions we engage in. It is not at all arbitrary to assume this of all other humans, despite the fact that not all humans will be able to instantiate every element of a typical person life, nor is it arbitrary not to assume it of poodles. To describe a

---

[11] To feel the force of the way in which our shared conditions of embodiment shape our interaction think of Shylock's monologue in Act III of *The Merchant of Venice*:

> Hath not a Jew eyes? hath not a Jew hands, organs, dimensions, senses, affections, passions? fed with the same food, hurt with the same weapons, subject to the same diseases, healed by the same means, warmed and cooled by the same winter and summer, as a Christian is? If you prick us, do we not bleed? if you tickle us, do we not laugh? if you poison us, do we not die? and if you wrong us, shall we not revenge? (William Shakespeare, *The Merchant of Venice*, III.i)

This speech will take on special salience in the next section.

typical poodle as having the same or greater capacities than a human with an atypical developmental trajectory is in fact misleading because this takes the capacities out of the context in which they are employed. A poodle can be left alone with food and water for long periods of time in a way that a human with cognitive deficits cannot be (although if the food and water are on a high counter a human with severe cognitive deficits might fare better than the poodle). The comparison is not simply a matter of something completely commensurate between the two cases like IQ; these are just different kinds of beings.

PLV thus has the implication that humans with atypical developmental trajectories are persons because they are accorded a place in person-space. I hope also to have shown that there are legitimate grounds for seeing developmentally disabled humans as persons that do not apply to other animals with cognitive capacities that are (by some measure) equivalent or greater. I also hope to have shown that there is a meaningful and legitimate sense of "appropriate" in which these individuals are rightly seen as appropriate loci of forensic concerns, and so to have answered the last challenge of the problem of multiplicity, the problem of definitional unity. In the next section we will turn to a very different kind of challenge, one that comes from cases in which it seems as if humans with typical developmental trajectories are not seen or treated as persons, and consider what PLV has to say about personhood in these cases.

5.3 Anomalous Social Position

A crucial move in showing why PLV sees humans with atypical developmental potential as persons is the claim that it is a deep and non-accidental part of human social infrastructure to view and treat all other humans as persons, and so to accord them a place in person-space, where they will live a person life. One might legitimately wonder whether, as a matter of empirical fact, this is actually true. History, it would seem, is full of examples where one group of humans treats another group of humans as non-persons and prevents them from living a person life. It is, in fact, depressingly easy to find examples past and present of social and cultural infrastructures that institutionalize the idea that those of a different skin color, national origin, ethnicity, religion, sex, social class, or sexual orientation from the dominant group should not be accorded a place in person-space or inducted into the life of a person. There are, moreover, a vast number of different ways in which this can happen, since there is no end to our creativity when it comes to dominating others.

In what follows I will refer to these phenomena collectively as "oppression." This is, of course, a complicated word and it is by no means obvious that we have a clear and generally agreed-upon understanding of just what oppression is. I do not here mean to imply any particular theory of oppression, but am instead using "oppression" as a kind of term of art to talk about the range of cases where there is systematic and institutionalized mistreatment of others to the point where we are tempted to say that they are not seen as persons. As mentioned earlier, oppression in this sense can run the gamut from some of the more subtle ways in which women are discouraged from pursuing technical disciplines to the humiliation and torture of prisoners at Abu Ghraib, slavery in the Antebellum South, the genocidal activities of the Nazis, the Rwandan Genocide of 1994, and any number of other atrocities. For this discussion, when I talk about oppression I will be thinking mostly of the extremely egregious kinds of mistreatment of humans by other humans found on the far end of the spectrum, since it is here that it seems most difficult to maintain the claim that human persons always see and treat other humans as persons.

Faced with the kinds of atrocities described above, PLV has two choices: On the one hand it can acknowledge that there are cases in which some humans living within a culture are not treated as persons, do not live person lives, and so are not persons. On the other hand it can argue that, appearances to the contrary, even in the most horrible cases oppressed humans are in fact recognized and treated as persons, and so live person lives. PLV takes the latter approach, and understanding why it does so will help further clarify the notion of a person life. Key to this position are the distinctions between treating someone as a person and treating him well, and between living a person life and thriving. One common way of understanding what it is to treat someone as a person is to treat him with dignity and respect. On the Kantian understanding we saw in Korsgaard's work, for instance, oppressing someone is fundamentally incompatible with treating him as a person. This is obviously not the concept of personhood that is operating in PLV.[12] The sense of personhood this view is after is more fundamental than the notion of moral selfhood, and so the idea of what it is to see or treat someone as a person will also be more fundamental. It is once again a matter of certain expectations about development and capacities. These expectations play out in a very different way in these scenarios than they do in the case of humans with atypical developmental prognosis; they are in fact expressed in the very mechanisms of oppression, which imply a recognition of the personhood of the oppressed.

The sense in which this is so is captured with great precision by Stanley Cavell in *The Claim of Reason*. Cavell describes a hypothetical Southern slaveholder

---

[12] Although, since persons as PLV defines them are supposed to be loci of *all* of the practical relations we associate with personhood, including autonomy, there will need to be some connection. For now what is important is that whatever the connection between autonomy and personhood according to PLV, it cannot and does not claim that to see someone as a person just *is* to see him as an autonomous agent or that to treat someone as a person just *is* to respect his autonomy.

who says he does not believe that his African slaves are human beings.[13] ("Human being" in this context carries the weight I give to "person" and is obviously not meant as a purely biological category. This slaveholder understands, for instance, that slaves and non-slaves can produce fertile offspring.) Cavell tells us that what this slaveholder "really believes is not that slaves are not human beings, but that some human beings are slaves."[14] He believes, that is, that it is permissible to treat some human beings (or persons) in the way he treats his slaves. Cavell illustrates what he means by this as follows:

> When he wants to be served at table by a black hand, he would not be satisfied to be served with a black paw. When he rapes a slave or takes her as a concubine, he does not feel that he has, by that fact itself, embraced sodomy.... He does not go to great lengths either to convert his horses to Christianity or to prevent their getting wind of it. Everything in his relation to his slaves shows that he treats them as more or less human—his humiliations of them, his disappointments, his jealousies, his fears, his punishments, his attachments...[15]

It is too simple to suggest that slaveholders or Antebellum Southern society saw African slaves as non-persons, beings totally unlike themselves. The actual nature of the interactions is far more complex and in many ways more horrible.

There are numerous examples that can be invoked to amplify this general point about oppression. An impassioned argument that women should not be granted suffrage because they are too emotional or not intelligent enough to participate in the choice of political leaders to be sure demonstrates a lack of fundamental respect for women. We will, however, find very few impassioned arguments against pigeon or hamster suffrage; the question just does not come up. Rape is frequently used as an instrument of torture and terror in civil wars and tribal conflicts, as is forcing a vanquished enemy to defile objects he holds sacred. Such tactics would be completely ineffective against nonhuman animals, and those who are keen to assert dominion over those animals are unlikely to think to try them. Returning to the example of Antebellum slavery we find the Slave Codes, laws that prevented slaves from testifying in court against whites, making contracts, leaving the plantation without permission, striking whites, buying or selling goods, owning firearms, possessing anti-slavery literature, and engaging in a variety of similar activities. Everything in these codes acknowledges that slaves are the kinds of individuals who *could* do such things and must be actively prevented from doing them. To acknowledge this, according to PLV, is to see slaves as persons and accord

[13] Stanley Cavell, *The Claim of Reason: Wittgenstein, Skepticism, Morality, and Tragedy*, New York: Oxford University Press, 1979. See especially pp. 372–89, although the book as a whole is really relevant here.

[14] Cavell, *The Claim of Reason*, p. 375.

[15] Cavell, *The Claim of Reason*, p. 376.

them a place in person-space, albeit a disenfranchised, unjust, and deeply undesirable place.[16]

It is, of course, not just an accident of history or upbringing that the oppressed are viewed and treated as persons in this way—a mere happenstance or convention. It happens because social infrastructure, daily interactions, and the attributes of individuals all constrain each other in the ways discussed earlier. Slaves in the Antebellum South were viewed as beings who might be able to fire guns, read and be inspired by anti-slavery literature, or testify in court for the simple reason that they were humans and so (in the typical case) capable of doing all of these things. It is not a decision or choice of those in power whether to see the humans they oppress as persons in the ways described above; they are forced to do so by the capacities of those they are oppressing. Oppressors who really did relate to a group of humans just as they do to domesticated cattle or cats would need to overlook the fact that the oppressed individuals can understand what they are saying, speak to one another, and strategize about how to resist or escape. Overlooking these facts would make it unlikely that they would long be able to maintain dominance over a group whose resources they have so badly underestimated. It would be untenable to take this attitude long term to a group of humans with standard capacities not (or not only) because it is immoral or irrational but also because it is not viable in the most basic practical sense.

It is also critically important to remember that the attitude and actions of the oppressors is only part of the story. There is a second set of attitudes and actions involved where there is oppression, and that is the one found among the oppressed. As discussed earlier, person-space is something that is present wherever there is a set of institutions and practices governing interactions among beings who typically possess the psychological capacities that stand behind forensic activities (i.e., self-consciousness and rationality). It is thus established not only by the dominant culture, but by subcultures within it. Even if oppressors *could* maintain an attitude

---

[16] This discussion may also help to amplify the point I made earlier about abortion (see Chapter 4, note 21). There are certainly many people who explicitly deny that fetuses are persons, and the fact that abortion is legal and relatively common in many societies may seem to imply that not all social infrastructures see human fetuses as persons. It seems evident that in many cases, at least, those who deny personhood to fetuses are operating with a conception of personhood where being a person implies a particular moral status—more specifically, one that would make terminating a pregnancy involving a person morally impermissible. PLV, however, involves a far more basic conception of personhood. Since, according to this view, seeing someone as a person is compatible with killing or mistreating him (and in fact is implied by certain reasons for killing and types of mistreatment) the mere fact that abortion is a practice does not entail that fetuses are not seen as persons in the sense at issue here. To the contrary, the fact that practices concerning the willful termination of pregnancy are usually the subject of a particular and strict kind of codification in most societies suggests that they are seen as persons.

in which they genuinely saw the oppressed as non-persons in the strongest possible sense (although I think, for the reasons already given, this is a deeply implausible hypothesis) there is still the question of how the members of an oppressed group see and interact with one another. *They* will talk to one another, seek to comfort one another, strategize, exchange information, disagree and factionalize, and otherwise interact as persons despite the limitations within which they must operate.[17]

None of this is to deny that oppression is deeply problematic or that it has massive costs to both oppressor and oppressed. Nor is it to deny that oppression is an assault on the personhood of the oppressed. I have emphasized the way in which social scaffolding supports the development of the capacities and activities that make up a person life. When social interactions are deficient or fail to offer the proper support, the ability to lead a robust and full person life will almost certainly be impaired. This is not only the obvious point that a life of slavery and oppression will be less *fulfilling* than an autonomous and self-directed life, but the further observation that the capacity to lead a recognizable person life will be attenuated. To anticipate a comparison I will develop later, we can think of the impact of an oppressive social context on the life of a person as analogous, in important ways, to the impact of a noxious or hostile physical environment on the life of an organism. An organism living in an environment that is insufficiently oxygenated or does not contain sufficient nutritional resources may not develop fully along the standard trajectory, and basic biological functioning might be compromised in a variety of ways. None of this prevents there from *being* a biological life (and so an organism)—at least for a while. Nor does it suggest that biological life is a matter of degree. It does, however, suggest that there are healthier and unhealthier lives. Something similar, I claim, is true in the kinds of cases of oppression we have been considering. The claim is not that a life of oppression is, from the point of view of constituting personhood, *equivalent* to a life with proper social support. It is only to say that it is not sufficiently different in the relevant respects to fail to be a person life.

PLV thus sees both humans with atypical developmental trajectories and humans with atypical social status as persons. The kinds of facts I invoked in discussing the two cases are, however, very different. To demonstrate that humans

---

[17]   There can, of course, always be individual sociopaths or sadists who somehow manage really not to see other humans as persons. This would, however, have to be extremely rare if a culture is to survive. Most forms of sadism and manipulation in fact involve seeing one's human victims as persons. It is this that makes their suffering more satisfying than that of other animals. In order to manipulate or dominate in these particular ways, moreover, one must, for reasons already given, understand the one being manipulated or dominated to be a creature acting from reasons. It is thus not evident that we have any clear cases in which someone truly views other humans always as non-persons, and even if we do, these cases are severely pathological and can be seen as the exceptions that prove the rule.

with atypical developmental prognosis live person lives I (like Lindemann) pointed to the fact that they are given names instead of numbers, sleep in beds, are dressed in clothes, and in many other ways engage in the kinds of day-to-day rituals and routines that persons do. Humans who are oppressed, however, may well not live this kind of life. In the most extreme cases oppressed humans may be given numbers instead of names, sleep on dirt floors, be denied clothing, and in other ways stripped of the signs of personhood that are enjoyed by their oppressors. I said that these individuals are persons living person lives because they are approached as beings with the *capacities* of mature persons—precisely the kind of interaction that is *not* possible with humans who have profoundly atypical developmental prognosis.

This may make PLV seem objectionably protean, helping itself to different fundamental criteria of personhood as needed. There is, however, a deep commonality between the two cases, and that is that in each the way we interact with the individual in question displays a fundamental expectation that they are beings like us who are able to live as we live. This expectation expresses itself very differently in the two cases. In the case of atypical developmental trajectory, it is expressed as a recognition of its inevitable frustration (to some, I realize, it may thus seem perverse to call this an "expectation" at all, but this can be taken as a technical term). The difference between our response to a dog and to a human with similar levels of cognitive capacity reveals this expectation quite clearly. In these cases the way in which the human is living a person life is found in the compensations, accommodations, and reactions that are aimed at making such a life as much like a typical human life as is reasonably possible. In the case of oppression, the expectation is seen in the means of oppression and the active attempts to block the kinds of actions that only persons can take.

To get at the general idea at work in both of these cases we need to appreciate the fact that a person life is not defined in terms of some particular set of activities. Defining a person life in this way is hopeless since, as I mentioned at the outset, each of us does different things in his or her life, and the details of human life vary greatly over time and place. To live a person life is rather to live within a social infrastructure that organizes the broad contours of daily life and interaction; the kind of infrastructure that can emerge only among beings that typically develop sophisticated cognitive and agential capacities. In fact, it is part of the very notion of a person life that the details of our lives can differ in significant ways from person to person—it is an expression of our agency, our aspirations, our ability to conceptualize contingency and choice, and a great many other features that define paradigmatic persons. To recognize the lives of the oppressed or those with atypical developmental potential as deficient or incomplete lives is to recognize the individuals living these lives as among those whose lives should be judged by the standards of a person life, and it is in this way that the cases are alike.

We have now seen why PLV claims that all humans in a culture are going to be persons. The next question to consider is whether and how the view makes room for nonhuman persons.

5.4 Nonhuman Persons

Since typical enculturated humans provide the paradigm cases employed in developing the conception of a person life, there is a serious question to be raised about whether the view automatically excludes the possibility of nonhuman persons. Much of the description of person lives so far has invoked activities that are deeply bound up with facts about our biology. Lindemann, you will recall, sees our form of life as tied so essentially to our embodiment that she excludes the possibility of nonhuman persons (while allowing that there may be other forms of life equally complex and morally significant). The role that developmental trajectory plays in my own understanding of a person life makes it even more difficult to see how persons could be anything other than human, given that we are unlikely to find exactly this developmental trajectory in other kinds of beings.

Appearances to the contrary notwithstanding, however, PLV does leave room for the possibility of nonhuman persons. To understand how it does, we need first to remind ourselves that there is an important sense in which PLV can be understood as a broadly Lockean picture of personhood. On this view, as on Locke's, the most salient and distinguishing characteristic of persons is their forensic capacities and all that follows from them. PLV differs from the traditional Lockean view, however, by focusing on the impact of these capacities at the social level as well as on the individual level. The forensic capacities are crucial to personhood on this view because they lead to and guide the development of the social and cultural infrastructure that characterizes person lives. In section one we saw that this infrastructure confers personhood on all humans, including those that lack forensic capacities, and that this conferral is non-arbitrary. It does not follow from this that personhood can be conferred *only* on humans however, nor that the possession of the forensic capacities by an individual is irrelevant to the question of whether she is a person.

What is necessary to being a person on this view is that one live a person life, which means engaging with others in person-specific ways codified in the social infrastructure, and taking a place in person-space. I have been emphasizing that whether or not an individual is accorded such a place is not a matter of convention, but a response to facts about the individual. In the case of humans with atypical developmental trajectories, humanness is sufficient for inclusion because our infrastructure is such that our animal functions and interactions are never *purely* animal (in a colloquial sense of that term) but are always infused with forensic significance and structure. This means that the life of any human will have such structure and significance even if she does not engage in the canonical forensic interactions. But a nonhuman who does possess the forensic capacities is also capable of engaging with others in person-specific ways and so of living a person life within the social infrastructure that defines such a life. Such an individual can therefore be a person. Indeed, if a nonhuman is capable of interacting in these ways we cannot *but* include her in person-space for reasons similar to those discussed in the last section. Since, as we have already noted, the form of our person-specific interactions is deeply connected to facts about our embodiment, there will undoubtedly be some limitations on how different from human embodiment the embodiment of a nonhuman person can be. Just where these limits lie is, however, a largely empirical question, and there seems no clear way to determine them a priori.

Both the circumstances under which PLV can allow for nonhuman persons and the complications caused by issues of embodiment can be made clearer by considering some examples. Let's begin with the case of a single, super-intelligent nonhuman animal and contrast this with the case of the pampered house pet discussed in section 5.2. I said that PLV denies personhood to the pampered pet despite the fact that its life can mimic a person life in superficial ways. A beloved poodle may be dressed in clothes, given jewels, sleep on a bed, eat in restaurants, and go to doggie daycare and a pet therapist, but the poodle is still not being seen as a person, I argued, because there are deeply different expectations for poodles and humans, even humans we have good reason to believe will in fact frustrate those expectations.

This case involves a dog with the typical capacities of a dog, but we can imagine instead an exceptional dog who, along the lines of Locke's rational parrot, is able to speak to us in a language we understand and seems for all the world to exhibit the capacities of a typical mature human person. Take, for instance, Mr. Peabody from the *Rocky and Bullwinkle Show*—a dog who is a famous inventor, goes to court for the right to adopt a boy (Sherman), and invents a time machine to amuse the lad after winning custody. Actually confronted by Mr. Peabody or someone like him I think few of us would have trouble accepting that he is a person or, to put the point more strongly, that we would be capable of seeing him as a non-person. He is able to play the same role in most of our interactions that typical human adults do, and it would be difficult if not impossible to see him as we see typical dogs (for what it's worth in this context, the cartoon courts did see him as person enough to grant him the legal right to adopt a boy).

Of course, we have many good reasons to doubt that we would ever encounter anyone like Mr. Peabody, and the scenario he presents is probably not even completely coherent (and this is even when we omit the element of time travel). Not only does our current understanding of the biological basis of cognition suggest that a Peabody-like animal is impossible, Peabody's embodiment is likely to be problematic in ways the cartoon fails to explore. He vocalizes like a human, for instance, and wears spectacles that stay put despite his having the wrong kind of ears to support them. His engineering of the "wayback machine" and the way he twists its dials seem to imply the presence of opposable thumbs where they should not be. In these and myriad other ways the cartoon ignores difficulties that would be encountered by a dog of Peabody's intelligence trying to fit into our cultural infrastructure.[18]

The importance of these whimsical observations is that they underscore the fact that according to PLV it is not just the *possession* of intelligence that is most relevant to personhood, but the expression of that intelligence in a form of life that employs it on a regular basis. In fact, it is hard to make sense of the notion of the relevant kind of intelligence without such expression, and it is difficult to fully envision how an animal with the embodiment of a dog could express that intelligence in a lived life (this, I take it, is Lindemann's point). At the same time, however, intelligence can express itself in surprising ways, and challenges arising from particular forms of embodiment that at first seem insurmountable can sometimes be overcome with ingenuity and technology. I am therefore unwilling to rule out entirely the possibility that in some way not yet imagined an animal embodied like a dog could demonstrate enough of the attributes of a mature person to live a person life. If it did, it would be a person according to PLV.

It is far less of a stretch, of course, to imagine an atypical nonhuman primate finding a place in person-space. It would be very difficult not to see a bonobo with exceptional cognitive capacities who started communicating in human language and expressing thoughts that implied self-conscious awareness, prudential reasoning, and agential capacity as a person. For the same reasons it is very difficult to deny personhood to a human with typical human capacities (something like this is the fantasy of the 2011 movie *Rise of the Planet of the Apes*). Bonobos can manipulate objects as we do, walk on two legs, have faces that express emotion in roughly

---

[18] In fairness, the cartoon is called "Peabody's Improbable History."

the way ours do, comfort one another through physical contact in the same ways we do, and otherwise live in ways that express the similarities between our embodiment and theirs. A bonobo with super intelligence would almost certainly be granted a place in person-space (even if a somewhat unusual one) and therefore would be judged to be a person by PLV.

The cases I have discussed so far involve nonhumans within human culture. Another kind of example worth considering is that of groups of nonhumans whose members typically develop capacities relevantly like those of the humans who present our paradigmatic cases of personhood, and so develop infrastructure and institutions of their own. According to PLV such beings would be persons provided that their cultural institutions were sufficiently like ours to allow for the kinds of interactions between us that make up a person life. Here, once again, the nature of embodiment is likely to set some limits, but once again the exact parameters of those limits are difficult to gauge a priori.

Science fiction presents numerous examples of nonhuman civilizations with which we can interact in all kinds of ways that typify person lives—enjoying each other's literature and myths, engaging in trade and negotiating tariffs and treaties, caring for each others' young, drinking together in intergalactic bars, teaming up for military and other adventures, sharing technology, and so on. It is, of course, telling that the aliens depicted in these portrayals usually appear fairly close to us in the basics of their embodiment. Intelligent balls of light energy that could not take human form, do not need sustenance from the environment, and do not reproduce in anything like the way animals do would undoubtedly have a social organization so different from ours that it is exceedingly difficult to see how we could understand their form of life or engage with them in forensic interactions. Here we are no longer talking about nonhumans with the capacities of persons, but rather about beings with other kinds of capacities that may be equally or more sophisticated than our own. Such beings would not be persons according to PLV although they may be highly intelligent. Lest this seem chauvinistic, we should recall that our goal is to understand the nature of beings like us and to explicate the conditions of their individuation. At some point we are no longer talking about "beings like us" and that is all that the denial of personhood amounts to in this context.

We should not, however, be too quick to overestimate how like us creatures must be in order to be able to live recognizable person lives. Think, for instance, not of aliens but of elephants or whales or dolphins. We know that these animals have a great deal of intelligence and complex social organization. So far as we know they do not have cultural institutions like ours, but it is not so far-fetched to imagine (and has in fact been suggested by some scientists) that some animals do have culture that has been invisible to us.[19] The question of whether other animals have cultures is controversial, but the possibility that, e.g., marine mammals could have a cultural infrastructure that allows forensic interaction is by no means incoherent. The institutions and practices that would make up whale or dolphin culture would need to be very different from those that make up human culture given the differences in embodiment and environment. But the possibility (now or in the future) of discovering a species of marine mammals with whom we could communicate well enough to negotiate the use of waterways or engage in other cooperative ventures does not seem ruled out from the start. Such creatures would, according to PLV, be persons. It is also important to note that if these creatures typically possess the forensic capacities and a cultural infrastructure of their own, then individuals among them who fail to possess those capacities would nevertheless be persons within their own infrastructure (and so, by extension, within ours) for the very same reasons that humans with atypical developmental trajectories are.

A different kind of question arises about the possibility of inorganic persons. Just as frequently as science fiction has imagined alien life forms with person-like lives and capacities, it has imagined androids and robots with similar lives and capacities. What does PLV say about the personhood of machine-persons? Matters are complicated by the fact that questions about the personhood of artificial life forms often stand proxy for questions about whether machines that act like persons are sentient. Questions about whether sophisticated inorganic machines of this sort are persons usually revolve around one of two different worries: either that although such machines are sentient and intelligent they will be arbitrarily ruled out as persons or that they will be counted as persons even though they lack sentience.

The first worry is the more easily answered. If androids or robots in fact had the capacities (including the psychological capacities) of human persons and were able to engage in forensic interactions with humans and one another but were not treated as persons, their circumstances would be materially like those of oppressed humans. Arguably many science fiction treatments of this possibility (e.g., *Bladerunner*, its source, *Do Androids Dream of Electric Sheep*, and *A.I. Artificial Intelligence*) use such scenarios at least in part to explore phenomena of

[19] See, for instance, Luke Rendell and Hal Whitehead, "Culture in Whales and Dolphins," *Behavioral and Brain Sciences*, 24(2), 2001, pp. 309–82 (target article and replies); H. Lyn, J. Russell, D. Leavens, K. Bard, S. Boysen, J. Schaeffer, and W. Hopkins, "Apes Communicate about Absent and Displaced Objects: Methodology Matters," *Animal Cognition*, May 17, 2013; J. David Smith, "Inaugurating the Study of Animal Metacognition," *International Journal of Comparative Psychology*, 23, 2010, pp. 401–13. For a selection of essays on both sides see Kevin N. Laland and Bennett G. Galef, eds., *The Question of Animal Culture*, Cambridge, MA: Harvard University Press, 2009.

the oppression of humans by other humans, and so highlight the senses in which such cases are parallel. The exact nature of the argument here depends upon many details, but if we are assuming the fundamental forensic capacities I suggest that ultimately it would be as impossible for us to deny the personhood of these capable machines as of capable humans. In order for the relevant interactions to occur we would need to have the same expectations of these androids that we have of persons and they would be able to create cultures of their own just as oppressed humans do.

The second worry is a bit more complicated. It depends upon the assumption that it would be possible to create a machine that could replicate the most sophisticated human behavior and interactions without sentience. My own view is that this possibility does not make sense, but I am not in a position to argue for it, so it is necessary to say something about PLV's position in such a case. The waters around questions of the possibility of machine sentience are deep and treacherous and I have no desire to enter them now. It is true that sentience is part of a typical person life. We have allowed, however, that atypical person lives can produce persons, and we have already seen a case in which a non-sentient human may nevertheless count as a person (that of PVS), although only in a degenerate sense. I would be inclined to say that if it is possible for there to be non-sentient androids with the capacity to engage in forensic interactions with human persons (in the sense that they, e.g., make, keep, and break promises, save for their futures, hold each other responsible, express remorse, are brought to trial when they break laws, are able to enter into contracts, show anxiety when their work is going badly, etc.) then these androids would be persons.[20] They are strange persons, but so are many humans, and PLV is meant to allow for a great deal of variation. As I said at the beginning, however, I do not think this case is actually coherent.

I will round out my discussion of anomalous person lives by considering one last case which might seem to describe a scenario in which PLV is forced to grant personhood when it is implausible to do so. Since humans without the forensic capacities can be viewed as persons simply because our social infrastructure is such that they are automatically taken as persons, we might wonder whether it is possible for some group of humans to develop a social infrastructure that for some reason also automatically views members of some group of nonhumans (say dogs) as atypical persons. I am not thinking here of a super-intelligent race of dogs like

---

[20] Think, for instance, of HAL in *2001: A Space Odyssey*. This is going to become an interesting and important question as technology that mimics human behavior in some sense (e.g., assistants with voice recognition such as Apple's SIRI that can follow some commands and remind the user of appointments) becomes more fully integrated into our daily lives.

Peabody, nor of a culture that sees animals as containing the spirits of ancestors or gods. The former case we have already discussed. The latter is not one in which the nonhuman animals *qua* animals are being seen as persons; the persons are instead the spirits that inhabit them. The case I am considering here is one in which there is no assumption that dogs are anything more than they seem to be—they are not taken to be inhabited by spirits or capable of speech or rational thought—but nevertheless the infrastructure takes them up into person-space as they do human infants with atypical developmental potential. To be a dog, according to this view, is to be a person with a certain kind of disability, not to be a different kind of thing.

If such a cultural infrastructure were to exist, PLV would be committed to saying that the dogs that lived within it would be persons. But this kind of social organization seems to me truly unimaginable. It is just not clear what it would mean for dogs to be seen as persons in this case. Humans with atypical developmental potential are treated as persons because the failure of these humans to develop the capacities of mature personhood is experienced as an expectation unmet. It is not evident what would be involved in having those expectations of ordinary dogs. Would the birth of every dog be viewed as a kind of surprise? Would there be foundations and research initiatives to determine what could be done to prevent dogs from being born with only the capacities typical of dogs? It is difficult to see exactly how this would work unless we think of a society made up of people like the character Peppermint Patty in the Charlie Brown comic strip who never quite figured out that Snoopy was a Beagle and continued to think he was a "funny looking kid with a big nose."[21] This is a mistake that in real life would force its own discovery just as the underestimation of oppressed humans would and it is unclear how an infrastructure of this sort could actually exist.

There are no hard and fast rules that can be given about exactly how similar to humans nonhumans must be if we are to be able to engage with them in the ways that are necessary for them to be brought into person-space and so to lead person lives. I hope to have shown, however, that there is plenty of room within PLV for nonhuman persons, and that despite the central role human embodiment and human biology play on this view, being a person does not simply amount to being a member of the species *homo sapiens*.

5.5 Summing Up

We now have in hand a preliminary picture of a person life as defined by PLV. A paradigmatic person life is a characteristic developmental trajectory that can be

---

[21] And Snoopy is a lot more person-like than your average dog.

understood on three interconnected levels: the level of capabilities and attributes, the level of activities and interactions, and the level of social infrastructure. The standard capabilities and attributes found in such a life are the biological and psychological capacities and attributes typical of enculturated humans at their various stages of development (although we have seen that one can be a person despite lacking some of these); the standard activities and interactions are those undertaken by and characteristic of enculturated humans, who serve as our paradigmatic examples (although we have seen that one can be a person without engaging in all of them); and the social infrastructure is the set of institutions and practices that grow out of the social organization of beings who typically possess the forensic capacities and set the norms that govern interactions among persons. These three levels depend upon, support, and constrain one another. In order to make the case that PLV can truly provide an account of our literal identity which draws an inherent connection between facts about identity and practical considerations, however, we will need a clearer understanding of how the view individuates person lives and defines the conditions of their continuation. This will be the topic of the next chapter.

6

Personal Identity

The previous chapter described the general features of a person life and provided a picture of what personhood amounts to according to PLV. Our task in this chapter is to clarify what this view says about the individuation and continuity of persons. It will be most effective if we undertake this task in two steps. First, it will be useful to get a general sense of how it can be coherent to individuate persons by their lives. There is an air of paradox that surrounds such an idea, since we might think that in order to individuate person lives we would first have to individuate the persons who lead them. Lives are, moreover, such complicated and multi-faceted things that providing a single list of necessary and sufficient conditions for one to continue seems hopeless. If we cannot provide such a list of conditions, however, we will need to have another schema for saying what the continuity of a person life entails. With this structure established we can think about how it applies more specifically in the case of person lives.

To address the structural questions it will be enlightening to look in some detail at a case in which it is common to define an entity's identity in terms of its life—the case of biological organisms. The first part of this chapter will thus depart radically from the topics we have been discussing to investigate some of the issues surrounding the identity of organisms, without reference to questions about personhood or personal identity. The goal here is by no means to resolve outstanding disputes about these issues, and our foray into questions of organic life and death will be largely superficial. It will, however, provide a useful model for thinking about person lives by introducing the possibility of thinking of *life* as a cluster concept. This model can then be applied to the notion of a person life, yielding a general picture of what the continuity of such a life entails. With a broad sense of what is involved in the continuity of a person life in hand we can then revisit some of the standard puzzle cases in the personal identity literature and see what PLV implies about identity in these cases. Importantly, we will see that the structure of the view requires rethinking the way in which hypothetical cases are employed and the kinds of answers they can be expected to yield.

6.1 Biological Life and the Continuation of an Organism

Our first step is to discuss the identities of organisms and the nature and continuation of biological life. These are, of course, enormous questions and can by no means be considered here in their full complexity. Fortunately, there is a very helpful discussion of these issues, tailored directly to our concerns, in Eric Olson's *The Human Animal*, where he argues that the identities of organisms should be defined in terms of their lives. In the course of this argument Olson offers some instructive and compelling analysis of these issues which will be valuable here.

To begin, he tells us that "every organism has a life, and it is hard to see how there could be a life without there being an organism whose life it was."[1] Taking inspiration from Locke and Peter van Inwagen, he thus proposes the following criterion of identity for organisms: "For any organisms x and y, x=y if and only if x's life is y's life."[2] He follows this up in *What Are We? A Study in Personal Ontology,* by saying that he is "inclined to believe that an organism persists if and only if its life continues."[3] When he speaks of a life, he says, he means "more or less what Locke meant: a self-organizing biological event that maintains the organism's complex internal structure."[4] He tells us further that "the individual biological life of a particular living organism is a special kind of event, roughly the sum of the metabolic activities the organism's parts are caught up in."[5]

Olson recognizes that this definition has an apparent paradoxicality of the sort described above. "Since I have not given an independent criterion of identity for lives," he says, "you may wonder whether giving persistence conditions for organisms in terms of lives is at all helpful or informative."[6] Since a biological life

---

[1] Eric Olson, *The Human Animal*, p. 137.

[2] Olson, *The Human Animal*, p. 138.

[3] Eric Olson, *What are We? A Study in Personal Ontology*, Oxford: Oxford University Press, 2007, p. 29. It is worth noting that things may be more complicated than Olson says. The case of cryptobiotic organisms suggests the possibility of being neither dead nor alive. See, e.g., Cody Gilmore, "When do Things Die?" in Ben Bradley, Fred Feldman, and Jens Johansson, eds., *The Oxford Handbook of Philosophy of Death*, New York: Oxford University Press, 2013, pp. 14–19. I am grateful to an anonymous reviewer for pointing this out and directing me to Gilmore's fascinating piece, and more generally for many very useful comments that have helped me to be more precise throughout the book and in this chapter in particular.

[4] Olson, *What are We?*, p. 28.

[5] Olson, *What are We?*, p. 136.

[6] Olson, *The Human Animal*, p. 139.

is defined in terms of the metabolic activities of an organism's parts, it is hard to see how such a life could be the basis for a non-circular definition of an organism. Olson claims convincingly, however, that what circularity there is in such a definition is not vicious. To do this, he offers an analogy which demonstrates the legitimacy and usefulness of definitions of this general form. We can often tell, he says,

whether the storm that hit Cuba yesterday and the storm that brought floods to Alabama today are the same storm or different ones; and our ability to know this doesn't involve any judgments about the persistence of material objects. We don't first need to find out whether the material object composed of all and only those particles caught up in the Cuban storm is the same as, or different from, the material object composed of those particles caught up in the Alabaman storm. There may not even be any such material objects.[7]

If this is true of storms, he argues, it should be equally true of lives. Just as we can identify and reidentify a storm without any independent way to identify all and only the matter that is caught up in it, so we should be able to identify and reidentify a biological life without an independent way to identify all and only the material parts which must be caught up in it. An identity criterion for organisms in terms of their lives can thus be "useful and informative."[8]

This analysis does not yet show, of course, that an *entity* can be constituted by a life. To do this we will need to say more about what makes something an entity.[9] It does show, however, that we are in principle able to individuate and reidentify salient loci of interaction by a string of events rather than through the reidentification of material substance and, to the extent that organisms are convincing entities, that in principle an entity can be constituted by a life. The crucial point here is that even though organisms and storms involve material parts that are acted upon in particular ways, fixing their identities does not require that we be able ahead of time to know which material parts these are. All that is necessary is to be able to follow the series of activities that makes up an event of the appropriate kind—a life or a storm. Thinking that we need somehow to be able to identify the material object (the organism) independent of its life is a mistake. This can be seen by the relevantly similar case of the storm, in which there is no presumption that there *is* any independent object, and so identity conditions are clearly set by the activities themselves.

We will have occasion to revisit these issues, as well as Olson's view of biological life, in a somewhat different context in the next chapter. For now, however, Olson's analysis (and analogy) can be used to give preliminary credibility to the idea that

[7] Olson, *The Human Animal*, pp. 139–40.
[8] Olson, *The Human Animal*, p. 140.
[9] I am grateful to an anonymous reviewer for pointing out the need to make this clear.

we might be able to define organismic identity—and eventually personal identity—directly in terms of a life. This is only part of the overall story, however. While
the analysis we have given supports the claim that a definition of an organism in
terms of a biological life *can* be informative it only *will* be informative if we are able
to say whether or not a life has continued in a given case and what continuation
involves in general. As it turns out, this is not a trivial task, as can be seen by the
vigorous and ongoing debate about when biological death occurs. Looking a bit
more closely at this debate will be useful in providing a model for thinking more
broadly about what it means for a life to continue.

Before beginning this discussion I want to be very clear on what I am and am
not doing. Questions about when organisms die—and in particular when human
organisms die—are heavily studied and deeply contested. These are questions of
immense ethical importance with significant policy implications. The arguments
and positions that have been put forth, especially in the last decades, are enormously sophisticated and complex. I add no new arguments to the debate about
biological death, nor do I draw any firm conclusions. Since my ultimate interest
is in the continuation of person lives, I will dip into this discussion only deeply
enough to extract some useful tools for thinking about that question.

Several different criteria have been proposed for the cessation of a human life,
but the two most central—and most salient to our current inquiry—are the cardiopulmonary criterion (or its updated version, the circulatory-respiratory criterion),[10] and the whole brain criterion. The former holds that an animal dies when
its circulatory and respiratory functioning ceases irrevocably; the latter that it dies
when it is brain dead. For most of human history there was little practical need to
choose between these two criteria since cessation of circulatory-respiratory function quickly brought about brain death and vice versa. The development of artificial life support, however, has called for a principled choice, since circulation and
respiration can now be continued without the relevant brain functioning.

The two criteria express different ways of thinking about what a life is. The
circulatory-respiratory criterion focuses on the fact that the many integrated functions that constitute the life of an animal all ultimately depend upon circulation
and respiration. When these functions cease the others will all terminate in rapid
succession. It is thus the fact that circulation and respiration are central to the network of life-functions that gives their cessation a special status. Most proponents

---

[10] For an explanation of this distinction see D. Alan Shewmon, "The Brain and Somatic
Integration: Insights into the Standard Biological Rationale for Equating Brain Death with Death,"
Journal of Medicine and Philosophy, 26(5), 2001, p. 469; or David Degrazia, *Human Identity and
Bioethics*, pp. 147–9.

of the circulatory-respiratory criterion consider the organism to be alive so long as these functions are carried out, whether they are carried out by organic hearts and lungs or by artificial life support (hence "circulatory-respiratory" rather than "cardiopulmonary").

Proponents of the whole brain criterion, on the other hand, argue that artificial life support only maintains the appearance of life. In determining a criterion of death they focus on the fact that life is self-directed and self-sustaining and hold that these capabilities reside in the brain. The brain is the command center from which the self-organization that defines organic life takes place, defenders of this view argue, and without such a command center there is no living organism properly speaking.[11]

There are troubling objections which can be raised against either view. As a counterexample to the circulatory-respiratory account it is pointed out that organisms appear to retain consciousness for several seconds after the sudden (and ultimately irreversible) cessation of cardiac function. Winston Chiong, for instance, refers to the case of someone who simultaneously suffers irreversible cardiac arrest and the cessation of respiration and says that on "any ordinary understanding of life, this double victim would clearly remain alive as long as he remains conscious; if he managed to mouth a few words or flail around before lapsing into unconsciousness, we would have little inclination to say that these words and actions were produced by a dead organism.... we would say instead that they were produced by an organism in the process of dying."[12] There is no denying the central importance of circulation and respiration, of course, but to those who insist that the cessation of these functions *constitutes* death rather than merely *causing* it, this is a forceful counterexample.

Against the whole brain criterion opponents raise compelling biological evidence that there is a great deal of integrative function that is not directed by the brain. Much self-organization and self-maintenance occurs after brain death. Examples include maintenance of homeostasis; elimination, detoxification, and recycling of cellular wastes; wound healing; infection fighting; and cardiovascular and hormonal stress responses to unanesthetized incisions (for organ retrieval).[13]

[11] For more in-depth discussions of the history of definitions of death see D. Alan Shewmon, "Recovery from 'Brain Death': a Neurologist's Apologia," *The Linacre Quarterly*, 64(1), Feb. 1997, pp. 30–96, and Degrazia, *Human Identity and Bioethics*, pp. 115–24.

[12] Winston Chiong, "Brain Death without Definitions," *Hastings Center Report*, 35(6), Nov.–Dec. 2005, p. 22. Shewmon arguably offers an understanding of respiration which is more complex than that implied here (see Shewmon, "The Brain and Somatic Integration," p. 464), but the subtleties of this question can be ignored for our purposes.

[13] Winston Chiong, "Brain Death without Definitions," pp. 21–2. Chiong is relying here on Shewmon's work; see, e.g., Shewmon, "The Brain and Somatic Integration," pp. 462–73. See also Degrazia, *Human Identity and Bioethics*, pp. 142–3.

Much of the relevant integrative and self-organizing work of the organism seems to take place in the spinal cord and even at the periphery, and so the theoretical justification invoked for taking the cessation of brain activity to constitute death seems to point instead to a broader, and not-easily-articulable, criterion.

It is worth mentioning here (and will become important later) that Olson's sympathies are with the arguments that favor the whole brain criterion of death. He argues that it is the coordination of life-sustaining functions that ultimately defines organic life. For this reason he concludes that the continued function-ing of the same brainstem is ultimately required for the same life, and hence the same organism, to continue. This means, for instance, that if someone's head were removed and both the detached head and the rest of the body were kept alive arti-ficially, the animal would survive in the head. The rest of the body would not be a living thing at all, Olson says, and this would be so even if it were kept functioning with an artificial brain. On this view, a brainstem kept alive in a vat would be a radically depleted animal,[14] while a human whose brainstem was replaced with a miraculous inorganic prosthesis that kept it walking and talking and acting just as it had would in fact no longer be alive.

Olson realizes that this view is not immediately intuitive, but tells us that in the end the sharp distinction between the activities of the brainstem and of the rest of the body can be justified:

Part of what makes something a living organism...is its capacity to coordinate and reg-ulate its metabolic and other vital functions. A living organism may be prevented from *carrying out* those functions. I might be unable to digest my food because of a blockage in my intestine; I might be unable to purify my blood because my liver or kidneys are damaged: I might be unable to draw air into my lungs because my windpipe is clogged, or because my diaphragm muscles are paralyzed. In that case I could not survive for long without some sort of outside intervention. The instructions that my brainstem sends out to the rest of my organs may not arrive at their intended destinations, or they may not have the effects they are designed to have ("intended" and "designed" by evolution, not consciously). Nevertheless, the control and coordination mechanisms are intact.[15]

Given the challenges to the theoretical justification for placing executive control in the brain, these counterintuitive results seem even more unpalatable. They also point to a rather troubling disconnect between the metaphysical and biological points of view (despite the fact that Olson says that he means by "animal" "what biologists mean by it"[16]). It is unlikely that even those biologists who adopt a whole

[14] Olson does not actually say this; his examples involve a whole head being kept alive. Given what he says about the role of integrative functions, however, and about brainstem transplant and the dis-pensability of the rest of the brain, he seems committed to this view and so I will attribute it to him.
[15] Olson, *The Human Animal*, pp. 133–4.
[16] Olson, *What are We?*, p. 27.

brain criterion of death would view a brainstem in a vat sending out impotent signals (or a whole severed head, for that matter) as an organism. From the point of view of a biologist, an intact and functioning brainstem-complement with prosthetic brainstem that has beating heart, circulating blood, and functioning endocrine system is likely to be at least as good a candidate for an organic life.

In light of the complexities that arise in debates about the criterion of death Chiong applies Richard Boyd's account of homeostatic property clusters to the concepts of *life* and *death* and suggests a view on which "the property of being alive (like the property of being a language or a game) involves a cluster of characteristics—none of which is in itself necessary and sufficient for an organism to be alive, but all of which contribute to an organism's being alive and tend to reinforce one another in paradigm cases."[17] This approach might raise difficulties if we are looking for a criterion of life and death that can be used, e.g., for purposes like determining whether organs can legitimately be harvested for transplant or whether someone is legally a widow. In these contexts we might need to define something more clear-cut that can settle policy. If, however, we are trying to characterize what truly ends a life in either biological or metaphysical terms this view is very appealing. The standard general definition of death for organisms is "the irreversible cessation of functioning of the organism as a whole." Conceptually this is what death must be, and biology suggests that there are a variety of ways in which organisms can continue to function as wholes, at least if they are given the proper support and deficits in ordinary functioning are made up with artifice.

In the paradigm case, organic life involves the functioning of all major organs and systems. In animals like us this means that the heart and lungs must be healthy, the liver, kidneys, and pancreas must operate as they are supposed to, the nervous system must direct and regulate metabolic activity, the immune system must function, and so on. The organism as a whole can be maintained through the loss of any one of these systems, however, so long as the crucial functions are taken up in some other way. Artificial life support systems, medications, dialysis, insulin injections, antibiotics, and antivirals can all do some of the work that natural systems are no longer capable of carrying out. Where these artificial compensations are not possible, the functioning of the organism as a whole may, depending on the centrality of the function lost, still continue to function for some time. The traditional approach to understanding death tempts us to define "life" in terms of that

[17] Chiong, "Brain Death without Definitions," p. 25. The work of Boyd's on which he draws is well represented in "Homeostasis, Species, and Higher Taxa," in Robert A. Wilson, ed., *Species: New Interdisciplinary Essays*, Cambridge, MA: MIT Press, 1999, pp. 141–85. Chiong's contribution is to apply this notion to the debate about biological death, and so it is his treatment of cluster concepts that is especially relevant for our purposes.

last function whose cessation signals the end of all function. But "lastness" may be merely chronological and not consistent from case to case. There are different ways of dying and they involve different kinds of specific last moments. This means that there are a variety of functions whose cessation might (or might not) undermine the integrity of an organism as a whole, depending on context and on which other functions are still occurring.

This understanding of biological life and death in terms of homeostatic property clusters is attractive not only in avoiding some of the difficulties encountered by the traditional criteria, but also in reminding us that we do not best understand life by asking when the animal is at last dead. If we think that there is some single function whose cessation always constitutes death, we will be tempted to try to understand life itself in terms of that single function. On reflection this is clearly a mistake. Even if we were to accept the whole brain criterion of death, for instance, we certainly do not want to understand organic life simply in terms of the functioning of the brainstem. In a healthy human animal, life involves a beating heart, circulating blood, the production of hormones by various glands, the circulation of blood, dilation and contraction of blood vessels, and the production of white blood cells, among many other events. All of these are part of the organic life of a human animal fundamentally, and not accidentally. Understanding the continuity of a life does not just mean knowing when it ends, and if we want to understand what is involved in the continuity of organic life we would do well to look at animals in the prime of health as well as those gasping their last.[18]

There is, of course, a great deal more that can be and has been said about biological life and death, but I will leave the debate here. We have, however, gained some important resources by considering these questions. First, we have been given a general model to help us understand the way in which a life can reasonably be taken to provide a means for individuating and reidentifying integrated loci (using Olson's storm analogy). Second, we have been given a useful model for thinking about the continuity of a multi-faceted life in Chiong's homeostatic property cluster analysis. Whatever the ultimate determination about how well this model works for providing an account of the continuation of a biological life, it is, as we will see shortly, very well suited for providing an account of the continuation of a person life. The usefulness for our purposes of this general understanding of a life does not, I hasten to point out, depend upon its success in the biological context.

---

[18] This is not, of course, to say that there are no studies of biological life that focus on understanding healthy animals—most, in fact, probably do. But when the question is about *persistence* the kind of analysis I have described is quite common. At any rate, the distinction between these two approaches will play a central role in our discussion of personal identity so it is important to lay it out.

I therefore now return to a consideration of person lives to show how this idea is applied there.

6.2 Person Lives: a Cluster Model

I have said that I will think of a person life in terms of property clusters[19] along the lines Chiong proposes for biological life. In this section we will consider in more detail just what this amounts to and what methodological implications it has for an investigation into personal identity.

According to Chiong, the property of being alive "involves a cluster of characteristics—none of which is in itself necessary and sufficient for an organism to be alive, but all of which contribute to an organism's being alive and tend to reinforce one another in paradigm cases." The relevant characteristics in the biological case include a functioning respiratory and circulatory system, ongoing metabolic and neurological activity, and the host of other biological functions that work together to maintain a healthy organism. If PLV is going to apply this model to person lives, it will be necessary to say which are the relevant characteristics and functions in a paradigmatic person life. We saw in the last chapter that the lives of persons involve biological, psychological and social functions working together, and that these different dimensions of our lives—dimensions which, as we have seen, are only artificially separable in paradigm cases—can be used to roughly categorize the functions that work together to make up a person life. In order to be able to give a slightly more detailed account of what a person life entails I will focus once again specifically on the lives of human persons, who serve as our paradigms of personhood anyway. The analysis I give can, however, be modified to apply to nonhuman person lives along the lines suggested in the last chapter.

Because they are human, the lives of human persons involve the activities and functions that are taken to define the human organism, but person lives include more besides. Human persons are also beings who in the standard case develop characteristic psychological capacities and features and engage in certain kinds of social interactions. Crucial to PLV is the recognition that in a paradigm person life these different systems and capacities are deeply intertwined. That they are interconnected is obvious. It is evident, for instance, that the psychological capacities of persons are intimately bound up with their biological functioning—so intimately

---

[19] "Property clusters" should be read as "homeostatic property clusters," which in this case means the set of relations and attributes that make up a person life. When I say that I have a "cluster concept" of persons or person lives this should be taken to mean that I think of them in this way. Of course, since the model is here being applied to a person life and not to natural kinds or biological lives, the details will be different from those offered by either Boyd or Chiong.

that some would question whether they are usefully distinguished. While we can therefore speak of a biological or psychological or social life within the context of PLV what we are referring to is not a separate life, but a particular kind of activity within a person life. The nature of the interactions among these features in a typical life is crucial to the view and so, although we touched on these issues in the previous chapter, it is worth exploring them a bit further.

Let's begin, then, by thinking about biological functions and how they fit into the life of a human person as a whole. The connection between biological and psycho/social features on which PLV focuses is not limited to the causal role that biological mechanisms play in producing psychological capacities, but involves many different levels of interrelation. Embodiment in a human body is, as a general fact, absolutely central to the specific organization that structures our lives, and our embodiment is inscribed in the institutions and practices that make up the person-space within which our lives are lived. As described in the previous chapter, social and cultural institutions develop as part of the natural history of humans, and at the deepest level reflect and express the biological facts of human existence. We have medical professions, exercise regimens, and other activities aimed at keeping us healthy; we have complicated practices surrounding sexuality and reproduction that impact a great deal of what we do every day and shape the social/cultural organization within which our daily activities take place. We worry about our mortality and that of those we love; artifacts of culture like organized religions, poems, stories, and philosophical treatises are dedicated to understanding the implications of our organic nature; systems of law and justice are built around an understanding of the kinds of damage that can be done to organic life by acts of violence.[20]

Our psychological and social lives are thus infused everywhere with our biology. Importantly, however, the direction of influence is not all one way, and it is crucial to appreciate that our biological lives and functioning are impacted in a host of ways by our psychological functioning and social context. It is not, after all, as if we have on the one hand immune response and on the other practices concerning vaccination, pharmaceuticals, and healthcare professions. Practices of immunization, sanitation, and medical treatment influence the functioning of our immune systems in a very direct way. Similarly, we do not have metabolic functioning on the one hand and practices of agriculture and food distribution on the other. There is ample evidence that the changes in diet brought about by the development of

---

[20] Think here of Shylock and his pound of flesh. Once again, I want to emphasize that for the moment I am focusing on human persons. Presumably the cultures of nonhuman persons would be built around the facts of their embodiment.

farming led over generations to changes in the human organism including, but not limited to, alterations in dental and jaw structure, skeletal structure, and digestive enzymes. Within a single life these practices can lead to increased vulnerability to heart disease and diabetes, early puberty, tall stature, and a variety of other biological attributes. We are, moreover, only now beginning to understand the plasticity of the human brain and the ways in which both brain architecture and neurological functioning are influenced by our social and cultural environments.

As far as I am aware no one denies that in the ordinary course of events the lives of human persons have biological, psychological, and social components, nor that these components interact in the ways I have described. Since PLV takes the cluster property model of person lives seriously it holds that these connections between the different aspects of our lives as ordinarily lived constitute a defining feature of personhood and personal identity. This is in contrast to traditional views which tend to see the ways in which the different aspects of our views are entangled with one another as a complication that prevents us from apprehending clearly what we truly are. Locke, for instance, tells us that we fail to appreciate that personal identity must be defined in terms of sameness of consciousness because we confuse questions about sameness of man and sameness of person. Olson, on the other side, tells us that the psychological approach has a hold on us because we have failed to keep our eye on the metaphysical question, confusing it with various psychological or social concerns. Neither allows for the possibility that the conditions of our continuity might incorporate both elements.

This difference in attitude toward the interrelations among the different aspects of our lives inspired by the property cluster model has methodological implications for discussions of personal identity. While these different activities usually occur together, they can also come apart in cases both real and imagined. In PVS, dementia, amnesia, the transfer case, teleportation, and other scenarios frequently invoked in the personal identity debate some of the functions that are part of a paradigmatic person life continue while others are lost or compromised. It is in these kinds of cases that the hard questions of personal identity emerge. The standard method for analyzing such scenarios is to ask whether the protagonist survives the vicissitude imagined and then to use the answer to that question to determine which of the functional continuities present in paradigmatic cases provides the real basis for identity. If someone can survive in a PVS, then we know that a person can continue when only biological continuity is in place and conclude that all along it was biological continuity that constituted our identities; if someone can (in principle) survive disembodied or transferred to a new organism in virtue of a transfer of psychological life, then we know that in the standard case it is psychological continuity doing the real work. It is thus traditional to view these puzzle cases as a way of conducting a sort of controlled experiment in which we disentangle features that tend to occur together (i.e., psychological, biological, and social continuities) in order to determine which of them is actually responsible for the relevant phenomenon (i.e., the survival of the person).

The property cluster understanding of a person life offers an alternative picture. Instead of assuming some one of the relations present in paradigmatic cases of continuation is the one that constitutes our identity, we can think instead of identity as constituted by their interactions with one another. On the standard approach the fact that biological, psychological, and social continuities are intertwined is seen as a complication which makes it difficult to determine which relation constitutes continuation. On the property cluster model the integrated functioning *is* the true nature of the relation that constitutes the conditions of our continuation. The existence of the individual types of continuity in their "pure" form is in fact a degenerate case of the more basic relation that contains all three.

Where the standard approach would thus encourage us to determine which of the standard continuities in a person's life is *the* relation that defines identity, the property cluster model of a person life encourages us to consider how these different types of continuity support one another and work together to sustain the integrated functioning of the person as a person and, on the flip side, to look at the ways in which different types of discontinuity compromise that integrity. In doing this we can use some of the same tools the traditional approach does, looking at what happens to a person in cases of actual anomaly and fantastic puzzle cases, but there is an important difference in what we will attend to when we look at these cases, and what kinds of conclusions we will seek to draw. Since the standard method does not focus primarily on the interactions among the different dimensions of our lives that occur in everyday life but instead on each dimension individually, the possible or predictable impact that a loss or attenuation of one set of functions will have on the others is largely ignored. This is so in both real life and imaginary cases. PVS, for instance, is not the cessation of psychological continuity in an otherwise completely healthy organism; neither is late-stage Alzheimer's disease. And amnesia almost never happens without the impairment of other kinds of cognition. In all of these cases there are biological changes that impact the functioning of an organism beyond the psychological symptoms but these are hardly ever discussed in philosophical reflection on them.

Things are similar in the imaginary cases. Very little attention is given in these hypothetical scenarios to the question of what kinds of psychological and social impact something like transferring a psychological life to a new organism might have, and this is often pointed out by critics of the method. The fact that being in a very different kind of body might have some disorienting results, and potentially profound psychological or social implications, is sometimes mentioned in passing, but is rarely a central and sustained part of the discussion of these cases.[21] On the method suggested by the property cluster model, on the other hand, these kinds of interactions and their implications for the functioning of the person as a whole are the primary focus of reflection in these cases. Our general model of the continuation of a person life thus suggests a new way of looking at the traditional cases. We can get a clearer idea of this new approach and the fruits it can bear, as well as a more concrete picture of what PLV says about personal identity in anomalous situations, by looking at some examples.

6.3 Puzzle Cases

To fill out the picture of diachronic identity found in PLV further I will look at variations on some traditional cases and describe PLV's position on the continuation of the person in each instance. I begin with a version of the transfer case from Chapter 1 (in which PLV renders a fairly straightforward judgment that the person survives in a new body), and end with the fission case (in which PLV renders a fairly straightforward judgment that the person does not survive at all). In between I will look at a variation on the first case which is somewhat more difficult for PLV to address and highlights the complexity of the methodology involved.

6.3.1 The simple transfer case

We can call our initial case the *simple transfer case*. This case is just the familiar transfer case introduced in Chapter 1 with a few additional details spelled out. The importance of these extra details will be explored in the next section by tweaking them. Here is the initial case:

Sometime in the future an environmental toxin reaches levels at which it begins regularly to cause liver failure in a large segment of the population. A technique is developed to clone healthy livers from an individual's own tissue, transplant techniques are improved, and liver transplants become common. Later the toxin begins to attack other organs, and these are regularly cloned and transplanted as well. Eventually, it attacks all tissue but the cerebrum (which is somehow protected). Fortunately, cloning technology has developed to the point where healthy whole cerebrum complements can regularly be cloned. Moreover, the development of clones can be accelerated and directed so that the result is an adult human body (minus cerebrum) that looks almost exactly like the individual from whom the genetic material was taken. The cerebrum of the diseased individual is then placed into the cerebrum-less skull of the cloned body, carrying with it the individual's beliefs, values, desires, memories, and so on. This operation inevitably and immediately leads to the end

---

[21] See, e.g., Parfit, *Reasons and Persons*, pp. 253–4.

of biological activity in the body from which the cerebrum was taken. Everyone refers to this operation as a "full body transplant" and sees it as the limiting case of the transplantation of individual organs. Just as it is assumed that a person survives when she gets a new liver or kidney or heart, it is assumed that a person survives when she gets a new body (or, strictly speaking, cerebrum-complement). After post-surgical recovery the patient typically returns to her family, friends, job, and hobbies.

In the case as described PLV has the implication that the original person would survive the cerebrum transplant. What is required for a person to continue is for a person life to continue, which is for a single locus of our person-related questions and concerns to continue. In this case it seems clear that there is such a locus that continues through the transplant. The person who emerges from surgery is the natural target of the questions, concerns, and relationships that applied to the original person. The intuition that this is so is nearly universal, acknowledged even by many who (like Olson) want to reject the value of this intuition for determining the answer to questions about our identities.

For PLV, the continuation of the same person just consists in the fact that the person before us now is viewed as, treated as, and acts as the same locus of practical concerns as the person who entered surgery for cerebrum extraction. What this case thus reveals is that in the appropriate circumstances a person can survive a particular kind of change of embodiment; the biological functions that are caught up in the person life at time t_2 may be discontinuous with those that were caught up in that same person life at t_1 without ending the person life. The circumstances in which this can happen are, however, very special, and several of the details of the simple transfer case are crucial if we are to be able to make this kind of straightforward judgment. One of these details—the fact that biological life immediately ceases in the body from which the cerebrum is taken—will be explored in detail in subsequent sections. For the moment I want to concentrate on the way in which the historical development of the transplantation technology is depicted, starting with the cloning of individual organs and ending, ultimately, with what is referred to as a "full body transplant."

The point of this back story is obviously to make it plausible that in the minds of those who inhabit the world depicted (and so, as readers of the story, in ours) the transfer of the cerebrum to a decerebrated skull will look merely like the extension of other kinds of transplants of a sort that already exist and are clearly person-preserving. This is important because it is essential to the judgment that a person survives a "whole-body transplant" that the transplant product is able to pick up the thread of the life of the person who enters surgery. This can happen only if the transplant product is accorded the appropriate place in person-space;

that is, if she is treated as and responds as the continuation of the original locus of concern.

In fact, once the case stipulates that the person who results from the transfer is treated as and responds as the original person the implication that the cerebrum donor survives as the whole body recipient follows immediately. In some sense, then, the survival of the original person in this case is a matter of fiat, since it is part of the *description* of the case that the person who wakes up from the transplant surgery is the same locus of person-related concerns as the person who went under the knife. If this is only stipulation, consideration of the case doesn't teach us much. To say "imagine a case in which a person undergoes this or that vicissitude (e.g., change in embodiment) *and* meets our criterion of survival," and then to point out that in such a case the person survives according to our criterion, seems a truly pointless exercise. But this does not adequately express the nature of the simple transfer case. The real question is not so much "Would the person survive in the case as described?" but rather "Is the case as described coherent and plausible?" If I say this is a case in which human embodiment changes as described *and* we all go on treating and interacting with the product as the original person, have I described a scenario that we can truly envision?[22]

To see what I have in mind here, contrast the simple transfer case with a different story involving a blood transfusion (from a body in which biological activity ceases immediately after blood is taken) into a unique recipient who, according to stipulation, is treated by everyone as the same person as the blood donor and picks up the thread of the original person's life. In the "simple blood transfer" case, unlike the simple transfer case, the stipulation that the blood recipient will be treated as and act as the original person is unmotivated and incoherent. There is nothing to make the attempts to treat the blood recipient as the original person "take" and such attempts would be bound to fail in something like the way that attempts to treat slaves as non-persons or ordinary dogs as persons would. Receiving a blood transfusion does not provide the resources someone needs to respond and act as the blood donor. Our practices concerning the direction of person-related concerns and questions are not determined completely by facts external to our social organization but they are, in the ways we have explored, constrained by and responsive to them.

The simple transfer case can work as an example of a person life continuing with discontinuities in organic life because the stipulation that practice would evolve in

---

[22] For a terrific discussion of these matters, to which I owe a great deal of what I say here, especially about fission, see Aleks Zarnitsyn, *Thought Experiments in Personal Identity: a Literary Model*, Doctoral dissertation, University of Illinois at Chicago, 2013.

such a way that a single locus of person-related concerns would continue through the transfer is not a mere stipulation, but rather a well-grounded prediction. This seems a natural way for our person-related practices to evolve should such technologies develop, and it is reasonably easy to imagine how we could seamlessly take up the relevant relations with the product of a whole-body transplant as described. It does need to be acknowledged, however, that this is only a prediction, and so judgments about whether a person would actually survive such a transplant are, in a certain sense, provisional. I mentioned much earlier that some have expressed reservations about the use of fantastic thought experiments, and I share many of these. They are the usual kinds of concerns—that it is not clear if we are truly able to imagine what we think we are imagining; that it is not evident that the worlds depicted are sufficiently like ours to tell us anything about persons as we know them; that intuitions about bizarre cases are easily manipulable; and so on. For all of these reasons we must be careful both to spell out the cases on which we reflect in sufficient detail to allow us to make relatively informed decisions about what they tell us and to be modest in our conclusions. It might be, for instance, that unforeseen pressures or developments would make it impossible to really treat transplant products of the sort described as if they were the original person. If that were the case, PLV would have to alter its judgment of the case, and conclude that even though we might predict that a person could survive such a transplant it turns out that actually they cannot.

It is important to be clear about what this implies, however. Since the claim that the transplant product would be easily and naturally seen as the original person seems quite compelling given what we know, we need to assume that if it turned out that she could not or would not be so treated it would be because the case is in fact materially different than what we are imagining and not just because the people in the imagined world happen, arbitrarily, to take a different attitude than we thought they would. Acknowledging that it is possible for us to mis-imagine a puzzle case in a way that renders our judgments erroneous is not the same as acknowledging that whether someone survives such a transplant is *merely* a matter of convention. Still, the role PLV gives to social interactions and attitudes in determining facts about personal identity does cause some complications, as we will see if we alter this case a bit.

6.3.2 The surviving animal transfer case

In the simple transfer case it was stipulated that a cerebrum transfer would always result in the death of the animal from which the cerebrum is taken. To push the issues that emerged in the last section a bit further let's consider instead *the surviving animal case*, in which the biological entity from whom the cerebrum is removed is kept alive in a vegetative state. This case presents a challenge. I have said that according to PLV a person who falls into a PVS survives as a vegetative human person. Just a moment ago, in discussing the simple transfer case, however, I said that according to this view the person whose cerebrum is removed would survive as the person with the old cerebrum and cloned body. It is thus not evident what the view can or should say in the surviving animal case, where the vegetative individual and the newly-cerebrated individual are both present. PLV seems committed to saying that *both* are the original person, but this is hardly coherent.

What PLV can and should say in the surviving animal case, as in all cases, depends in large part on how the social infrastructure surrounding the case develops. The challenge stems from the fact that it is much more difficult to predict in this case than it was in the simple transfer case just how the products of this kind of operation would be treated or perceived and whether they would be able to pick up the thread of the original person's life. For this reason it is much more difficult to say anything definitive about the survival of the person.

There are two main possibilities for the resolution of this case, each of which raises tricky issues for PLV. In one, the outcome would be largely like that of the simple transfer case. Our practice might evolve so that, for all of the reasons given in the discussion of simple transfer, the person life of the original person would continue in the individual with the cloned body and original cerebrum. In this scenario the decerebrated being in a vegetative state would not be the focus of person-related concerns and questions but would be seen, perhaps, as the discarded husk of the original person, something with the status of a diseased heart or liver removed in a transplant and replaced with a healthy organ. I think that it is not just coherent, but perhaps even likely, that this is how our practice and perception would develop if such transplants became possible (although, and this is not a trivial matter, it takes some work to make up a story about why the vegetative individual would be kept alive if this were so). The intelligibility of this scenario calls for some explanation on the part of PLV, however. If in real-world PVS the vegetative individual in the hospital bed is Father, who worked hard his whole life and traveled the world before he took ill, how can Father become nothing more than medical waste just because the cerebrum taken from his skull is placed somewhere else?

There is a straightforward answer to this question from the perspective of PLV: the difference is that in the former case the vegetative individual is accorded the place of Father in person-space while in the latter he is not; that place is given now to the individual with the cloned body and Father's cerebrum. But this answer is not by itself very satisfying. Throughout my discussion of PLV I have been insisting that seeing and treating someone as a person is not a matter of arbitrary choice but a response to facts about the world, and the same will also have to be true about seeing him as the *same* person if PLV is to be plausible. Since there is no obvious intrinsic difference between the vegetative individual in the real-life case of PVS and the vegetative individual in the science-fiction scenario I have described, it seems as if the *only* distinguishing feature is found in our attitudes towards them. If this by itself can make the difference between judgments of identity in the two cases the worry that PLV is unpalatably conventionalist is sure to reemerge. This is a serious worry, and demands a rather complex answer.

The best response to this concern is not to deny that there is a measure of conventionalism in PLV, but rather to show that it is limited to very special circumstances in which it is not as objectionable as it might at first appear. The salient feature is that the individual who is counted as continuing the person life in the case of real-world PVS is not a typical person, but a person in marginal and unusual circumstances. I argued that person lives continue in PVS, but it was always a part of this argument that these lives are attenuated and minimal. No one is under the illusion that the person life of someone with PVS continues in just the same way as a typical person life. PVS is a degenerate case of personhood in the best of circumstances. It is because of this that it makes sense to say that there is some room for interpretation, and that we might intelligibly take a different attitude toward someone in this condition in the surviving animal transfer case than we do in the real-life case.

To see why this is so, it will be helpful to recall that on this view a person life is understood via a cluster concept and to remind ourselves of two important implications of thinking of life this way. One is that there is no single set of necessary and sufficient conditions required for a life to continue. A life is a set of integrated and usually mutually-supporting functions. When too many of these functions cease the overall integrity of the life can no longer be maintained and the life ends. So long as enough functions continue the life goes on. It may not always be the same functions whose continuation maintains a life, however. A second implication is that lives can continue more or less robustly. As functions are lost, the hold on life becomes more tenuous. An organism in which many life functions are compromised may be just barely alive, holding on by a thread. Both of these aspects of the property cluster model are important to a satisfying analysis of the present case.

The kind of life at issue here is a person life, defined in terms of the constellation of different functions, biological, psychological, and social, that make up the life of a person. A person in a PVS has a seriously compromised biological life, but an even more compromised person life. Most of the functions that define such a life are lost when someone is in a vegetative state. Not only is there mitigation of biological functioning, there is a complete or almost complete loss of psychological functioning, and social relations are drastically compromised as the person in a vegetative state can be only the recipient of social attentions and not an active participant in interactions with others. This is important because at these margins there is always some room for interpretation and disagreement. We have seen this quite vividly in the case of biological life. While we can all agree that a healthy human is alive, there is real dispute about a brain-dead human on artificial life support. Even those who believe that there is a unique correct answer to the question of whether the human on life support is a living organism or not can understand how there could be disagreement and confusion here. Wondering whether such a being is really alive is coherent in a way that wondering whether a perfectly healthy adult is alive is not.

The significance of this fact for present purposes lies in the way that it sets natural limits on the conventionalist aspects of PLV. According to this view, being accorded a continuing place in person-space is required for a person to continue to exist. I have emphasized that whether or not we accord someone a place in person-space is not truly a matter of choice, but a response to how things are in the world as we experience it. The remaining person-life functions of someone in a PVS are so minimal that, unlike the case of an adult human with typical cognitive functioning, it is coherent to question whether that person life is really continuing. With the technology that we have now, in industrialized nations in the early twenty-first century, our practice is to treat those who fall into a PVS as minimally continuing a person life in the ways I described earlier. But we recognize the tenuousness of such a life. Importantly, this is a situation where available infrastructure plays an important role. We mentioned earlier that before the development of effective artificial life support technologies the dispute between whole brain and circulatory-respiratory criteria of organic death had no purchase, since the one always led inevitably to the other. Similarly, without the means of maintaining those in a PVS the question of whether the person life continues in such a state does not really arise.

To say that there is a conventionalist element in PLV with respect to cases of this sort thus does not commit us to saying that choices in the paradigmatic cases of personhood and personal development are conventional. The property cluster picture of person life also helps us to understand how the existence of the clone-bodied recipient of the cerebrum in the surviving animal case can legitimately make a difference to our identity judgments concerning the vegetative individual. This is because on this picture it is not some particular relation that determines the continuation of a life, but rather a critical mass of the usual relations. The specific relations that constitute continuity can be different in different instances. In the case of real-world PVS we have continuity of a minimal set of functions and nothing else, and this is sufficient to say that the person life (barely) continues. In the surviving animal case we have a situation in which this same set of minimal continuities exists but there is also another locus in which something like the full range of continuities consists, with only a disruption in the biological continuities. In this case it makes sense to say that the locus is where the larger and more significant cluster of functions is, even though it would be where the minimal functions are if those were the only continuities.

As always, it is useful to think of an analogous case concerning biological life. Someone with a severely damaged heart may remain biologically alive, but profoundly compromised, with devastating effects on all life functions. Suppose a healthy heart becomes available and is transplanted into the ailing organism which renews its health and vigor, and that for research purposes and by some technology the diseased heart is kept alive and beating elsewhere. The original heart, in the context of the original organism, may well have been the core of the ongoing life. After the transplant, however, the life is where the nexus of restored biological functions take place, and not in the diseased heart that used to stand at its core.[23] Similarly, when someone falls into a PVS, the vegetative individual will be the locus of relevant person-related concerns, but if a transplant leads to a revival of the lost functional continuities in the clone-bodied individual that individual will become the locus of concern. The analogy is not perfect, and the case is admittedly strange, but so are cerebrum transplants in which the original body is kept alive in a vegetative state. Once we are in the realm of science fiction we need to tread carefully and be mindful that it is difficult to draw confident conclusions. These cases can, nevertheless, help us to see how unusual the circumstances must be before the conventionalist elements of PLV kick in, and this should help to mitigate concerns about this aspect of the view.

The discussion so far has assumed that in this case the clone-bodied person will be treated unambiguously as the original person. There is, however, another way in which this case might unfold. Throughout the discussion of PLV I emphasized that we are largely unable to see living humans as non-persons, and that this fact is written into the social and cultural infrastructure that supports personhood. This may run so deep that we are in fact unable to see the cerebrum-complement as mere tissue rather than as a person. This is especially likely if we try to attend to some of the biological realities of the case and admit that a cerebrum transfer would likely not in itself generate complete psychological continuity since some support for

---

[23]   Some might well reject this analysis of the biological case, but nothing much turns on it and it is meant only to clarify the structure of the claim.

psychological functions seem to involve more peripheral systems.[24] At the same time, no matter how we see the vegetative individual, it would almost certainly be impossible not to see the cloned individual as somehow continuous with the original person, and so also a locus of at least some of the relevant person-related concerns. This means we are left with two distinct entities, each of which is viewed as a continuer of the original person. This possible development raises a different kind of problem for PLV than the problem of conventionalism we just considered, as the view now seems forced to acknowledge the possibility that someone could be identical to each of two future people who are not identical to one another.

The best response to this difficulty is to say that in such a case PLV would actually have the result that the original person is identical to *neither* the decerebrated individual nor to the clone-bodied individual, but in fact ceases to exist. This is because a person is, by definition, a unified locus of our person-related concerns, and there is no such unified locus where concerns are spread between two individuals. On the surface this response is likely to sound like an attempt to save the view by stipulation—insisting that relations to a future person that would count as survival if they were unique do not if they are multiple for no other reason than their brute multiplicity—and this seems to bring us back to the reductionist view of persons discussed in Chapter 1, with all of its challenges. This is not quite the case, however. The claim is that the multiplicity of relevant loci changes the *nature of the concerns* that can be directed at them in such a way that it is not possible to have the original person-related concerns toward any individual in this situation. The structural similarity between these issues and questions considered in depth and revolutionized by Parfit should be clear, and my response to this case has some similarities to, but also fundamental differences from, those Parfit offers. Since the relevant challenges arise more cleanly and directly in the case of fission than they do in the surviving animal case, I will explore them more fully in that context.

6.3.3 Fission

There are many different versions of the fission case, but for (a kind of) simplicity we can focus on Parfit's or, even better, on the case in which a person splits like an amoeba into two qualitatively identical beings. In either version we are left with two continuers of the original person who are distinct from one another. According to PLV a person life, and so a person, continues as long as a unified locus of our person-related questions and concerns continues. This clearly does not happen in the fission case. After fission there are two easily identifiable loci and

---

[24] I discuss this issue in "The Brain/Body Problem," *Philosophical Psychology*, 10(2), June 1997, pp. 149–64.

it does not seem possible to treat them as a single person in any straightforward way that mirrors the singleness of persons as we know them. There are thus two people after the split, according to PLV, and neither of them is the original person. To see how this claim could be justified we need only consider what it would be like to try and find the pre-fission locus of concern in the post-fission products. It is not even clear how this would be done.

One possibility is that the two products together would be seen as a unit of our person-related interests so that interacting with either would count as interacting with the whole. If I owe Ben money and he fissions, perhaps I can now pay back either of the resulting Bens; if Ben promised to help me move before fissioning perhaps *at least one* of the post-fission Bens would be obligated to help me, but it wouldn't matter much which one. It does not seem viable to take this approach within the infrastructure of personhood as it now exists, for obvious reasons. Each of the fission products has the capability to be an independent locus of concern and interaction, and ultimately treating them as one will lead to incoherence. If post-fission Ben is my student, I cannot teach the material to Ben_1 and expect Ben_2 to produce the relevant information on the exam; if it is Ben_1 who got his pilot's license or finished his surgical residency then it is Ben_1 and not Ben_2 that I want flying my plane or operating on me; if Ben_2 has an infection it will not work to give antibiotics to Ben_1.

While there will undoubtedly be an uncanny amount of overlap between the two fission products, and thus many circumstances in which one can be treated in just the same way we would treat the other, all the considerations that link human personhood to embodiment in a single organism in the everyday case will interfere with treating the Bens as a single entity. It is important to note that the argument I am making does *not* depend on the logical form of identity (i.e., since Ben_1 ≠ Ben_2 it cannot be the case that Ben = Ben_1 and Ben = Ben_2), but only on the fact that after fission the kinds of independence that Ben_1 and Ben_2 have from one another makes it impossible to treat them as a single locus, and so that they cannot jointly serve as the locus of our concerns and questions about Ben, the person who existed before the fission.

We might think that the two continuers could *each* be treated as Ben. That is, since each has the same psychological make-up, memories, and proclivities that Ben has in the ordinary case, each can be treated as Ben, and so Ben, a single person, can continue as two loci of concern and attention. A double success, as Parfit reminds us, is not the same as a failure. On reflection, however, it is clear that this could not work at all. If I promise Ben I will help him move I now have to help both Bens move; if I owe Ben money I now have to pay them both the amount I owe (although if they owe me money they both have to pay, which is somewhat less disconcerting). If Ben is my graduate student and is entering the job market I now have to write a letter for each Ben, perhaps undercutting both of them by putting them in direct competition. If Juliet is in a committed and exclusive relationship with Ben, after the fission she will need to be in such a relationship with both Bens. Clearly this is untenable. As Kathleen Wilkes points out, it would be difficult at best to manage institutions like schools, marriages, and prisons in such a world.[25]

To round out the space of logical possibilities we could, in theory, treat one but not the other of the fission products as Ben. It is very difficult to believe that this could be sustainable, however, for the very same reasons that truly treating slaves or women as non-persons is not sustainable. The fact that there really are no relevant differences between the two products in this regard, and so that any choice between them really would be entirely arbitrary, basically takes this option off the table. Ben's parents or children or partner—if they are like parents and children and partners as they have been throughout history—will not be able to treat Ben₁ but not Ben₂ as their child or parent or partner. To do so their psyches and relationships would need to be arranged in ways very different from the way ours are. And this, ultimately, is the bottom line of PLV's analysis of the fission case. It might well be the case that, should fissioning become possible and common, the social and cultural infrastructure would shift and adapt to create a set of practices that makes sense for fissioning beings. What we can see from reflection on the case, however, is that those changes would need to be truly profound—so profound that it is questionable whether they would still count as *personal* or inter*personal* practices.[26]

I am therefore committed to rejecting Parfit's claim that fission is a "double success" where this means that it preserves, and in fact doubles, all of "what matters" in identity. Parfit's insistence that it does so is based on the argument that since the existence of one of the fission products would contain all of what matters in survival, and the two are qualitatively identical, each must contain all of what matters. Since there are two of them, he argues, we must have what matters twice over.[27] On the surface this argument sounds compelling, but it is not as straightforward as it first appears. Parfit's argument assumes that the only attributes that can matter to

---

[25] Kathleen Wilkes, *Real People*, p. 11. Other philosophers have also noted that in cases of fission the effects of doubling may undermine agency and our ability to live our lives in one way or another. Peter Unger, for instance, discusses this in *Identity, Consciousness and Value*, pp. 268–86, and Lynne Baker discusses it in *Persons and Bodies*, pp. 126–30.

[26] This raises a difficult question about whether the fission products could be persons. It certainly seems as if they would have to be given my arguments of the previous chapter, but if there are no interpersonal practices how can they be? This is a complicated issue and I will return to it at the end of this section. I am grateful to an anonymous reviewer for pointing out that this is a question in need of an answer.

[27] Parfit, *Reasons and Persons*, pp. 256–8.

survival are intrinsic. At best the intrinsic features of the two fission products are each identical to the intrinsic features a unique survivor would have in the case where only one of the fission products survives. The relation of each survivor to his environment and to other people is, however, drastically different from the relation a unique survivor would have to his environment and to other people. If fundamental person-specific relational properties are taken into account the relation of the fission products to the original person is *not* the same as the relation of the unique survivor; fission is *not* the same thing, only doubled.

Parfit does allow that fission will have some impact on a person's life. It might be disconcerting, he says, to have to share one's identity with someone else (although it might also have its advantages). Such changes might impact the quality of life, he allows, but he denies that they are the kinds of changes that could undermine survival.[28] This description misunderstands the nature of the change involved. There are, of course, many changes in rights, responsibilities, and relationships that take place within the life of any single person. A person may be hired and then fired from a particular job, enter into a marriage and later get divorced, make money and lose it, and so on. Parfit's suggestion seems to be that this is roughly what happens to the original person in a case of fission. Since fissioning may complicate employment, marriage, and the distribution of savings, he implies, it will bring on the kinds of losses and opportunities that are found in ordinary life. It should thus be viewed as a change of circumstance rather than a failure to continue.[29]

PLV insists, however, that the nature of the change that fission would bring about is very different from ordinary change. To understand this we can make use of something like the distinction between questions about the moral self and questions about the practical locus drawn in Chapter 1, as well as the conception of being an appropriate target of practical concerns that we have developed over the last several chapters. The sorts of changes Parfit talks about are changes within the history of a single locus. We can ask if Ben is still in the same job or marriage or still in the chips as he was the last time we saw him, and the answer might well be "no; everything's changed for him since then." But it might also be "That's not Ben you're thinking of; that's Jack. Ben was in jail and penniless then." In both cases the answer to the question is negative, but they are quite different kinds of negative answers. In the first case the locus is the appropriate locus to ask about, but the details have changed; in the second the negative response indicates that

---

[28]   Parfit, *Reasons and Persons*, p. 264.
[29]   Of course, in some ways it is a failure to continue on Parfit's view insofar as there is no one after fission identical to the original person. Here I mean that it is not a failure to continue on his view insofar as it is not like death.

we have individuated the wrong locus and so cannot even get started with a useful discussion of details. In the case of fission the changes in circumstance—marriage, employment, finances—are not simply that. These changes result from the fact that there is no longer an appropriate, unified locus in which to track the continuity of circumstances. The first kind of negative reply to the question about Ben assumes the coherence of a positive answer; in principle Ben might have kept his job or stayed married or rich. In the case of fission the existence of a double undermines the coherence of a simple "yes" answer. There is no single "Ben" who might have continued these relations. One might be tempted to say that the question could be asked about either, but the existence of the other guarantees that it cannot be asked in the straightforward way in which it could be asked if there were a unique continuer.

It is also true, however, that it seems appropriate to raise these questions about either (or both) of the fission products in a way that it is not appropriate to raise them about some completely disconnected person, and that is what makes Parfit's analysis seem so compelling. Obviously there is a close connection between each of the fission products and the original person. Each carries the memories, affections, skills, and knowledge of the original, and so each has by hypothesis everything that is needed to continue these relations—except for uniqueness. Moreover, some kind of relationship will obviously hold between the fission products and intimates of the original person. The original person's children will not, for instance, simply be indifferent to the fission products because there are two of them, nor will the fission products be indifferent to the children.[30] Nevertheless it will not be possible to have just the same relationship, only with "two dads." This is not like divorce and remarriage; it is something far more fundamental.

Presumably what would emerge between fission products and the children of their progenitor would be an intense and complicated relationship of a sort that does not exist in our world, where people do not fission. The closest approximation in our world is perhaps something like the kind of relationship someone might have with the adult child or close sibling of a lost loved one—someone in whom we can find some of the looks and quirks and sensibilities of the person we have lost, and to whom he has transmitted some of his memories, wisdom, skill, and perspective. While I disagree with Parfit that fission gives us what matters in survival twice over, then, I agree wholeheartedly that going out of existence by dividing is not at all the same as ordinary death. This is equally true from the perspective of the person about to undergo fission, the fission products, and those

[30] An adult child getting married, for instance, need not regret the fact that her father didn't live to see her wedding if both fission products are present at the ceremony.

who interact with all three. There are different ways of ceasing to exist; destruction is one way, but metamorphosis is another, and they do not have the same emotional valence or implications. This is true even in our world. According to Olson a zygote is not identical to a fetus; when a fetus develops the zygote ceases to exist. Surely, however, there is an immense difference between a zygote that ceases to exist by dying and one that ceases to exist by becoming a fetus; just ask an expectant mother. Similarly, and perhaps more relevant here, is the standard view that when an amoeba divides it ceases to exist and gives rise to two daughter organisms. Again, this is very different from death.[31]

In the fission case a person leaves an extremely close kind of progeny of a sort that we just do not have in our world. The closeness is such that it is clearly wrong to speak of the person as *simply* ceasing to exist. At the same time, however, the person who splits in two does not continue to exist because he becomes two people. Because we do not split like amoebas our entire cultural and social infrastructure—the infrastructure that supports personhood—is built around the unity of the loci with which we interact. If we encountered a single instance of doubling we undoubtedly would not know how to react, and if it became common we would become different sorts of beings with an entirely different (and to me not-yet-imaginable) social organization and another way of life. This is not just a question of redefining "marriage" or restructuring bank accounts and employment contracts. The ability to double is a deep biological change and would undoubtedly lead to a radically different kind of psychological organization. Such beings might come to be, but they will probably not be persons.[32]

This brings us back to the difficulty postponed earlier. It will not be immediately obvious how my claim that fission products would not be persons could be consistent with my claims in previous chapters that infants, the demented, and even those in a PVS are persons, and that we cannot deny personhood to adults with typical

---

[31] It is perhaps worth mentioning that another approach to the fission case altogether is that taken by four-dimensionalists, who argue that persons are four-dimensional beings and in fission there are two people present all along, who share a stage before splitting. (See, e.g., David Lewis, "Survival and Identity," in *Philosophical Papers*, Vol. 1, pp. 55–72 or John Perry, "Can the Self Divide?" *The Journal of Philosophy*, 69(16), September 7, 1972, pp. 463–88.) This is an interesting and, in many respects, fruitful approach, but it obviously will not alter the analysis here since there is still no single locus of interaction in the case as four-dimensionalists describe it, and four-dimensionalists therefore still cannot provide a way of preserving our person-related practices in a case of fission.

[32] It is important not to overstate the certainty of this result. As with the simple transfer case, we need to be open to the possibility that practice would evolve in ways we cannot foresee. Perhaps our concept really is malleable enough to treat the fission products somehow as a single unit. While this seems deeply unlikely, it cannot be ruled out entirely, and if it happened we would survive fission. We must remember, however, that this could happen only if social infrastructure changed in ways that are very, very difficult to imagine and are perhaps even incoherent.

capacities. Despite appearances to the contrary, consistency is possible because I allow for the possibility of intelligent creatures with capacities in some ways like ours but different enough that we cannot really engage in interpersonal interactions with them. Since we are paradigmatic persons, I said, these creatures will be something else—something like persons, but not persons. The fission products are thus denied personhood in a very particular way which may be less unmotivated than it originally appears.

This conclusion may still seem unmotivated in the case of fission. Since I have just suggested that fission products might plausibly interact with the intimates of the original person in some of the ways that are characteristic of interpersonal interaction it may be puzzling that I now claim that such interaction is not possible. The response to this seeming inconsistency is a bit complicated and admittedly somewhat counterintuitive. PLV's actual position on personhood in fission is that if fission is a rare occurrence, personhood is likely preserved, but if it is common it probably is not. Let me explain. If fission is unusual our infrastructure would probably remain as it is and the products of fission would need to make their lives conform to the institutions of non-fissioners so far as possible. This would undoubtedly involve the fission products interacting with others as persons whose lives have in some sense started anew at the moment of fission, but which are nevertheless shaped by the life of their predecessor in a way that is much more direct and complete than the way in which our lives are usually shaped by our ancestors. These fission products would thus most likely live as persons and so be persons, but they could not, for reasons already given, be the same person as the original.

If fission became common, however, social infrastructure would need to change as well. If it were typical in a society for individuals to split like amoebas one or more times in their lives institutions and relations could not be as they are now, and so the society that evolved would be sufficiently different from ours that it is likely (but not a priori necessary) that we would not be able to interact with them effectively. Many of our most central interpersonal interactions presuppose uniqueness.[33] Much depends here on the details of the fission and of the changes in social organization and lifestyle that go with it. The question of whether the

---

[33] The 2004 television series *Battlestar Galactica* depicts interactions between humans and human-oid "cylons" who are very like humans except that there are a limited number of models and many copies of each, which exist simultaneously. When one token dies it is resurrected in a new, qualitatively identical body into which its consciousness is uploaded, and consciousness is shared (to at least some extent) between tokens of a single model. The plot contains interesting examples of the ways in which interaction breaks down in this situation, and also how it might be possible. Significantly, however, effective interactions only truly become possible when the cylons start distinguishing among tokens of a single model.

products of fission are new people or something else thus cannot be answered without much more detail.

The idea that someone's personhood might depend upon the frequency with which others fission may seem implausible, but if we consider carefully what is being asserted I hope it will seem less so. The claim is not that the very same thing (a fission product) might be a person if there is only one case of fission and not be a person if fission is common. It is rather that the fission products will be very different in the two cases because the environmental context in which we find ourselves determines (at least partially) what we develop into. Personhood, it must be recalled, is not defined exclusively in terms of attributes at a moment, but rather in terms of a life that depends upon attributes in a context over time. In the case of fission the difference in context between a world where fission is common and a world where it is rare will almost certainly lead to different paths of development and hence to different lives. The crucial point for present purposes, however, is that whether fission products are persons or not, they are almost certainly not the same person as the person who underwent fission.

We have now seen how PLV addresses some of the key hypothetical cases employed in philosophical discussions of personal identity. We could, of course, go on multiplying cases and generating new questions for discussion. We might consider, for instance, what happens when we transplant a cerebrum into a body that is physically very unlike the one from which it is taken, or when we replace a diseased cerebrum with an inorganic but functionally equivalent duplicate. Some of the cases we could generate will, admittedly, be very difficult for PLV to analyze. While this is a useful and important exercise, the cases already discussed give a fair representation of the way in which PLV addresses questions of persistence and deals with the tricky puzzle cases that are standard in the literature. I hope also that this discussion has helped to make features of the view that may at first seem problematic (e.g., the fact that there is room for some conventionalism or that what Parfit considers extrinsic features can play a role in judgments of personal continuation) appear less so by examining some of the details of their application.

6.4 Summing Up

In this chapter I have provided an understanding of what is involved in the continuation of a single person life. I have not provided necessary and sufficient conditions for the continuation of such a life because I do not think that there are any. A person life, I have argued, should be thought of as a homeostatic cluster of properties and relations which, in the paradigmatic cases, support one another. In a full and healthy person life there are biological, psychological, and social functions that work together to provide the distinctive kind of life that beings like us live. It can and does happen, however, that sometimes some of these functions are lost or attenuated, leaving some but not all of the continuities that are typically present in place. Provided that enough of the typical functions remain in the right circumstances to sustain an identifiable locus of interaction in person-space, the person life has continued and so has the person. When loss or change is such that we are left without an identifiable locus, the person life has ended, and so has the person. There are, however, many different ways in which a locus can be sustained and many different ways in which it can disintegrate, and so there is no straightforward answer to the question of which functions or relations are necessary for the continuation of a person.

My account of personal identity thus allows for a certain amount of give in answers to the question about what will occur in any particular case, and this has implications for the standard method of reflection on hypothetical cases. Sometimes we just will not be in a position to say what will happen in an imagined scenario. It is important to realize, however, that the kind of uncertainty described here is not the same as that associated with Parfit's reductionism and discussed in Chapter 1. PLV does allow that a person life can continue in a more or less robust and healthy way, just as a biological life can. And just as with a biological life, at the margins there will be some questions that are difficult to resolve and on which there will be disagreement. The uncertainty within PLV, however, comes from a lack of relevant information. We do not know how practice will evolve or how we will be able to view the products of strange and hitherto unseen vicissitudes and, because the continuation of a person life depends upon the continuation of a unified target of our person-specific concerns and questions, without that information we do not know whether a person life continues in these cases. I have emphasized that our practices do not depend solely (in fact, depend very little) on our decisions and conventions, but depend rather upon facts about us and the world we live in. We do not know all of these facts about ourselves or about imagined worlds, and so we are not able to predict exactly what will happen in them. The consolation, however, is that this epistemological situation is hardly unique to our understanding of persons and applies to many systems with far less complexity.

The last two chapters have provided an overall sense of the basic positions of PLV on personhood and personal identity. It should be clear that PLV is a view that inherently links facts about personal identity to (the full range of person-related) practical considerations. It should also be clear that the unity of a person as defined by this view, although it is a practical unity, is more fundamental than that which is defined in accounts of the moral self and other obviously metaphorical understandings of "personal identity" and has more of the form of a literal question about the identity of an entity. None of this yet shows that it should be taken as an account of our literal identity, however, and the challenges to doing so that come from animalism remain unanswered. Now that we have an understanding of the view we are ready to address these questions and challenges head on.

7

Ontology

Our main task in this chapter is to show that PLV is legitimately understood as a question about our literal identity. The standard way of thinking about such a question is as a question about the numerical identity of a substance. I will therefore argue that PLV can be considered an account of our literal identity by showing that it can plausibly be seen as giving the conditions for the numerical identity of a substance. In the course of making this argument, however, I will also describe a different way of thinking about the question of literal identity and explain why I prefer it to the more traditional understanding.

The easiest way into an understanding of how PLV can reasonably be seen as an account of the numerical identity of a substance is to consider why someone would deny that it could be. The most forceful reasons for such a denial are, I think, found in the arguments for animalism. As we saw in Chapter 2, animalists raise extremely powerful challenges to any view that rejects the claim that each human person is strictly identical to a human animal, showing how taking persons to be distinct substances with their own persistence conditions leads to a raft of problematic implications. If PLV is to be a viable account of our literal identity, these challenges must be addressed. I will therefore organize the discussion in this chapter around addressing the animalist objections, showing that PLV can be coherently and plausibly meet the challenges animalists raise.

7.1 Animalist Objections

Let's begin with a review of the animalist arguments against taking *person* as a substance concept that we saw in Chapter 2. These arguments are directed most immediately against psychological accounts of personhood and personal identity, and some of them do not find as much traction with PLV as they do with traditional psychological views; PLV is not, for instance, subject to the fetus and vegetable problems in the way that views which employ a basically Lockean conception of personhood are. The central animalist objection, however, which we can call the "coincidence problem,"[1] remains a problem for PLV. The coincidence problem points to a metaphysical awkwardness verging on incoherence which results if we insist that persons are substances but are not identical to human animals. Since it seems that human animals are undeniably substances (although we will revisit this claim later) this claim has the implication that when we encounter human persons we are encountering two distinct but materially coincident substances.

Olson, as we saw in Chapter 2, points out that it is difficult even to make sense of the idea that a single material composite could comprise two distinct substances. Before trying to answer the animalist concerns, let's examine them in a bit more detail. On the views Olson opposes, it is supposed to be possible for persons and humans to be materially coincident but distinct because the person and animal that share their matter have different persistence conditions (on the traditional view, psychological for persons and biological for animals). It is not clear, Olson says, how this difference could emerge from a single set of material properties. How, he asks, could one of these substances come to have properties that the other does not? Wouldn't any property belonging to one automatically belong also to the other? To bring this worry home he imagines a duplicating machine that can make a molecule-for-molecule replica of any object. If we put a human person, call him Jack, into the duplicating machine, Zack, a perfect replica, emerges. If Jack is two things—a human and a person—then it seems Zack must be as well. The machine must have made a human Zack and a person Zack. But what did the machine do differently, Olson asks, when it made the person and when it made the human? What extra did it add to the person to give it different persistence conditions?[2] This difficulty generates a great many other more specific problems such as the "too many thinkers" problem. Since the animal and the person are identical in all but dispositional attributes, it seems that if the person is able to speak and think, so is the animal, resulting in two thinkers of each thought and two utterers of each sentence.

This difficulty obviously applies just as directly to PLV as it does to traditional psychological approaches. According to PLV the biological life that constitutes an organism is a part of the person life that constitutes the person, and so there will be complete material overlap between the human and the person. In light of this it is tempting to conclude that it is just a mistake to think of the person as another

---

[1] It should be clear that the "coincidence problem" is not directly related to the "coincidence model" of the relation between personal identity and practical considerations discussed in Chapter 1.

[2] Eric Olson, *The Human Animal*, pp. 99–100.

thing. A much simpler way of describing the situation is to say that there is one entity—the human animal—that takes on the attribute of personhood in virtue of being involved in certain kinds of social interactions. Compelling as this picture is, however, it is not without its own difficulties. Being a person, at least as PLV defines it, cannot be seen simply as an attribute of a more basic entity. A person on this view is not a set of characteristics or capacities; it is a locus of interaction, and a locus that can transcend the life of a single organism (as in a cerebrum transplant). Olson, we have seen, suggests that we can think of *person* as a kind of office. This is a helpful metaphor, but in the end only a metaphor. *Organism* might equally be seen as an office occupied by different matter at different times (although there are of course differences between the way in which this metaphor would apply to an organism and to a person). To move forward with the account of personhood and personal identity PLV presents we thus need a way to respond to the difficulties raised by the material coincidence of human animals and human persons. I turn next to a consideration of some of the responses PLV might offer.

7.2 Responses to the Animalist Objections

The coincidence problem and attendant difficulties arise because it is taken for granted that: (1) a literal account of personal identity must provide the conditions for the numerical identity of a substance; (2) human animals are substances; and (3) there is no coherent way for persons to be substances materially coincident with human animals yet not identical to them. Pressure could be put on any one of these assumptions, and in what follows I will eventually challenge all three. The philosophical literature already includes a highly-developed challenge to the third assumption in the form of the constitution model of persons, and I will start there. While I take a great deal from the sensibility of the constitution model, I will ulti-mately retool the insights I find there into a challenge to the first two assumptions in a way which incorporates an alternative understanding of what it means to offer a literal account of personal identity.

7.2.1 Constitution

One of the most successful replies offered to animalist challenges to the psycholog-ical approach is the constitution view.[3] According to this view the relation between human persons and human animals is that the former are *constituted* by the latter.

---

[3] Another important approach to explaining the relation between human persons and human ani-mals is that offered by Jeff McMahan, who argues that persons are parts of organisms (see McMahan, *The Ethics of Killing*, pp. 92–4).

A detailed and influential version of the constitution view as a response to animalism has been developed by Lynne Rudder Baker. Constitution, Baker says, is a ubiquitous relation of the kind that holds between statues and the clay out of which they are sculpted, flags and the bits of cloth out of which they are sewn, dollar bills and the pieces of paper on which they are printed, and so on. A statue constituted by a lump of clay is not identical to the lump of clay because they have different persistence conditions—the lump of clay can continue to exist after the statue is destroyed. Nevertheless, the relation between the statue and the clay is more intimate than distinctness since they are materially coincident and have each other's properties derivatively. The statue for instance, may be, *qua* statue, extremely valuable and this makes the lump of clay derivatively valuable in virtue of constituting the statue. The lump of clay, meanwhile, may be, *qua* clay, enormously heavy, and this gives the statue the derivative property of being heavy. Similarly, Baker says, persons are not identical to human animals, but are connected to them by this especially intimate relation.

Baker's account of personhood is strictly psychological. To be a person on her view is to possess what she calls a "strong first-person perspective." Roughly, this is a sophisticated form of reflective self-consciousness that allows us, for instance, to articulate concerns about our own continued existence and about our relations to others and to the world. To have a strong first-person perspective one must be "able to conceive of oneself independently of a name, or description, or third-person demonstrative. It is to be able to conceptualize the distinction between [one]self and everything else there is. It is not just to have thoughts expressible by means of 'I,' but also to conceive of oneself as the bearer of those thoughts."[4] Human persons are persons who are constituted by human animals. The typical story of a human person begins with a human that is not yet a person (i.e., an embryo) but will, if all goes well, ultimately develop a first-person perspective. When this happens a new thing comes into existence, a person, just as when a sculptor molds a piece of clay a new thing, a statue, comes into existence.

This strategy will obviously need to be applied somewhat differently in PLV, which has a different conception of personhood. There is no reason, however, why PLV cannot adopt a version of the constitution model, saying that human persons as defined by this view are (typically throughout their entire earthly existence) constituted by a single human animal. In some ways this view would be more

---

[4] Lynne Rudder Baker, *Persons and Bodies*, p. 64. She has actually changed her view a bit and now allows that human infants under the right circumstances can be persons (see, e.g., *The Metaphysics of Everyday Life*, pp. 75–82). This change does bring PLV and Baker's view closer together in many interesting ways, but not in ways that are significant for the discussion here since the relevant relation is still constitution.

intuitive than Baker's, since it is not subject to the modified versions of the fetus and vegetable problems which hers is,[5] but it also faces problems Baker's version does not. PLV does not, for instance, offer a decisive change of state through which a person is brought into the world as it is in Baker's view by the development of a first-person perspective.[6] The PLV version of the constitution model would say that a human animal is a substance that comes to constitute a different substance, a person, in virtue of the fact that it exists in the social and cultural infrastructure of person-space. This makes finding a separation between persons and human animals even more difficult on this view than on Baker's.

Key to the response that the constitution view offers to animalism is the fact that according to this approach the human person and the animal that constitutes it—like the statue and the lump of clay out of which it is constituted—have a relation to one another that is intermediate between identity and distinctness. The two are not identical, since the person has non-derivative properties that the human animal has only derivatively (and vice versa). They are also not simply distinct, however. When an individual (x) comes to constitute a different individual (y), Baker says, they become a unity, and "the identity of the constituting thing is submerged in the identity of what it constitutes. As long as x constitutes y, y encompasses or subsumes x."[7] There is one thing: y-constituted-by-x. This single thing, which is most fundamentally a y, can have properties of both y's and x's, but it has the former directly, in virtue of *being* a y, and the latter "derivatively," in virtue of being *constituted by* an x.

This analysis speaks directly to Olson's concerns about coincidence. Olson is mistaken, Baker says, to view the relation between persons and human beings as coincidence. In a human person there are not two separate and independent entities—a person and a human animal—there is one single entity, a person, who happens to be constituted by a human animal. For each thought there is only one thinker, the person-constituted-by-human, and for each sentence only one utterer. According to the constitution view of human persons, she says, "the 'animal' and you are not two separate things, one of which is a duplicate of the other. Your body is not a duplicate of you; it constitutes you... If x constitutes y, then x and y are not two independent things that rather mysteriously come to coincide. You and 'the

---

[5] Although, it should be noted, she provides responses to these objections.

[6] Although Baker does allow that this can happen gradually and the origins of a person may be vague (see, e.g., *The Metaphysics of Everyday Life*, p. 132, and "When Does a Person Begin?"), it is worth noting that Olson also allows that the beginnings of a biological life may be vague (see, e.g., *The Human Animal*, pp. 91–2).

[7] Baker, *Persons and Bodies*, p. 33.

animal' are…things of primary kinds that are a unity in virtue of being constitutionally related."[8]

Olson, for his part, finds the claims of the constitution view "too good to be true."[9] He is unsure of the true content of the claim that on the constitution model "*A* [the animal that constitutes me] and I, though numerically different, are one person," and goes on to add that "whatever it means, I do not see how it could help me to know that I am not *A*."[10] His worry seems to be the following; as long as the animal exists—submerged or not—it must have all of the same capacities that the person does. It is materially coincident, and so has a brain which functions just as the person's brain does (in fact, the brain is presumably native to the animal and not the person). Given this, it is hard to see why we would not need to say that the animal, submerged or not, is also having all of the thoughts that the person does. So when I think "I am not an animal" I still have no way of knowing whether I am a person thinking a true thought or an animal thinking a false one. Ultimately, he says, there are either two things present or one, and the idea of unity without identity is too mysterious to do the work it is claimed to do.

At bottom, the dispute about the viability of the constitution model seems to rest on a host of extremely fundamental metaphysical disagreements. One which is particularly important is a profound division in ontological sensibilities that includes differences on the question of whether relational properties can be essential properties. Persons, Baker says, have different relational properties from human animals and in virtue of these and these alone can be distinct primary kinds with different persistence conditions, even without material changes. This is something Olson seems to deny. This difference depends on an even deeper one. Baker's is a "metaphysics of everyday life" which she characterizes also as "big-tent metaphysics." Metaphysics, she says, is "the study of fundamental reality" and fundamental reality "include[s] all the objects and properties whose omission from ontology would render an account of reality incomplete."[11] She continues, "Big-Tent Metaphysics looks to a metaphysics of Fs to tell us the *nature* of Fs, what is *distinctive* or unique about Fs, and what is *significant* about Fs. What we consider to be real should not be independent of what we consider to be important. Else, why bother with metaphysics?"[12]

---

[8] Baker, *Persons and Bodies*, p. 192–3.

[9] Olson, *What Are We?*, p. 60.

[10] Olson, *What Are We?*, pp. 61–2.

[11] Lynne Rudder Baker, "Big-Tent Metaphysics," *Abstracta*, Special Issue 1, 2008, p. 10. For a greatly expanded version of this picture see *The Metaphysics of Everyday Life*, pp. 3–48.

[12] "Big-Tent Metaphysics," p. 10.

In daily practice we divide the world into objects, the "medium-sized dry goods" of everyday life. These divisions, Baker says, form the basis for our ontology. The substances to be found in our world are the substances that we identify and interact with on a daily basis, and the division of the world into objects that informs our lives is to be taken seriously as a revelation of the ontological structure of the world. There is, of course, a great deal that needs to be worked out to fill in this view, and Baker's development is full of subtlety and detail. The crucial point to appreciate for our purposes, however, is that the constitution model of the relation between human animals and human persons depends upon the generous ontology that Baker supports.

The animalist perspective on these questions is quite different. The contrast can be seen in Olson's characterization at the beginning of *What Are We?* of the question he will be exploring. He tells us that he is "not asking about our conception or understanding of ourselves—about what we take ourselves to be. This is metaphysics, not anthropology." He continues, "What we ordinarily take ourselves to be may be wildly mistaken."[13] There are, of course, many ways in which we can be and often are mistaken about ourselves. It is an implication of Baker's view that one way in which we cannot be mistaken is in our assessment of what we most fundamentally are—what fundamental kind we belong to. Olson does not only think that we can be mistaken in this way, but that the psychological approach to questions of personal identity is based on just such a mistake. It is thus worth pausing for a moment to consider in more detail the kind of inquiry in which such a mistake is possible. A natural initial picture of what happens when we misunderstand ourselves in this way is something like this: we latch on to a substance in ignorance of its true nature or persistence conditions and christen it as the target of our inquiry. We then ask ourselves what this particular individual standing before us truly is. Sometimes we get this right, but other times we get it wrong, pouncing on some salient aspect rather than on the entity's true metaphysical nature. In the case at hand, the target is ourselves; those who defend the psychological approach mistakenly conclude that the target we have identified is a person with psychological persistence conditions, the argument goes, when in fact it is a human animal with biological persistence conditions.

If this is how these investigations are supposed to work, however, a question arises about exactly how we are able to individuate legitimate targets of inquiry in the first place. It is a presupposition of this picture that we are not entirely competent to individuate substances or to track them over time. If we were, a mistake of the kind described here would not be possible. This means that if we can make

---

[13] Olson, *What Are We?*, p. 14.

such a mistake, there is no guarantee that what we have set ourselves to study is a single, unified object at all. We carve up the world and individuate objects of inquiry according to the features that are salient to us. In the case of ourselves, this often involves psychological or ethical features. Baker assumes our competence at dividing the world into objects and at identifying the distinctive and special aspects of the Fs we identify in our world. On Olson's approach, however, it is a possibility that we may be thoroughly mistaken about ourselves, or any object of inquiry, because there is no guarantee that the divisions that are important to us reflect the way in which the world is actually carved up into independent substances. This means that our inquiry, if it is to be a genuine metaphysical inquiry about substances, cannot start from our individuation of objects into targets of inquiry but must begin instead from more general reflection on what kinds of substances there actually *are*. Determining what kinds of things there really are in the world will reveal what may be proper objects of inquiry, and not the other way around.

This general methodological picture plays an important role in the defense of animalism. As we have seen, one of the most serious problems it identifies with the psychological approach turns out to be that *person* is not a convincing substance concept while *organism* is paradigmatic. In other words, a *person* is not a plausible kind of thing to be while a *human animal* is and this, in the end, is how we can know that we must be most fundamentally human animals rather than persons. In a very helpful discussion toward the end of *What Are We?* Olson articulates this general principle by endorsing the idea that there is a connection between general ontological commitments and accounts of personal identity. He offers the "bold conjecture" that "there is an intimate connection between the question of what we are and the question of when composition takes place or what material objects there are."[14] If we have a principled metaphysical account of the circumstances under which parts combine to make a complex substance, we will have a way of determining what kinds of substances there actually are and this will in turn reveal the actual possibilities for the kinds of things we might be. The compositional theories most congenial to animalists, Olson suggests, are those that yield a sparse ontology. Peter van Inwagen's account of composition is an example of such a theory. Olson describes van Inwagen's position as one in which "things compose something if and only if their activities constitute a biological life—a self-organizing event that maintains the internal structure of an organism."[15] According to this view, philosophical reflection provides arguments for believing that, roughly speaking, the

---

[14]   Olson, *What Are We?*, p. 229.   [15]   Olson, *What Are We?*, p. 226.

only true substances are particles (or things not much larger than particles) and organisms, and since we are not particles we must be organisms.

Neither Baker's ontology nor the sparse ontology congenial to animalism is by any means uncontroversial, and both Baker and Olson acknowledge this fact. The differences in basic orientation between the two positions are so profound that it is not clear how they could finally be resolved. According to Olson, however, the constitution view would not solve the basic problems of the psychological approach, even if we accepted its ontology. If a human animal is a substance then it does not cease to exist when it is "subsumed" into a person, he says, and no matter how intimate the relation of constitution, if it is not identity the person and human must be distinct. All this, by Olson's count, still leaves us with too many thinkers.

Ultimately, I think, the argument between Baker and Olson rests on whether, formalisms notwithstanding, we can make sense of a relation in which objects and the substances of which they are constituted are neither exactly identical nor exactly distinct. It seems that some people can make sense of this idea while others cannot and there is no definitive way to demonstrate that one position or the other is the correct one. To this extent we are left with something of a stalemate, and so with grounds for the defender of a constitution model of PLV to insist that she has a way of explaining the relation between human persons and human animals against which the animalist has no conclusive objections (and for the animalist to make the corresponding claim). This strategy for responding to the animalist challenges could, of course, be pursued still further by providing further arguments that the metaphysical presuppositions of the constitution approach are superior to those of animalists, but what we have learned about the ontological presuppositions of animalism suggests a second strategy which is somewhat more straightforward and in important respects, I hope, more decisive.

From the animalist perspective the constitution theory of human persons will continue to run into difficulties because both *human animal* and *person* play the role of substance concepts, and where there are two substance concepts there are two substances, no matter how intimately related. While one strategy for responding to this difficulty is to deny this claim as constitution theorists do, another is to simply concede that persons are not substances. This is likely not an attractive option for Baker, since showing that *person* is a primary kind is an important objective for her. Our goal, however, is somewhat different; it is to show that the question of personal identity addressed by PLV is a literal one. This might be done by showing that it is a question about the numerical identity of a substance, but it can also be done by showing that there is a natural and plausible way to construe a different kind of question about personal identity as a literal question. The ontological presuppositions of animalism point a way toward developing this second strategy, as we will see in the next section.

7.2.2   Literal questions without substances

For the sake of argument, let us accept the compositional principles and general metaphysical outlook that are favorable to animalism, taking van Inwagen's theory as a representative. On this account, most of the medium-sized objects that make up our lives are not really objects at all. Strictly speaking there are no apples, or chairs, or kidneys, or shoes, or wedding albums; there are only particles and organisms. This view, Olson points out, "has the startling implication that there are no nonliving composite objects."[16] This has the further implication that most of the questions that we ask and sentences that we utter are not actually about substances at all. If I ask whether the shoes are made of leather, for instance, or whether the wedding album survived the fire, or the apples are still on the sideboard, I have failed to find a substantial target for my inquiry.

It would be problematic, to say the least, if this meant that the answers to all questions about everyday objects were the same—"no" or "that is not a well-posed question." The situation in which, after the fire, there is something I can thumb through to look at photos of the day I was married on the one hand, and the situation in which all that is left is a heap of ashes on the other, are importantly different. According to van Inwagen's compositional minimalism, however, in a strict sense there was never a photo album to begin with, and so there is never "still a photo album" after the fire. Van Inwagen insists, however, that this need not imply that we must give up our ordinary way of speaking or the kinds of questions we regularly ask and answer. We can preserve ordinary discourse by, roughly speaking, viewing our everyday claims as paraphrases of claims about the arrangement of particles in space rather than as claims about actual substances.

Van Inwagen himself suggests that the meaning of our terms is context-dependent. Taking the example of a sentence like "there are apples on the sideboard if you want one" he tells us that there is no single meaning of this sentence but that it "expresses different propositions in different contexts of utterance. When the sentence 'There are apples' is uttered in what David Lewis calls 'the philosophy room,'" he says, "it may well express a proposition whose falsity is consistent with the truth of the proposition that would be expressed by typical utterances of 'There are apples on the sideboard if you want one.'"[17] In other words, when we

---

[16]   Olson, *What Are We?*, p. 226.

[17]   Peter van Inwagen, "Reply to Reviewers," *Philosophy and Phenomenological Research*, 53(3), September 1993, p. 711.

are immersed in the business of everyday life the utterance tells us that there are particles arranged apple-wise on the sideboard, and it is true if there are and false if there are not. In the philosophy room, however, this utterance tells us that there are substances of a certain kind on the sideboard which is false even if there are particles arranged apple-wise there, since there are no apple-substances (or, for that matter, sideboards).

Van Inwagen emphasizes that his metaphysics does not depend on this specific resolution: "The salient point of this philosophy of language is that it is possible for utterances of sentences like 'Some of her chairs are very good nineteenth-century copies of Chippendales' to express truths even if there are no chairs."[18] Those who do not like context-dependent meaning can, he says, equally well fix the meaning of this kind of sentence and say that it is *always* strictly speaking false. All that can reasonably be demanded of a philosophy of language in conjunction with his metaphysics, he continues, "is that it somehow, in some principled way, sort 'good' sentences containing the material-object count-nouns of ordinary speech (sentences like the 'Chippendale' sentence) from 'bad' ones—like 'Some of her chairs are made of cheese.'"[19] There are various ways of describing this division. If we insist that the sentences are always false we can find a different way to describe how we separate the wheat from the chaff. The crucial point is that the metaphysics he defends does not rule out a principled way to formulate and address a question like "Did the wedding album survive the fire?" to which the correct answer is "yes" if there is still an arrangement of particles such that we can grab it off the shelf and flip through it, and to which the correct answer is "no" if where such an arrangement of particles once stood there is now only an arrangement of dust and ash particles.

My proposal is that since most of the things we interact with and talk about in our daily lives are not substances on this view there is no reason that persons need to be either. The ontological status of persons, in other words, can be seen to be the same as that of apples, wedding albums, shoes, chairs, and kidneys. Just as we can meaningfully ask questions about the identity and continuation of these everyday objects (Are the apples still on the sideboard? Are those the reproduction Chippendale chairs you got at the auction last year? Does he still have the same kidneys or did he finally get a transplant?), so we can meaningfully ask about the identity of persons. And just as there are right and wrong answers to questions about the identities of apples, chairs, and kidneys, there are right and wrong answers to questions about the identities of persons. Apples, and chairs and kidneys, although

---

18 Van Inwagen, p. 712.   19 Van Inwagen, p. 712.

not substances, are also not properties or phases of some more basic substance, and answers to questions about their identities are not ethical questions or merely linguistic questions or simply questions about what we think; they are questions about the world.

The question of personal identity addressed by PLV can thus reasonably be said to be a literal question of identity in just the same way that the question of whether the wedding album survived the fire is a literal question. If we concede the sparse ontology associated with animalism, there is a great deal of room between questions about the numerical identity of substances and questions about properties or ethics or what we think or how we speak. In this ontology as described, the distinction between literal and metaphorical questions of identity need not be construed exclusively in terms of a contrast between metaphysical questions about substances on the one hand and everything else on the other. Even outside of the philosophy room, wholly within the context of ordinary speech, we distinguish between literal and metaphorical assertions about identity. If someone spills a sticky drink on your wedding album you may protest that they have "destroyed it," but we all recognize that "destroyed" means something different here than it would mean if you said that the album, reduced to a heap of ash, was destroyed in the fire. Similarly, when we say that Kate is a "different person" from the angry teenager hauled off to prison we all recognize that we mean something other than what we mean when we say that the person you saw at the restaurant isn't Kate, it's her sister (or, that that isn't Kate, it's Juliet who has had a full body transplant with Kate as the donor).

A modified strategy for addressing the problems of material coincidence is thus to avoid the problem of coincident substances by allowing that persons are not metaphysical substances at all, but rather part of the world of everyday objects. These objects are connected to our interests and practices because they reflect the way in which we carve up the world based on features that are especially salient to us. Questions about the identities of everyday objects, including ourselves, are questions of *literal* identity, however, insofar as they are settled by facts about the world and insofar as what is salient to us is not a mere matter of choice or convention but a fact about us. When we talk about persons—what they do, what they think, their identities—we are speaking from within the world of everyday objects, and this means that persons are neither identical to animals nor distinct substances from them; they belong to a different mode of discourse.

This strategy does give us a way to see questions of personal identity as literal while conceding that persons are not substances, but it is open to the following objection: There is an obvious difference in the sparse ontology under consideration between everyday objects like apples and wedding albums on the one hand

and persons on the other. Apples and wedding albums are arrangements of particles in a region of space in which there is no genuine substance. Persons, however,
are arrangements of particles in a region of space in which there is a substance—a
human organism. More than this, the substance that is in that region of space is
composed of exactly the same particles as the person, arranged in exactly the same
way. It may thus seem that the view I have been describing is subject to a version of
the very coincidence problem it is developed to resolve. Somehow a single group
of particles arranged in a particular way is supposed simultaneously to constitute a
metaphysical substance (a human animal) and an everyday object (a person), and
one might wonder how this is done and where the difference can be located.

An initial reply to this objection is to say that the difference between persons
and animals is not found in some feature of the collections of particles that constitute each, but rather in the context in which we are asking about the one or the
other. When we are in the philosophy room asking a metaphysical question about
a region of space and what it contains the answer is that it contains a particular
kind of substance, an organism, and the persistence conditions of that substance
are biological. When we ask the same question within the context of everyday life,
however, the answer is that the relevant region of space contains a person, and
the conditions of the continuation of that person are those described by PLV. In
the end, then, the situation of persons really is just parallel to the case of an object
like an apple. When we ask what the relevant region of space contains in the philosophy room the answer is "a bunch of particles"—something that strictly speaking has no persistence conditions. When we ask in everyday life the answer is "an
apple" and there are conditions that determine when it is proper to say it is still
there and when it is not. The two contexts involve different questions that yield
different correct answers about conditions of continuation, even though we are
talking about the same matter in the same configuration in both instances.

This reply will only get us so far, however. The problem is that human animals are
not just abstract metaphysical substances but also objects of everyday life. It is not
only a complete commonplace that we are human animals, but also a central and
explicit part of PLV. In ordinary discourse we might well say that what occupies the
region of space in which our parent or child or friend stands is a human animal. It
is thus not so easy to confine human animals to Lewis's philosophy room, where
they will not interfere with the ontology of everyday life, and there will be a problem answering the animalist challenge so long as we allow both that we are animals
and that *animal* is a substance concept. Since it is not an option for PLV to deny
that we are animals, the only remaining possibility is to reject *animal* as a substance
concept. There are many forms that this rejection might take, but perhaps one of
the most straightforward is compositional nihilism. We might argue that there are

no genuine composite objects at all, and that human animals have the same ontological status as persons and apples and wedding albums. Although nihilism is not
exactly the position I will defend in the end, it is a useful first approximation, and
a good starting point for discussing the possibility that *animal* is not a substance
concept.

Olson discusses the possibility of nihilism as an approach to understanding our identity in *What Are We?* He argues that it is a coherent position and
not self-refuting as it might initially seem to be. Although he does not see this as
entirely straightforward and unproblematic, he also suggests that nihilists might
employ some version of the general strategy of paraphrase described above to
make sense of the truth of everyday statements about persons such as "there are
many people in London" even if there are, strictly speaking, no people.[20] Despite its
basic viability, however, he does not find the view congenial. The main objections
Olson raises to nihilism are that it is depressing and possibly pathological. It is
depressing because most of our hopes, dreams, and aspirations concern *ourselves*
and *other people*, not collections of particles. Nihilism thus involves the dashing
of these hopes. He gives the example of marriage. "Imagine that one of my strongest desires is to be married," he says, "As it happens, I believe that I *am* married." If
nihilism is true, he continues, his desire is not really met: "The desire to be married
is the desire to be married *to* someone, and nihilism implies that there is no one to
be married to."[21] "Pathology" in the sense he uses it here signifies a philosophical
claim that is impossible to live by. Olson worries that nihilism might be pathological in this sense because our reasons for acting are always ultimately to benefit
someone or something. Since nihilism has the implication that there is no one or
nothing to be benefitted, we have no reasons for doing anything, including defending nihilism. Olson admits that he is not entirely sure of the soundness of this last
argument, but sees it as at least giving us reason for pause.[22]

These observations do not pose a very deep problem for the view, however. If the
question we are considering is what there really is in the world from a strictly metaphysical point of view then our interests and emotions should be largely irrelevant
to our investigation, as Olson himself repeatedly reminds us. The fact that a state of
affairs would be depressing does not, alas, make it false, and the fact that we cannot
live in accordance with the truth demonstrates an existential failing on our part
but does not alter the facts, at least not if we are thinking about metaphysical facts
in the way that is presupposed by the arguments for animalism. If, on the other

---

[20]   Olson, *What are We?*, pp. 192–202.
[21]   Olson, *What are We?*, p. 204.
[22]   Olson, *What are We?*, pp. 208–10.

hand, we are thinking about our ordinary way of looking at the world, I doubt that the fact that persons are not metaphysical substances would be depressing to most people. It might well be so for Olson and for some others, but it seems obvious that most young men and women who dream of being in a romantic relationship do not really care about whether their betrothed is a true substance or a bunch of particles arranged person-wise. The young woman of traditional romantic stories does not, it is true, pine for the bunch of particles next door, but then neither does she pine for the substance next door; she pines for the boy next door, and being married to him, whatever his metaphysical nature, *is* being married to someone. These considerations alone do not seem to provide sufficient grounds for rejecting the possibility of nihilism.[23]

Adopting compositional nihilism does not yet completely resolve our quandary, however, but seems only to push the difficulty out of the realm of the metaphysical and into the realm of the everyday. I have claimed that there are literal questions to be asked about the objects of everyday life, questions whose answers do not depend solely on what we think or care about, but rather on facts about the world. I have further claimed that persons are among these ordinary objects. But so, it seems, are human animals. If persons and human animals are both objects, how-ever (even in the everyday sense), and *we* are supposed to be both, then problems analogous to the problem of coincidence will still arise within the realm of the everyday and we will need to refine our strategy still further.

7.2.3   The priority of persons in everyday life

While the rules of everyday life may not be quite as strict as those in the philosophy room, it cannot be a place where anything goes. If everyday life is going to contain questions about the literal identities of the "objects" found within it, it will need to make a distinction between objects and attributes within its own ontology, even if this is not the strongly metaphysical one with which Olson and van Inwagen oper-ate. If this is the case, and if we take humans to be objects of everyday life and take persons to be distinct objects of everyday life, we will have some explaining to do. The persons of our day-to-day lives are supposed to be distinct and unified indi-viduals according to PLV. When I interact with my son or my colleague I am not interacting with a human animal and with a person, but with only one thing. If we say that human organisms are objects of everyday life, it will be almost irresistible

---

[23] Of course, positive arguments for the claim that organisms are substances of the sort one finds in defenses of sparse ontologies would count as different and additional arguments against nihilism, and I suspect Olson is relying on the strength of these here as well. Since those arguments are not definitive, however, and since I will be moving my analysis in another direction, I will not engage them directly.

to say that persons are not. In the everyday world, as in animalist metaphysics, it will seem that the *thing* is the animal. The claim that there are two things—an animal and the locus which is the appropriate target of practical concerns—is implausible in any context, metaphysical or everyday. So, if a human animal is a something and we are human animals then it would seem to follow that the locus which is the appropriate target of practical concerns just is a human animal. If I want to insist that persons are *objects* of everyday life I will thus need somehow to argue that human organisms are not objects of everyday life after all, and this, counterintuitive as it sounds, is what I intend to do.

According to PLV persons are loci of interpersonal interaction whose integrity as unified wholes results from complex and dynamic interactions among biological, psychological, and social processes. I have argued that when we encounter other humans we experience them first as persons, and cannot help but do so. This means that in order to see a human person as an animal or organism we must abstract from the totality of our experience. My suggestion is that we take this fact seriously in understanding the ontology of everyday objects. According to this proposal a "human animal" or "human organism" is not a thing in its own right, but rather a particular perspective we take on ourselves and our lives, one that attends only to our purely biological functions. The perspective from which we talk about human organisms is a theoretical one which necessarily involves willfully ignoring central and defining features of human persons as we encounter and interact with them. The biological viewpoint is, moreover, always only partial because *in vivo* our biological functions are connected in intricate and intimate ways with our psychological and social lives and cannot be cleanly separated from them if we want to fully understand even our biology. This is not to say that abstracting in this way is not extremely useful for particular purposes or that *organism* is not a helpful concept. It is only to insist that these facts alone do not imply that when we talk about an organism we name an object of everyday life. The difference in interpretation I am pointing to here is subtle, but it is quite profound.

The content and importance of this interpretive move may become clearer if we consider that the abstraction I am describing can occur at different scales and levels of specificity, and so can be found even within a purely biological perspective. It is quite common, for instance, to isolate a particular biological system for study. A medical student might be shown a diagram of the circulatory system that consists of the outline of a human form with the heart, veins, and arteries sketched in. Such a diagram may be extremely important for pedagogical purposes, and it may be a highly accurate representation of the actual circulatory system, but it is incomplete. Not only do actual organisms possess, e.g., a neurological system and an endocrine system *in addition to* the circulatory system; a full understanding of even the circulatory system will ultimately require knowing how it interacts with these other systems. Likewise, looking at human persons from a purely biological perspective is undeniably useful, but it provides a similarly incomplete picture of what we are. The fact that we can study the circulatory system or nervous system or endocrine system in isolation, and that we give each its own name, does not imply that there are three distinct entities whose relation to the biological organism as a whole must be explained. In the same way, the fact that we can concentrate exclusively on the collection of biological functions in a person life and describe this as "the organism" or "animal" does not mean that there is an additional *thing* other than the person herself.

The integrity of human persons as we know them involves the interaction of many processes. We can focus on different subgroups of these processes, zooming in at finer (e.g., circulatory system) and coarser (e.g., organism) levels of detail. The important point is that we need not and should not imagine that there is an entity corresponding to each of these subgroups. Lest it seem that I am treating biological functioning as a special case we should recognize that "psychological subject," "agent," "social interlocutor," and related concepts are also abstractions from the totality of a person. This is what leads to the situation outlined in the introduction where there are many different conceptions of *person* at work, all of which have some legitimacy and none of which is complete. We can now see that none of the dimensions of personhood named above is an independent entity or locus; they are rather strategically limited ways of thinking about the individual persons with whom we interact. The person is the whole that arises from the interaction of all of the different kinds of functions and systems, and according to PLV this is what we are most fundamentally.

This analysis suggests a different understanding of the relation between literal and metaphorical questions of personal identity questions than is standard. If we assume that literal questions about our identity are to be defined in terms of a single kind of relation, metaphorical questions of identity will just be distinct questions that are called questions of "identity" because of some figurative or structural similarity to the question of literal identity, and an answer to the question of what constitutes identity in one of these more metaphorical senses will have no direct bearing on the question of what constitutes our literal identity. On the view described here, however, metaphorical identity questions are in fact just circumscribed questions about one aspect of that identity. In this picture "metaphorical" is really the wrong word to describe these questions, which are better understood as "incomplete" or "partial" questions of literal identity.

In ordinary speech, of course, we do say that animals are entities and treat them as loci of interaction. In doing so, however, we are not necessarily making assertions about the fundamental nature of these loci or implying that the conditions for maintaining their integrity are purely biological. The sense in which we call human animals objects in everyday speech is compatible with the heartfelt cry of John Hurt (portraying John Merrick) in *The Elephant Man*—"I am not an animal! I am a human being! A man!" Clearly the meanings of "human being" and "man" here are not the same as "organism"—any more than claims that Southern slaveholders did not see African slaves as "human" is intended to convey the idea that slaves were misclassified as belonging to some other species. In these instances "human being" and "man" mean much the same as "person" means in PLV. And while we of course also acknowledge that we are human animals (Merrick's denial notwithstanding), this does not in itself amount to asserting that we are fundamentally organisms or that organisms are entities, any more than the mere fact that we say we are persons by itself amounts to asserting that we are fundamentally persons or that persons are entities (although I believe we are and they are).

In determining the ontology of everyday objects we should not look exclusively to what we say but to the context in which we say it and, more importantly, to what we do. In previous chapters we have seen that in our social and cultural infrastructure and in our practice we treat humans first as persons and not as organisms. We can treat other humans solely as organisms only for short periods of time and only in special circumstances. When we encounter a human person we do not proceed and act as if there are two loci—a person and an animal—but treat and perceive her as a complex, multi-dimensional, integrated being. The people we know are of course animals, but they are also subjects, agents, and a great many other things. PLV denies none of that, but it does insist that they are, in the sense just described, fundamentally persons, which means that they are fundamentally all of these things. This is just what the homeostatic property cluster conception of personhood allows us to represent. It is this way of thinking about persons that allows us to explain how we can survive either in PVS (which may make it look like we are fundamentally biological organisms) or in a simple transfer case (which may make it look like we are fundamentally psychological subjects). We are fundamentally both of these things, but can survive on the strength of one or the other set of functions in extreme and unusual cases.

The answer to the problem of coincidence that I have proposed is that we are fundamentally persons, and that "human animals" are not basic kinds of everyday objects, at least if "human animals" are conceived as something different from persons as we have just described them. There is a bit more work to be done, however, to show that this move will really meet the animalist challenge, as I will explain in the next section.

7.2.4 What about oysters?

As we have seen already on a couple of occasions, rethinking the question of personal identity as a question about objects of ordinary life rather than substances does not automatically resolve every aspect of the animalist challenges concerning coincidence. Some problems raised in connection with the claim that persons and humans are both substances reemerge within the arena of everyday life. I will conclude my discussion of the relation between human animals and human persons by looking at one such problem. The issues that stand behind this worry run very deep, and the response I provide will flesh out the change in perspective I am suggesting yet further.

In *The Human Animal* Olson suggests that the most promising strategy for psychological theorists is probably to argue that *person* is our substance concept and *human animal* is not a substance concept at all.[24] While he thinks this is probably a nominally defensible position, he also thinks that it will be a rather tough row to hoe. Living things seem to constitute a natural kind, with like persistence conditions. If we deny that *human animal* is our substance concept then it seems that we will need also to deny more generally that *animal* is a substance concept and that things which are organisms have their persistence conditions in virtue of being organisms. This leaves us with a tricky question about what to say about the identities of oysters and rosebushes and *E. coli*. Olson puts it this way:

> If not all animals have the same or even similar persistence conditions, we ought to wonder what it takes for non-rational or non-thinking animals—those animals that aren't also people—to persist through time. What does it take for an oyster to persist for example? We might have thought that an oyster persists just as long as those biological functions that keep it alive carry on—as long as it continues to metabolize, breathe, digest, and so forth, or as long as it remains capable of doing those things... .
> ... the proponents of the Psychological Approach (if they think we are animals) are likely to have a hard time saying much about the persistence conditions for those animals to which the Psychological Approach does not apply.[25]

Although this objection is raised against the psychological approach and uses the idiom of substance concepts, an only slightly modified version raises equally tricky questions for the view I have been describing.

Oysters, rosebushes, and even *E. coli* are objects of our everyday world, and they are typically described as animals, organisms, and living things. If PLV denies that "human organism" names an entity it is difficult to see how it can non-arbitrarily claim that oysters are fundamentally organisms. If they were, an organism would be a kind of object of the everyday world and there would be no reason a human

---

[24] Olson, *The Human Animal*, pp. 120–3.   [25] Olson, *The Human Animal*, p. 123.

organism should not be one. I have insisted repeatedly that the ontology of eve-ryday life is not merely conventional but is responsive to and constrained by facts about the world, so moving from discussion of substances to discussion of every-day objects does not relieve us of the burden of following this logic. Denying that humans have biological persistence conditions means denying that oysters have biological persistence conditions. But if biological organisms are in general not objects of everyday life, then what is an oyster and what constitutes its persistence conditions?

The answers to these last questions are in some sense relatively straightforward, but will not provide much immediate satisfaction; on the view I am proposing oys-ters are, most fundamentally... well... oysters, and they persist in virtue of the con-tinuation of a single oyster life. If an oyster life is not a biological life, however, we will need to say more about what it is, and about what more an oyster life contains besides organic functions. The answer to this question depends upon what we take a biological life to be. We got a brief look at this issue in the previous chapter, but we have not yet considered it systematically. The issues here are complicated because animalism is using biological facts to metaphysical purpose, so the understand-ing of a life, and of the way in which a life makes an organism, will need both to be biologically accurate and suited to defining the numerical identity of an organism. It is not clear, however, that purely biological conceptions of a life and the meta-physical aims of animalism always pull in the same direction. Seeing where and how they are in tension will be immensely useful in understanding what an oyster life entails.

The animalist picture of a biological life tends to focus on the vast number of incredibly complex electrical and biochemical activities that go on inside the skin of an organism, and this seems to be Olson's basic view of organic life, for instance. In characterizing such lives he tells us that "at the microscopic level and below, an organism is the site of frenetic activity," that "the flow of matter and energy through an organism is subject to a complex set of internal controls," and that "the goal-directed nature of living things is grounded in an underlying biochemical structure of unimaginable complexity."[26] The features he takes to define biological life involve the buzz of processes that move matter around to maintain the form and function of the organism as a whole. The idea that an oyster can really be noth-ing other than an organism implies that it is an entity that is constituted by its bio-logical life, and it is useful to consider how such constitution occurs. This will take some time and may seem a bit of a digression, but it will ultimately bring us back to the question of what an oyster might be if not an organism.

---

[26]   Olson, *The Human Animal*, pp. 127–8.

The view of life just described suggests a particular way of thinking about how an organic life constitutes an entity. On this picture a life makes an entity by constructing it out of parts. Organic life is the process of taking bits of matter and molding them to the shape and purpose of the organism as a whole. Again, Olson's description is helpful: "When a life draws a molecule into itself, it breaks that molecule into smaller pieces and reassembles them according to its needs. After extracting such chemical energy from them as it can, it expels their remains in a less ordered form."[27] There is obviously something right about this picture, but I want to challenge it as incomplete. It suggests that an organic life is simply equivalent to inner biochemical processes operating at the molecular level and that it constitutes an organism by modifying, shaping, and holding together particles of matter through these activities. While it is undeniable that this is part of the story, it is less obvious it is the whole story.

To see why this is so it will be useful to start with an analogy. The view I have been describing models the ways in which the activities of organic life constitute an organism by importing a simple and familiar picture of how entities are constructed out of parts. Suppose, for instance, I am building a Lego castle. I take the various bricks and snap them together in a particular way, putting the right bricks in the right numbers in the right places, and thereby constitute a new object—a castle. We might think of the activity involved in a biological life as something like the brick-snapping activity involved in my castle building. A life takes the relevant materials (e.g., salts, minerals, vitamins, lipids) and configures them in just the right way to create an organism with a particular shape and appearance (a rabbit, say, or a lion, or a bacterium).

Of course, the Lego picture cannot be quite the right one for organisms because Lego constructions are relatively static, and one of the most characteristic features of an organism is that it is a material object whose matter is always changing. For this kind of analogy to be useful we thus need to imagine a kind of magic Lego castle whose bricks constantly shift, fall out, or disintegrate, sometimes in response to internal pressures and sometimes in response to external assaults (e.g., a malicious sibling constantly trying to dismantle the castle to use the bricks in her own project). In the case of this kind of magic castle the activities involved in constituting the castle as an object are somewhat broader than those in the case of the static castle. In the static case we can plausibly make a distinction between activities that are preparatory to building the castle (e.g., activities like reading the instructions or procuring and sorting the pieces that will be needed) and activities involved in the construction itself (i.e., snapping the bricks together). In the case of the magic

---

[27] Olson, *The Human Animal*, p. 137.

castle, by contrast, such distinctions are artificial. Here the castle needs to be not only built but maintained, and this means a perpetual cycle of procuring the necessary materials, putting them into place, and protecting against environmental assault. Given these dynamics, interactions with the environment such as finding new bricks and guarding against destruction and disintegration are just as much a part of maintaining the structural integrity of the castle as the activity of reconfiguring bricks and snapping them into place once they have been found.

There are still other important disanalogies with organisms, of course. In the case of the magic Lego castle, the builder is separate from the entity constructed. Organisms, by contrast, are self-constituting and self-maintaining. In order to preserve their integrity they thus need to do the work not only of putting parts into place and repairing parts that break, but also the work of procuring the necessary materials from the environment and guarding against destruction from the outside. And organisms do, in fact, do both kinds of work. The former set of activities are, for the most part, carried out by the internal biochemical processes with which biological life is often identified, and the latter are carried out via life-sustaining behavioral interactions with the environment. Both sets of activities are absolutely essential to maintaining the form and function of the organism. An animal must be able to find food as well as to digest it and to evade predators as well as to heal wounds and fight infections. In fact, the question of which life-sustaining functions are carried out by internal biochemical processes and which through behavior can have different answers from species to species; mammals regulate body temperature though complex internal homeostatic mechanisms, while reptiles do so largely by seeking the appropriate environment. Even in mammals, moreover, temperature regulation ultimately involves behaviors like finding or building shelter or undertaking seasonal migration. In very simple organisms, in fact, the line between behavior and inner process is sometimes hard to draw, as for instance in chemotaxis.

The life of an organism involves a host of different, interrelated systems, some local and some global, working at different levels (e.g., cellular, systemic, behavioral) to maintain form and function. These different systems and processes are interconnected and interdependent. Behaviors in complex mammals are driven by activity in the brain and the workings of the endocrine system, but the development of the brain and the function of the endocrine system are determined by various environmental cues and stimuli. The biochemical processes of organisms do not evolve in a vacuum, but in an environment, and the inner processes function to maintain the organism only when that organism is able to interact with the right kind of environment in the right ways. Interactions with the environment feed the internal machinery and keep it going and this in turn allows the organism to keep interacting fruitfully with the environment. It is not evident why one set of processes should be given priority over the other in defining biological life.

None of this is to say that there are no clear boundaries between an organism and its environment. Here I am largely (though not entirely) in agreement with Olson when he says that "a life must contrast with its surroundings," adding that "this is not meant to be an empirical claim from biology, but part of the concept of a life."[28] The point is rather that many parts of a life must be understood as interface with an environment rather than as entirely internal processes, something few biologists are likely to deny. The role of these interactions in biological life is recognized in the fact that the biological sciences comprise not only biochemistry, neurobiology, anatomy, and cell biology, but also evolutionary biology, ecology, and zoology (including ethology). There is, moreover, an increasing appreciation among biologists that these subfields must ultimately talk to one another if biological life is to be understood. Before explaining why this result is important for our purposes, I will consider and dismiss a few ways in which someone might try to resist it.

There are a variety of distinctions one might draw to try to make the case that metaphysically speaking it is the inner processes alone that do the real work of constituting an organism, but none is defensible in the end.[29] One could, for instance, argue that inner processes are constant while behaviors like hunting, feeding, shelter building, and fighting are intermittent, and that this means that only the former can truly constitute the organism. But many inner processes are also intermittent, and on a short enough timescale none is truly constant. What is essential is that the appropriate processes occur at the appropriate time—hunting when food is needed, fighting or retreat when there is a threat, digestion when nutrients are taken in, immune response when there is an infection, and so on. Processes like heartbeat and respiration are relatively constant compared to others, but it is not clear why this alone should do the metaphysical work of dividing identity-constituting processes from those that occur after constitution. As already discussed, these processes, stable as they are, could not constitute an entity if enough of the other intermittent processes did not also take place.

One might also try to argue that inner processes differ fundamentally from survival behaviors because the cessation of the former cause the end of a life immediately and directly, while the latter result in the end of a life only after they have led to the shutting down of inner biochemical functions. This suggests that

---

[28] Olson, *The Human Animal*, p. 138.
[29] I do not see any evidence that biologists are driven to make these kinds of distinctions since the issue here is a metaphysical and not a biological one.

inner processes actually constitute biological life while behaviors only support it by supporting those functions. This claim is not so straightforward either, however. An animal with diabetes or an inability to absorb nutrients from its food will die more slowly than an animal that fails to evade a predator and has its jugular punctured, or makes a foraging mistake and ingests a powerful neurotoxin. The force of "immediately" thus cannot be simply a matter of the time it takes for death to occur.

It is open to the defender of an internal-process picture of life to respond by pointing out that the jugular puncture and neurotoxin cause instant death because of their disastrous and immediate impact on inner biochemical processes and to remind us that they would not be deadly if they did not have such an impact, but this is not a very helpful solution for the friend of the view that biological life consists only in inner biochemical processes. Since an animal can clearly survive the cessation of *some* inner processes for quite a long time, the claim is now no longer that biological life is constituted by *all* of the inner processes but only those inner processes whose cessation causes immediate death. Our discussion of criteria of death in the previous chapter revealed just how difficult it really is to select some process or set of processes that makes the ultimate difference between life and death. Even if we could, if this is how we are thinking of biological life the claim that it is the biological life and only the biological life that constitutes an organism is no longer remotely plausible. Brain activity or circulation/respiration do not in themselves create objects; they are part of a cluster of activities that together constitute and maintain the shape and form of an organism. It thus seems that the best way of understanding the entity-constituting nature of organic life is in terms of the full range of characteristic functions and activities that work at different levels to maintain the form and function of the organism.

This expanded conception of biological life points the way to answering our question about the identity of oysters and the nature of an oyster life. It turns out that all living things have characteristic lives that involve not only the humming of internal machinery but particular kinds of relations to their environments; oysters, bacteria, and rosebushes are no exceptions. In more primitive living things, both internal functions and the range of characteristic interactions with the environment are relatively simple. The correlation between the levels of complexity in these two sides of biological life is, of course, non-accidental. As living beings become more phylogenetically complex both their inner functions and their interactions with the environment become correspondingly more diverse and complicated. Oysters have relatively simple inner mechanisms and also a correspondingly simple behavioral repertoire; chimps have more complex inner mechanisms and similarly complex interactions with their environment and with each other. It is for this reason that when we look at a creature like an oyster we may tend to think of it as having no kind of life distinct from the functioning of its inner biochemistry. Nevertheless, each kind of living thing does have a set of characteristic behaviors and a characteristic role in the ecosystem as a whole, taking up some kinds of resources and providing others. In this sense there is a great deal that an oyster, or rosebush, or *E. coli does* in the biosphere and these activities and roles help to constitute it as the kind of locus of interaction that it is in much the same way that the activities that make up a person life help to constitute a person as the kind of locus it is.

The question that got us started was the question of what the persistence conditions of an oyster could be if not the continuation of a biological life, and what an oyster could be if not an organism. We have seen, however, that there are two ways to think about biological lives and organisms. One is to define a life in terms of inner biochemical processes and functions and the organism as the material form within which these operate. On the other, more expansive, idea organic life includes characteristic self-sustaining interactions with the environment and with others as well as inner biochemical processes, and the organism is a unified locus of such interactions. My assertion that organisms are not objects of everyday life must thus be somewhat qualified. If we take the first understanding of biological life I will want to say that it is just as incomplete to describe an oyster as an organism as it is to describe a person as an organism and that organisms of this sort are indeed not objects of everyday life. In both cases the focus on inner processes is an abstraction from the full life of the entity. If we take the broader understanding of organic life, however, then oysters are indeed organisms, but this poses no problems for PLV's claim that we are fundamentally persons. On the broader understanding of organisms it turns out that person lives follow much the same pattern and include many of the same components as organic lives. The difference is that the kinds of interactions that define their lives are immensely complex compared to those that define the lives of oysters, rosebushes, and *E. coli*, and that they are mediated through cultural infrastructure and social institutions.

This may make us wonder whether we should not, on the expanded picture of organic life, concede that persons are also organisms—just very complex ones—and that what I have been calling a person life is just the organic life of a human. We could do this, of course, but it is not the most accurate or illuminating way of describing the position PLV is trying to stake out. In the case of humans (as we described in Chapter 5) a new kind of complexity is added to behavior and to interactions with the environment stemming from the co-evolution of reflective self-consciousness, symbolic representation, cultural and social infrastructure, and explicit normative judgments. These elements add dimensions to person lives that are not, so far as we are aware, present in the lives of any other animals. There are important respects in which the lives of enculturated humans are radically different from those of other biological beings.[30] The development of culture and of social infrastructure changes the character of a life so that social functioning takes on a special kind of significance and is more salient in many ways than the inner biochemical processes typically associated with organic life. This is why creatures with vastly different physiognomy who share the same kind of social organization can all be persons; they share the most central and distinctive characteristics of our lives, and are loci of the same kind we are. But it is crucial to see that there are continuities between person lives and the lives of other animals as well. Like all living things, human persons are unified loci constituted by the activities that make up their characteristic lives. And, like all of the other living things we encounter in daily life, some but not all of those activities involve electrical and biochemical processes.

This analysis also helps us to see why animalism does not have any real advantage when it comes to providing uniform persistence conditions for all living things. To begin with, we can see that even if we focus only on the narrow conception of biological life there is no real uniformity. The inner biochemical workings of humans, oysters, and rosebushes in fact vary greatly from one another. For instance, a functioning brainstem is, according to Olson, crucial to the continuation of a human organism, but this precise mechanism obviously cannot be required for the continuation of rose bushes or oysters. There are, to be sure, some commonalities among these different types of organisms; to the extent that living things are made up of cells and there are consistencies in cellular functioning there will be some overlap of life functions. If the question at issue is what is required for the *organism* as opposed to its individual cells to continue, however, we will find marked differences in the answer depending upon what kind of organism we are asking about. It is of course possible to make the persistence conditions of all living things uniform if we describe these conditions at a very general level—if, for instance, we define those conditions as something like "the continuation of the functions that allow the entity to preserve and maintain the form and functions characteristic of organisms of that kind." But if this is our definition it is trivial to make the persistence conditions of persons the same as those of all other living things by simply replacing the word "organism" with "being"; the persistence of a person requires the continuation of the processes necessary to continue maintaining the form and functions that characterize the life of a being of that sort—a person.

---

[30] At least as far as we know. And if we turn out to be wrong about this it only means, as I argued in Chapter 5, that there are more kinds of persons than we thought.

Because different kinds of living things have different characteristic lives and the characteristic lives of persons have unique features, PLV can recognize the continuity between human persons and other kinds of living things without neglecting the real and important differences between them. It can also provide a coherent account of how it is possible for us to be fundamentally persons, even though we are human animals. Human animals (understood in the narrow sense that animalists use) are not distinct entities from human persons, but a way of thinking about them. There are not two distinct entities where there is a human person, but one structurally complex and highly integrated locus of interaction.

7.3   What was the Question?

The preceding analysis suggests a way for PLV to make claims to providing an account of our literal identity without running afoul of the coincidence problem. In the course of making this case, however, the exact ontological status claimed for persons may have become somewhat murky. At the beginning of the chapter I said that although I would provisionally take the literal question of our identity to be a question about the numerical identity of substances, in the end I would provide a somewhat different formulation. That formulation has emerged over the last sections. Rather than telling us what makes a person at time t_1 numerically the same substance as something at t_2, PLV explores the conditions of the integrity of persons understood as unified loci of interaction and everyday objects. The difference between these two questions is subtle—in some ways more a difference of emphasis than anything else—but it will be helpful in understanding what we have accomplished to articulate these differences in a bit more detail.

I have described the ontological status of persons as that of the ordinary objects of everyday life within a sparse ontology. The idea this is meant to convey is that persons have integrity as unified entities that comes from their ability to play a particular role in the transactions of ordinary life, and that this does not depend upon any further or deeper principles of composition (although it does depend upon facts about the world). An apple is an object of everyday life because I can put it in my pocket to eat later, count it as one of the seven I need for a pie, trade it for your potato chips, and so on.[31] Persons are objects of everyday life because they can interact with each other and with the environment in particular ways as a single unit. The unity of both the apple and the person are directly connected to facts about both the matter of which they are composed and the structure of their

---

[31] I do not mean to imply that it is human activities only that define a locus. Apples are loci for other kinds of animals as well insofar as they can, e.g., transport and store them as units.

environments. If these facts were different in relevant ways they would no longer function as units.

I also suggested that organisms are not substances and so adopted a view that I said was approximated by nihilism as Olson understands it. One reason that I say nihilism is only an approximation of this view is that the name suggests that the only way entities can be real is if they are substances in a particular metaphysical sense. If they are merely particles arranged in a way that constitutes a practical locus—like an apple or wedding album—they are not, on this view, true objects. This is not just a terminological issue; understanding objects in this way suggests that if we accept nihilism as Olson describes it there are no genuine facts about the individuation and continuity of the objects of everyday life; it is all just a matter of what we say or of what is important to us. My repeated arguments that personhood and personal identity as defined by PLV are not merely conventional represent a denial of this claim. It is not up to us what conditions must be met for there to be a unified locus of interaction, or for a single locus to continue.

My insistence on genuine facts about the integrity of a locus may seem to indicate that I am talking about substances after all; I am just disagreeing with Olson about what a substance is. Baker, for one, sees the objects of everyday life as metaphysically primary kinds whose individuation and persistence conditions can be set by relational properties, so why not just say that I am endorsing Baker's conception of substance? My views on these issues are indeed very close to Baker's, and obviously owe a good deal to her. Her particular description of the metaphysics of everyday objects is, however, at once more liberal and more conservative than the one I am describing.

Baker's position is more liberal than mine because it allows for a greater range of ways in which something can become an object than I am inclined to. According to Baker a new entity is born whenever we are confronted with important new causal properties—for instance when a stone is designated as a war memorial or a piece of cloth is raised as a flag. To my ear it sounds wrong to say that in everyday life these transformations bring new entities into existence rather than saying, for instance, that a stone has become a war memorial or a piece of cloth is being used as a flag. Baker does not provide a general account of when changes in causal properties are sufficient to bring about a new object and makes it clear that not just any such change will be entity-producing (using an anvil as a doorstop, for instance, does not bring a new entity into existence; it is simply using an anvil in a new way). I wish to place slightly more definite constraints, however, constraints which would rule out some of the claims Baker makes about when new entities are brought into existence. The kind of changes in causal powers that are relevant to constituting new entities, on my view, are specifically those that give something the capacity to interact with the environment as a unified whole. The ability to draw protestors or tears does not make a rock-turned-war-memorial any more of a single unit than it was before—it makes it a unit that can do new things. The same is true when a piece of cloth is used as a flag. The biological, psychological, and social functions of a person, however, allow her to act as a unified locus of interpersonal interaction, and so constitute her as a thing.

Baker's account is also more conservative than mine because it shares with animalism a notion of a strong *de re* essentialism and a presupposition that in looking for an account of personhood and personal identity we are looking for the single defining feature that will determine persistence conditions. Baker, like Olson, is looking to define the numerical identity of persons. If this is our goal we will seek a list of necessary and sufficient conditions for being a person and for the continuation of the same person. This obscures the possibility of taking genuine unified loci to be conceived of as homeostatic property clusters, as I say persons should be. More generally, thinking of the question of our identity in terms of the identity of a locus allows us to avoid unnecessary restrictions imposed by taking the question as one about numerical identity. Numerical identity as it is usually understood is a logical notion that sits awkwardly with anything other than an absolute simple. As soon as we look at complex entities we run into the many well-known puzzles and paradoxes of borderline and difficult cases. The logical form associated with the integrity of a locus is more versatile. This is not to say that there will be no puzzles or hard cases if we approach the question this way, but we will have a wider range of resources for addressing them. The question of the integrity of a locus, like the question of numerical identity, should allow of a "yes" or "no" answer each time we ask it—either a single unified locus remains or it does not. But built into this question is a recognition that there are a variety of different ways in which a locus can stay together or come apart.

7.4 Summing Up

Our objective in this chapter has been to show that PLV is rightly understood as an account of our literal identity and, in the course of doing so, to clarify what forms such an account might take. The most powerful reasons for claiming that PLV addresses a metaphorical rather than a literal identity question come from animalist arguments. If we say that persons are not identical to human animals but are instead distinct entities with their own persistence conditions, the argument goes, we will have difficulty providing a coherent account of the relation between persons like us and the human animals with which they are associated; this is what we have been calling the coincidence problem. Since we are undeniably human animals, the animalist reasons, the best way to avoid this problem is to realize that "person" should not be taken to name a kind of thing but rather a property or function of some more basic thing (in the case of human persons, a human animal). Any question about the continuation of a person *as* a person is not, therefore, a question about the literal continuation of an entity but rather a question about whether an entity continues to possess particular attributes or is still in a particular phase of its existence.

Since PLV denies that persons are identical to human animals (in the animalist's sense) it must face the coincidence problem. I have described two different ways in which we might respond to this challenge, arguing that we are in fact more fundamentally persons than human animals and so that it is our personhood that sets the conditions of our literal continuation. One possibility is to accept that literal questions of identity are questions about the numerical identity of a substance and insist that our substance concept is *person* and not *human animal*. The relation between persons and animals could then be described as one of constitution along the lines developed by Lynne Baker (although employing a different conception of personhood than hers). On this view we are persons constituted by human animals. A second possibility, which I prefer for a variety of reasons, is to argue that the question of our literal continuation need not be viewed as a question about the numerical identity of a substance in the metaphysically-loaded sense employed by most animalists. Instead it should be interpreted as a question about the integrity of a unified locus which we can track and interact with as a single unit. Using this conception we can see persons as complicated biological-psychological-social loci more fundamental than the animalist's "organisms," which are viewed as abstractions.

While different in technical details, the two strategies I have outlined for responding to the coincidence problem share a rejection of the strong independence model of the relation between facts about personal identity and practical considerations. Standing behind the arguments for animalism is a supposition that metaphysical facts are necessarily independent of practical considerations. If we want to answer questions about what there is in the world, the thinking goes, our interests and practices are irrelevant and we should take an entirely theoretical stance. The constitution model rejects this assumption insofar as it depends crucially on the claim that relational and practical properties can be essential properties—a claim Baker makes explicitly. This assumption is also denied in the refiguring of the question of literal identity as a question about the integrity of a locus of interaction rather than as a question about the numerical identity of a substance. This alternative understanding of the question highlights the way in which the relational significance of an object can be inextricably tied up in the conditions of its continuation.

The difference in fundamental sensibility and perspective between animalism and these other views thus runs extremely deep, involving disagreement about the very nature of a metaphysical fact, and so it is a difference not easily resolved. It seems clear, however, that PLV and animalism offer competing accounts of what we most fundamentally are, at least in part by disagreeing about what "fundamental" means in this context. To this extent, PLV addresses the question of our literal identity, and we have met our goal of providing an account of our identity in which facts about our literal identity are inherently connected to practical considerations.

Conclusion

The arguments of the previous chapter provided the last piece necessary to show that PLV does indeed meet our goal of providing an account of personal identity according to which facts about literal identity are inherently connected to practical considerations. Meeting this goal has required us to rethink some of the standard methods and assumptions found in much of the philosophical literature on personal identity, and now that our task has been completed it is worth taking a moment to review how we got here and what we have learned along the way.

In Chapter 1 we made a distinction between the dependence model and the coincidence model of the relation between personal identity and practical concerns. This opened up the possibility that a practically-based account of personal identity need not make the limits of the person coincide with the limits of particular practical interests or judgments, but could instead define a unit which is the appropriate target of those interests and judgments. Chapter 2 confirmed that we need to assume the existence of such a unit to explain our person-related practices, and Chapter 3 argued for expanding our understanding of those practices beyond the sophisticated forensic concerns invoked in the Lockean conception of personhood, replacing the notion of a forensic unit with that of a basic practical unit. Chapter 4 gave us the tools to think about a kind of synchronic and diachronic holism of the relation that constitutes this unit, so that we were able to envision the possibility of a single relation which delimits a unified locus that is an appropriate target of the many and varied practices and interests associated with personal identity. All of these results taken together pointed the way to a practically-based account of personal identity both basic enough and general enough to achieve our aims.

The development and explication of PLV in Chapters 5 and 6 required, in addition to the application of the resources gathered in the first four chapters, two additional moves. One was a reconception of how to go about offering an account of personal identity. The standard assumption seems to be that when we set out to explicate the conditions of personal identity what we need to do is isolate the relation that is really doing the work from among the various relations and connections found in uncontroversial judgments of identity. In the unproblematic cases of identity we encounter every day there are usually many different kinds of connections and continuities present, and it is obvious that not all of them must be in place in order for a person to continue. It is thus natural to think that what must be done to discover the basis of personal identity is to distinguish the relation which actually constitutes identity from those that are merely co-present with that relation. One might attempt to do this through the use of hypothetical cases that serve as thought experiments or, alternatively, by excising practical considerations and looking for what is metaphysically necessitated for the persistence of a substance. Either way the goal is to find the one relation (or small subset of relations) in the jumble of a person's life that is necessary and sufficient for the continuation of that person.

In developing PLV I have viewed the problem differently. In particular, I have entertained the possibility that what actually constitutes the continuation of a person is not some one of the relations found in the tangle of intertwined connections present in paradigmatic cases of personal identity, but rather the tangle itself. On the standard approach it is as if we are interested in understanding what makes a length of rope whole and continuous and decide to do this by looking for the one strand such that if it holds the length of rope is continuous. This method will leave us with many puzzles. It will, for one thing, be possible to make a case for almost any strand being *the* strand that does the work of holding the rope together, since the continued integrity of almost any strand will make the rope (barely) continuous. We are thus left with no clear means of choosing which is the strand that "truly" constitutes the continuity of the rope. Moreover, even if we do identify some strand as the one that constitutes this continuity, we will be left with a puzzle about why the continuity of ropes matters to us in the way it does, since a rope held together by a single thread cannot do many of the things that we want and expect continuous lengths of rope to do (e.g., secure loads or work as part of a pulley system). In the case of ropes, it is clear that these puzzles arise because we have asked the question in the wrong way. If we want to understand the continuity of a rope and to explain why ropes can do what they can do when they are whole we will need to understand the way in which the various strands work together in a typical rope.

The strands of a person's life are obviously far more complicated and diverse than those of a rope, but I have argued that a similar principle applies. According to PLV the continuity of a human person consists in the interactions among the different biological, psychological, and social attributes and functions which support and mutually reinforce one another in everyday life. Providing an account of personal identity thus involves developing an understanding of how these different attributes and functions work together as opposed to prizing them apart to find the one which uniquely constitutes the continuation of the person. Using Boyd's notion of a homeostatic property cluster (as applied to biological lives by Chiong), we were able to show how a view of this sort could provide an informative account of our identity without specifying necessary and sufficient conditions for our continuation. We were also able to see how a person can in principle survive the loss of almost any of the standard functions and relations that make up a paradigmatic life if enough remain (or enough external support is available) to maintain an integrated unit of interaction. The different conceptions of *person* we employ should thus be viewed as descriptions of different aspects of personhood, and the different accounts of personal identity that flow from them not as competing accounts of a single phenomenon, but rather as articulations of one of the many relations that together constitute our continuation.

The second key move in developing PLV was to put emphasis on the social conditions of personhood and personal identity, and in particular on a social and cultural infrastructure that not only mediates interpersonal interactions, but supports them and makes them possible. The attributes that make us persons on this view reside not only in individuals, but also in the institutions and social organizations that emerge from the interactions of beings who typically possess higher-order or "forensic" capacities. This infrastructure is a crucial element of the personhood of every person, even those who do possess the forensic capacities, since it creates a "person-space" in which such individuals can be accorded a place and so live person lives. The centrality of social relations in this account naturally raises worries about conventionalism, and these were addressed at length. The social organization of our lives is not arbitrary, I argued, but responsive to facts about us and about the world.

The role given to social and cultural infrastructure in this view also required some reinterpretation of what is accomplished by reflection on hypothetical puzzle cases. It is a consequence of the social emphasis of PLV that the outcome of these cases does not depend exclusively on what happens to the individual whose adventures are described. The outcome depends also on what happens to the social context within which the kinds of changes described in these cases occur and the ways in which these vicissitudes impact the structure of person-space there. This means that our judgments in such cases must always be tentative. We are predicting how things would work in the space of interpersonal interactions were someone to change in some particular way, but whether these predictions would actually come true in the eventuality depends upon a great many details that cannot all be known in advance. Hypothetical cases thus cannot yield direct and definitive results of the sort we hope for controlled experiments to do. Since some of our predictions of outcome are more secure than others, however, when used properly these cases can be very helpful in reflecting upon the question of what kinds of social organizations are coherent for beings like us.

The Person Life View as described in Chapters 5 and 6 is clearly a view according to which facts about personal identity are inherently connected to practical considerations. To show that it is legitimately considered an account of our *literal* identity, Chapter 7 addressed the animalist challenge to any view that holds that human persons can have different persistence conditions from human animals, showing how PLV can meet this challenge. While I described two different responses PLV might give, my favored reply made use of all of the elements that went into developing the view. The change from a coincidence model of the relation between personal identity and practical concerns to a dependence model gives PLV a logical structure that is relevantly like that of an account of the numerical identity of an entity rather than that of a particular practical judgment. The expanded conception of the practical makes PLV more basic, and hence more plausible as a literal account of identity, than a Lockean view would be. The conception of a person as a homeostatic property cluster showed how our "biological lives" could be understood as a part of our overall person lives, and the notion of *organism* as an abstraction from a more basic unity, which is the person. This response to the animalist challenge also involved rethinking the question of how best to conceptualize the structure of a "literal" question of our identity, concluding that it is perhaps better conceived as a question about the integrity of a functional unit than as a question about the numerical identity of a substance.

To the extent that my arguments have been convincing, I have thus shown that it is possible to provide an account according to which facts about our literal identity are inherently connected with practical considerations. There is, however, an outstanding question which has yet to receive a direct response, and that is the question of why we should think it is desirable to provide such an account in the first place. There are, as we have seen, those who deny that we should appeal to practical concerns and judgments in trying to answer metaphysical questions about our literal continuation. From their perspective it is not an obvious advantage for a view of identity to be tied to practical considerations, especially if our attempt to incorporate these considerations distorts our theoretical perspective.

The most straightforward answer I can offer to the question of why it is desirable for an account of the identity conditions of beings like us to be intrinsically bound up with practical concerns is that the people who populate our world just *are* loci of person-related practices and interests, and this is something that a satisfying account of the conditions of their identity will have to recognize. Persons are by their nature practically-salient beings. This will sound, I realize, like nothing more than an assertion of the view that strong independence theorists deny, but it is an assertion grounded in the details that have emerged during the development and defense of PLV. I have argued that we do see (and cannot help seeing) one another as unified targets of interpersonal interaction, and that this is not arbitrary but depends upon features of ourselves and of the world. There is no reason not to take that fact seriously in fixing the phenomenon we are trying to explain. If the account we are offering is supposed to be an account of the identity conditions for people as we know them, it will have to be an account in which a person's identity is bound up with her practical significance. If the account we are offering need not be about the identity conditions for people as we know them, then it is no longer clear in what sense it is an account of the identity conditions for beings like us.

These observations are unlikely to sway the committed defender of the strong independence model. In the end the choice between that perspective and the one I am urging turns on metaphysical and metaphilosophical questions so fundamental it is unclear that there is a standpoint from which they can be cleanly adjudicated. Wherever one ultimately stands on these fundamental issues of method and ontology, however, at the very least the question of what constitutes the identity of a basic practical unit—the unified target of interaction to which our myriad person-related interests and practices apply—is an important question of great interest which has gone largely unrecognized in philosophical discussions of personal identity. PLV, for all of the faults it undoubtedly possesses, is uniquely suited to addressing this question, and so to providing a particular kind of insight into the people who fill our lives in all of their bewildering and magnificent complexity.

References

Alston, W. P. and Bennett, J. (1988). Locke on People and Substances. *Philosophical Review*, 97(1), 25–46.

Baker, L. R. (2000). *Persons and Bodies: A Constitution View*. Cambridge: Cambridge University Press.

—— (2005). When Does a Person Begin? *Social Philosophy and Policy*, 22(2), 25–48.

—— (2007). *The Metaphysics of Everyday Life: An Essay in Practical Realism*. Cambridge: Cambridge University Press.

—— (2008). Big-tent Metaphysics. *Abstracta*, 1, 8–15.

Baumeister, R. F. (2005). *The Cultural Animal: Human Nature, Meaning, and Social Life*. New York: Oxford University Press.

Boyd, R. (1999). Homeostasis, Species, and Higher Taxa. In R. A. Wilson (ed.), *Species: New Interdisciplinary Essays* (pp. 141–85). Cambridge, MA: MIT Press.

Bradley, B., Feldman, F., and Johansson, J. (2013) (eds.). *The Oxford Handbook of Philosophy and Death*. New York: Oxford University Press.

Cavell, S. (1979). *The Claim of Reason: Wittgenstein, Skepticism, Morality, and Tragedy*. New York: Oxford University Press.

Chiong, W. (2005). Brain Death without Definitions. *Hastings Center Report*, 35(6), 20–30.

Cockburn, D. (1991) (ed.). *Human* Beings (Royal Institute of Philosophy Supplements 29). New York: Cambridge University Press.

DeGrazia, D. (2005). *Human Identity and Bioethics*. Cambridge: Cambridge University Press.

Donald, M. (2001). *A Mind so Rare: the Evolution of Human Consciousness*. New York: W.W. Norton.

Fireman, G. D., McVay, T. E., and Flanagan, O. J. (2003) (eds.). *Narrative and Consciousness: Literature, Psychology and the Brain*. New York: Oxford University Press.

Frankfurt, H. G. (1988). *The Importance of what we Care About: Philosophical Essays*. Cambridge: Cambridge University Press.

Gendler, T. S. (2000). *Thought Experiment: On the Powers and Limits of Imaginary Cases*. New York: Garland Pub.

Gilmore, C. (2013). When do Things Die? In B. Bradley, F. Feldman, and J. Johansson (eds.), *The Oxford Handbook of Philosophy and Death* (pp. 14–19). New York: Oxford University Press.

Goldie, P. (2009). Narrative Thinking, Emotion, and Planning. *Journal of Aesthetics and Art Criticism*, 67(1), 97–106.

Gordon-Roth, J. (2013). *A Reconsideration of Locke on Persons as Modes*. Unpublished doctoral thesis.

Häggqvist, S. (1996). *Thought Experiments in Philosophy*. Stockholm: Almqvist and Wiksell International.

Hutto, D. D. (2007) (ed.). *Narrative and Understanding Persons* (Royal Institute of Philosophy Supplements 60). Cambridge: Cambridge University Press.

Inwagen, P. van (1993). Reply to Reviewers. *Philosophy and Phenomenological Research*, 53(3), 709–19.

Korsgaard, C. M. (1989). Personal Identity and the Unity of Agency: A Kantian Response to Parfit. *Philosophy and Public Affairs*, 18(2), 101–32.

——(1996). *The Sources of Normativity*. Cambridge: Cambridge University Press.

Laland, K. N., and Galef, B. G. (2009) (eds.). *The Question of Animal Culture*. Cambridge, MA: Harvard University Press.

Lamarque, P. (2007). On the Distance between Literary Narratives and Real-Life Narratives. In Daniel Hutto (ed.), *Narrative and Understanding Persons* (Royal Institute of Philosophy Supplements 60) (pp. 117–32). Cambridge: Cambridge University Press.

Lewis, D. (1983). *Philosophical Papers*, Vol. 1. New York: Oxford University Press.

Lindemann, H. (2001). *Damaged Identities, Narrative Repair*. Ithaca: Cornell University Press. (Published as Hilde Lindemann Nelson.)

——(2002). What Child is This? *The Hastings Center Report*, 32(6), 29–38. (Published as Hilde Lindemann Nelson.)

——(2009). Holding on to Edmund: The Relational Work of Identity. In H. Lindemann, M. Verkerk, and M. Walker (eds.), *Naturalized Bioethics: Toward Responsible Knowing and Practice* (pp. 65–79). New York: Cambridge University Press.

Locke, J. (1975). *An Essay Concerning Human Understanding*, ed. P. H. Nidditch. Oxford: Clarendon Press. Locke, *Human Understanding*

Lyn, H., Russell, J., Leavens, D., Bard, K., Boysen, S., Schaeffer, J., and Hopkins, W. (2013). Apes Communicate about Absent and Displaced Objects: Methodology Matters. *Animal Cognition*, May 17. <http://link.springer.com.proxy.cc.uic.edu/article/10.1007/s10071-013-0640-0/fulltext.html> (accessed October 6, 2013).

McMahan, J. (2002). *The Ethics of Killing: Problems at the Margins of Life*. Oxford: Oxford University Press.

Nelson, K. (2003). Narrative and the Emergence of a Consciousness of Self. In G. D. Fireman, T. E. McVay, and O. J. Flanagan (eds.), *Narrative and Consciousness* (pp. 17-36). New York: Oxford University Press.

Olson, E. T. (1997). *The Human Animal: Personal identity without Psychology*. Oxford: Oxford University Press.

——(2007). *What are We? A Study in Personal Ontology*. Oxford: Oxford University Press.

Parfit, D. A. (1984). *Reasons and Persons*. Oxford: Clarendon Press.

Perry, J. (1972). Can the Self Divide? *Journal of Philosophy*, 69(16), 463–88.

——(1975) (ed.). *Personal Identity*. Berkeley: University of California Press.

——(1976). The Importance of Being Identical. In A. Rorty (ed.), *The Identities of Persons* (pp. 67–91). Berkeley: University of California Press.

Reid, T. (1975). Of Mr. Locke's Account of our Personal Identity. In J. Perry (ed.), *Personal Identity* (pp. 113–18). Berkeley: University of California Press. Reid, "Of Mr. Locke's Account"

Rendell, L., and Whitehead, H. (2001). Culture in Whales and Dolphins. *Behavioral and Brain Sciences*, 24(2), 309–24.

Rorty, A. O. (1976) (ed.). *The Identities of Persons*. Berkeley: University of California Press.

Rovane, C. (1997). *The Bounds of Agency: An Essay in Revisionary Metaphysics*. Princeton: Princeton University Press.

Schapiro, T. (1999). What is a Child? *Ethics*, 109(4), 715–38.

Schechtman, M. (1990). Personhood and Personal Identity. *Journal of Philosophy*, 87(2), 71–92.

—— (1996). *The Constitution of Selves*. Ithaca: Cornell University Press.

—— (1997). The Brain/Body Problem. *Philosophical Psychology*, 10(2), 149–64.

—— (2001). Empathic Access: The Missing Ingredient in Personal Identity. *Philosophical Explorations*, 4(2), 94–110

—— (2005). Personal Identity and the Past. *Philosophy, Psychiatry, and Psychology*, 12(1), 9–22 and 27–9.

—— (2008). Diversity in Unity: Practical Unity and Personal Boundaries. *Synthese*, 162(3), 405–23.

Shewmon, D. A. (1997). Recovery from "Brain Death": a Neurologist's Apologia. *Linacre Quarterly*, 64(1), 30–96.

—— (2001). The Brain and Somatic Integration: Insights into the Standard Biological Rationale for Equating Brain Death with Death. *Journal of Medicine and Philosophy*, 26(5), 457–78.

Shoemaker, D. W. (2007). Personal Identity and Practical Concerns. *Mind*, 116(462), 317–57.

Shoemaker, S., and Swinburne, R. (1984). *Personal Identity* (Great Debates in Philosophy). Oxford: Blackwell.

Smith, J. D. (2010). Inaugurating the Study of Animal Metacognition. *International Journal of Comparative Psychology*, 23, 401–13.

Snowdon, P. F. (1991). Personal Identity and Brain Transplants. In D. Cockburn (ed.), *Human Beings* (Royal Institute of Philosophy Supplements 29) (pp. 109–26). New York: Cambridge University Press.

Sorensen, R. A. (1992). *Thought Experiments*. Oxford: Oxford University Press.

Strawson, G. (2004). Against Narrativity. *Ratio*, 17(4), 428–52.

—— (2011). *Locke on Personal Identity: Consciousness and Concernment*. Princeton: Princeton University Press.

Strawson, P. F. (1959). *Individuals: An Essay in Descriptive Metaphysics*. London: Routledge.

—— (1962). Freedom and Resentment. *Proceedings of the British Academy*, 48, 1–25.

Unger, P. K. (1990). *Identity, Consciousness and Value*. Oxford: Oxford University Press.

Uzgalis, W. L. (1990). Relative Identity and Locke's Principle of Individuation. *History of Philosophy Quarterly*, 7(3), 283–97.

Velleman, D. (1996). Self to self. *Philosophical Review*, 105(1), 39–76.

Verkerk, M., and Lindemann, H. (2009) (eds.). *Naturalized Bioethics: Toward Responsible Knowing and Practice*. New York: Cambridge University Press.

Wilkes, K. V. (1988). *Real people: Personal Identity without Thought Experiments*. Oxford: Clarendon Press.

Wilson, R. A. (1999). *Species: New Interdisciplinary Essays*. Cambridge, MA: MIT Press.

Wittgenstein, L. (1953). *Philosophical Investigations*. Oxford: Blackwell.

Zarnitsyn, A. (2013). *Thought Experiments in Philosophy: a Literary Model*, Doctoral dissertation, University of Illinois at Chicago.

Index

Printed and bound by CPI Group (UK) Ltd, Croydon, CR0 4YY